The Chambers of Memory

DEVE • R01203 08627 **'SYCHIATRY**

A Series of Books Edited By

Anthony L. LaBruzza, M.D.

The books in this series address various facets of the role of psychiatry in the modern world.

Using DSM-IV: *A Clinician's Guide to Psychiatric Diagnosis*
Anthony L. LaBruzza and José M. Méndez-Villarrubia

Filicide: *The Murder, Humiliation, Mutilation, Denigration, and Abandonment of Children by Parents*
Arnaldo Rascovsky

Return from Madness: *Psychotherapy with People Taking the New Antipsychotic Medications and Emerging from Severe, Lifelong, and Disabling Schizophrenia*
Kathleen Degen and Ellen Nasper

The Chambers of Memory: *PTSD in the Life Stories of U. S. Vietnam Veterans*
H. William Chalsma

Winning Cooperation from Your Child! *A Comprehensive Method to Stop Defiant and Aggressive Behavior in Children*
Kenneth Wenning

Brainstorms: *Understanding and Treating the Emotional Storms of Attention Deficit Hyperactivity Disorder from Childhood through Adulthood*
H. Joseph Horacek

Twisted: *Inside the Mind of a Drug Addict*
Carl Adam Richmond

The Essential Internet:
A Guide for Psychotherapists and Other Mental Health Professionals
Anthony L. LaBruzza

Building a Neuropsychology Practice:
A Guide to Respecialization
Marvin H. Podd and Donald P. Seelig

The Chambers of Memory

■ ■ ■ ■ ■ ■ ■ ■ ■ ■ ■ ■ ■

PTSD IN THE LIFE STORIES
OF U.S. VIETNAM VETERANS

H. W. Chalsma, Ph.D., Psy.D.

JASON ARONSON INC.
Northvale, New Jersey
London

Director of Editorial Production: Robert D. Hack

This book was set in 11½ pt. Century Expanded by Alpha Graphics of Pittsfield, New Hampshire.

Library of Congress Cataloging-in-Publication Data
Chalsma, H. W. (H. William)
    The chambers of memory : PTSD in the life stories of U.S. Vietnam veterans / by H. W. Chalsma.
        p. cm.
    Includes bibliographical references and index.
    ISBN 1-56821-691-2 (alk. paper)
    1. Post-traumatic stress disorder. I. Title.
RC552.P67C48   1998
616.85'21—dc21   97-26346

Printed in the United States of America on acid-free paper. For information and catalog write to Jason Aronson Inc., 230 Livingston Street, Northvale, New Jersey 07647-1726. Or visit our website: http://www.aronson.com

The present volume is based upon the videotaped life stories of thirty-one U. S. combat veterans of the Vietnam War. They all suffer from Post-Traumatic Stress Disorder (PTSD). They are the real authors here.

CONTENTS

▪ ▪ ▪ ▪ ▪ ▪ ▪ ▪ ▪ ▪ ▪ ▪ ▪

PREFACE

■ ■ ■ ■ ■ ■ ■ ■ ■ ■ ■ ■ ■

PTSD AND HUMAN EXPERIENCE

PTSD is the abbreviation for the standard diagnostic manual's Post-Traumatic Stress Disorder. PTSD is only the most recent label for the damage done to the body and to the sense of personal history and self-concept, or personhood, that follows overwhelming psychological trauma. It was not introduced in the *Diagnostic and Statistical Manual of Mental Disorders* until 1980. The DSM, now in its fourth edition (1994), is nothing more than a kind of reverse cookbook consisting of symptom checklists. Nevertheless, its formulation of post-traumatic conditions may serve as a broad overview of the profound impact of psychological trauma on the individual. Symptoms are divided into three clusters. First, there are the reexperiencing phenomena, such as flashbacks, nightmares, and intrusive thoughts associated with traumatic events. Second, there are avoidance behaviors, like social isolation, withdrawal, difficulty being in crowds, and especially an inability to form close, lasting relationships. Finally, the DSM covers what it refers to as hyperarousal, exemplified by the "exaggerated startle response." Here in this last grouping are also paradoxical reevoking behaviors, where parallel experiences are sought out to trigger the intense arousal of traumatic events. Combat veterans speak frequently about periods in their lives when they have looked for danger without knowing why (barroom brawls, for instance) and experienced once again the rush associated with the violence and danger of warfare. Recent research on PTSD has tended to focus on what is considered to be the biological substrate of post-traumatic conditions. There is even an animal model that goes back at least as far as Harlow's tortured monkeys. Foa and colleagues (1992) provide a more recent formulation, finding that unpredictability and uncontrollability are critical features of trauma. Nothing describes the combat experience in Vietnam more succinctly.

PTSD is really a generic designation, whereas the actual human experience of the devastating impact of psycholgical trauma, whether it is engendered by war trauma, childhood abuse, or any other traumatic experience, yields a broad spectrum of disturbance that amounts to a disruption of selfhood. As Jonathan Shay (1994) writes, "I do not believe the official PTSD criteria capture the devastation of mental life after severe combat trauma, because they neglect the damaging personality changes that frequently follow prolonged, severe trauma" (p. 169). Then, too, the detached clinical criteria ignore the profound disturbance of memory that accompanies the post-traumatic conditions. PTSD is an anxiety disorder, certainly; it may also be seen as a disordering of memory. How is one to deal with flashbacks, nightmares, and intrusive thoughts, when their impact overwhelms ordinary narrative memory and there is no way to assimilate these more physiological events into a story line? No wonder the veterans so often turned to treating themselves—with alcohol and street drugs. In addition, it is clear that the psychic phenomena to which the DSM refers only in its second edition are as old as the human race. For instance, Shay (1994), in his fascinating book *Achilles in Vietnam*, examines accounts of Vietnam veterans and parallel passages from Homer's *Iliad*. Erich Maria Remarque's novel on the lives of the infantrymen of World War I, *All Quiet on the Western Front* (first published in 1928), could serve just as well as a characterization of what war trauma means to the veteran. Putting experience like that into words is no easy task. Remarque's narrator notes, for instance, "It is too dangerous for me to put these things into words. I am afraid they might then become gigantic and I be no longer able to master them. What would become of us if everything that happens out there were quite clear to us?" (p. 165 in the 1991 edition). This, too, is PTSD, of course.

GENESIS OF THE PROJECT

It was early in my stay as a psychology intern at the National Center for PTSD, West Haven, Connecticut, that I was speaking to Dr. Hadar Lubin, Unit Chief, herself a former citizen of Israel and a veteran of the Israeli army. It turned out that, like me, Dr. Lubin was fascinated by people's stories and by the role of testimony in the healing process. She was also an associate of Dr. Dori Laub, who is, with Geoffery Hartman, co-founder of the Yale University Video Archive of Holocaust Testimonies. Having learned of my intention to base a dissertation on trauma narratives, Hadar said, "Do it here, and videotape the interviews." That immediately became my plan, resulting ultimately in the thirty-one videotaped life stories of U. S. combat veterans of the Vietnam War upon which this book is based. Soon after Hadar Lubin gave her gracious invitation to do the work at the unit with the veterans, I went to the video archive of Holocaust survivors' testimonies, which is open to the public, and viewed several of the over 3,000 tapes there. This was an astonishingly affecting experience. I came away moved *and* impressed with the control with which the narrators spoke their stories. The narratives that I viewed showed the teller speaking into the camera, with very little involvement of the interviewers, who seemed mostly intent upon disappearing from the process. I attempted to imitate as closely as possible this approach, just setting the stage for the story with a few comments as guidelines. As listener, however, I found myself far from disappearing. The experience of being witness to the trauma narrative is one that has, I can testify, a fundamental impact. Sitting with thirty-one veterans as they told their stories sometimes to, sometimes past the camera was a formative one; I am not the same person for having been a part of all this. I sensed a bond with every one of the veterans. This constitutes experiential research of the most powerful kind. It was a privileged position, and a gift; it was an initiation experience as well. Part of this ritualized entry into the veterans' lives was a sense of entering into the community to which they belonged, the community of veterans of the war and that highly coherent healing community that the unit constituted. Of course, communities are held together by stories; the stories of warriors occupy a special place in the binding together of villages, of clans and tribes, and of nations. What follows is my attempt to hear their individual stories as one story, while honoring each narrator's own struggle to make sense of a life marked by overwhelming combat trauma.

ACKNOWLEDGMENTS

■ ■ ■ ■ ■ ■ ■ ■ ■ ■ ■ ■ ■ ■

There are so many people I must thank for assistance in the prepa-
ration of this study. The members of my dissertation committee come
first of all to mind: Lorraine Mangione, Ph.D., Robinson Welch,
Ph.D., and William Lax, Psy.D. Bill Lax in particular guided the
work with a steady—and gentle—hand from the first. Later invaluable editorial guidance came from Bob Hack, Cindy Hyden, and
Cathcrine Monk of Jason Aronson Inc. Without their assistance this
book would never have seen the light of day.

I owe a special dept of gratitude to Hadar Lubin, M.D., and David
Johnson, Ph.D. Dr. Lubin invited me to undertake the original project at the National Center for PTSD, West Haven Medical Center,
and, importantly, suggested videotaping the life stories of the veterans. Dr. Johnson was the creator of the unit, a unique healing community, and my primary supervisor there. In fact, all staff persons
were invariably supportive and helpful. Dori Laub, M.D., was also
generous in his encouragement and, as co-founder of the Yale Video
Archive of Holocaust Testimonies, is one of the leading advocates of
the video recording of the narratives of survivors of overwhelming
trauma.

■ ■

There are any number of writers whose works contributed in ways difficult to specify, but I feel it necessary to mention at least of few of these. First and foremost is Inger Agger (1994), a Danish clinician working with the victims of trauma. Her elegant little book, *The Blue Room*, was a constant inspiration. James Young's (1988) enlightened study of the writings and other forms of documentation by and about survivors, *Writing and Rewriting the Holocaust*, was an inspiration especially in its intellectual honesty and the subtlety of its analysis. Lawrence Langer's (1991) *Holocaust Testimonies* is based on the Yale tapes and sets a high standard for writings on video testimonies, not to mention Langer's profound understanding of trauma and how it interacts with survivors' narratives. Dori Laub's writings, of course, were instrumental in fashioning an approach to the material upon which this book is based. Jonathan Shay's (1994) *Achilles in Vietnam*, a study based on parallel texts in Vietnam veterans' stories and Homer's *Iliad*, is especially significant in its unique perspective on the warrior's archetypal story. The list could go on, particularly when it comes to the Vietnam literature. Robert Mason's (1993) *Chickenhawk* is one of the best of the books to come out of the war, along with Philip Caputo's (1977) *A Rumor of War*, Tim O'Brien's (1969/1973) *If I Die in a Combat Zone*, and, for military history, Harold Moore and Joseph Galloway's (1992) classic account of the first major battle in America's involvement in the war, *We Were Soldiers Once . . . and Young*.

Closer to home, my wife, Tracy L. Smith, M.S.W., served as constant supporter and first critic of both the collection of the videotapes and the work of writing. Her insightful comments along the way were invaluable.

Finally, I feel a debt of gratitude that I cannot put adequately into words to the courageous and honorable men who contributed their stories so generously.

1

BEFORE THE STORY BEGINS

■ I am afraid to forget. I fear that we human creatures do not forget cleanly, as the animals presumably do. What protrudes and does not fit in our pasts rises to haunt us and makes us spiritually unwell in the present.

J. Glenn Gray, The Warriors

■ Thwarted, uncommunalized grief is a major reason why there are so many severe, long-term psychological injuries from the Vietnam War.

Jonathan Shay, Achilles in Vietnam

■ We were men who had gone to war. Each of us had his story to tell, his own nightmares. Each of us had been made cold by this thing. We wore ribbons and uniforms. We talked of death and atrocity to each other with unaccustomed gentleness.

Ron Kovic, Born on the Fourth of July

■ We who have experienced war directly have a responsibility to share our insight and experience concerning the truth of war. We are the light at the tip of the candle. It is very hot, but it has the power of shining and illuminating. . . . We know what war is. We also know that the war is not only in us; it is in everyone—veterans and non-veterans. We must share our insight, not out of anger, but out of love.

Thich Nhat Hanh, Love in Action

1

The active involvement of the U.S. in the Vietnam War ended in the Spring of 1973, when the last U.S. soldiers and 591 prisoners of war left the country. The Vietnam War goes on in the hearts and minds of American combat veterans, in their flashbacks and nightmares and in their haunted memory of traumatic events they experienced as 18- and 19-year-old adolescents ten thousand miles from home. Then, after a tour of twelve or thirteen months that seemed to lie outside of time, the survivors came back. There was no welcome home for them, no parades. On the contrary, returning home they were spat upon and reviled at West Coast airports, only to be subsequently marginalized and forgotten by society. The military did not help them in any real way; there were no debriefings, no attempts to heal their psychic wounds. Having endured experiences beyond words, they were simply afforded the routine change of clothes, perhaps a steak dinner, then a taxi back to the airport to catch a plane home. Their families didn't want to listen either. "Forget it," they were told, "put it behind you." This cruel rejection only served to deepen the damage to their already ravaged souls. Returning warriors, after all, are traditionally treated better than that.

The returning warrior is traditionally met by his people and treated as a hero, defeated or triumphant. His wounds are cared for by loved ones; he is washed of the blood and grime of battle. He is given rest. Inevitably, as in the Native American traditions, his suffering and his triumph are recognized—and treated—ritualistically. The warrior moves by ritual stages back into the society of his people; his standing, in fact, will be enhanced by his service in battle. At some point, there will be an opportunity, probably more than one, to tell his story. Around the campfire, the old and the very young will gather, and the returning warrior will tell his tale of war. Sadness and joy can be shared; grieving and laughter can mingle in the telling and the listening. In this way, a community that has been wounded and torn by warfare may restore itself and find meaning by way of telling and retelling. The warrior will be recognized and

2

heard by his people. An account of the warrior's experiences contributes to the tradition of his people, and he becomes himself a figure in that tradition. Jonathan Shay (1994), a V. A. psychiatrist with extensive experience working with Vietnam veterans, takes note in his book *Achilles in Vietnam* of the damage wrought by the closing off of this ritual sharing of the burden. Ron Kovic (1976), himself a wounded warrior who recounts his struggles during and after the war in his *Born on the Fourth of July*, recalls the fellowship among Vietnam veterans, something they had to wait all too long to achieve and an unburdening that they had first to fashion for themselves. The gathering together and intermingling of stories in this book will (it is hoped) achieve a small part of this reintegration process for the veterans who contributed their stories and to those who will hear them, even while substituting a video camera for the campfire. (The videotaping of these narratives was originally part of a dissertation project carried out at a V. A. hospital; it is described in some detail in the afterword.) The veterans responded to the invitation to contribute their stories with generosity and (it is not too much to say) love, though the stories they told are painful and fraught with anxiety, anger, and sorrow.

These narratives are all exemplars of what may be called the self-narrative, that genre we all use, one way or another, when we speak of ourselves and of our lives. The stories we tell, whether they are life stories or just anecdotal treatment of the day's events, have impact and, indeed, create meaning through the arrangement of their parts, the expressiveness of language, their overall shaping, and, of course, their teller's knack for spinning the tale. This is, it seems, a talent with which we are born. Susan Engel (1995), author of a study of the emergence of narrative in childhood, *The Stories Children Tell*, demonstrates that telling stories is something human creatures do from the first, quite naturally and spontaneously. Engel shows how even at an early age children use language to organize their internal world and lay down the narrational structures they will use throughout life. She speaks of "the cooling function of storytelling, and the role it plays in helping to gain mastery over emotions" (p. 40). Though Engel's focus is on childhood's normative emotional experience, the point is quite relevant to the trauma narratives of adults: telling and retelling permit working through and a sense of mastery over otherwise unmanageable material.

If your experiences are beyond words they remain formless. In fact, they lodge in your gut; they stay with you as the visceral traces of overwhelming events. One of the Vietnam veterans whose stories make up Al Santoli's (1981) *Everything We Had* put it this way: "Before I went over I knew a couple of friends that came back. I asked, What was it like? and they didn't know how to explain it and I didn't know what I was asking. And I ended up being the same way. Almost mute" (p. 133). Muteness speaks to the absence of an accounting in words and to that of which you know but cannot speak. In addition, there are the gaps in memory that many Vietnam veterans experience; many of the veterans speak of a time when their memory of their war experiences is sketchy at best. For Jim E., this was the period of a month or more after the beginning of the Tet offensive, January 31, 1968, preceded for him by a series of traumatic search-and-destroy missions and a long period of extremely heavy combat. For Ed W., it was most of his last four months in country and after a series of overwhelming events, two of which he relates on his tape.

Trauma memory's distressing reexperiencings are seemingly distinct from the kind of narrative memory that ordinarily sorts through the flow of events, experiences, and emotions to construct a life story or simply an adequate account of the day's events. Traumatic memories, on the other hand, are highly literalistic, repetitive, and disorienting. The content of flashbacks, nightmares, and intrusive thoughts consists of the elements from which a narrative account could be made, but they appear rather in the form of sensory information—the sights, sounds, and smells, often of amazing complex-

4

ity and vividness. By comparison, stories are distillations of experienced reality. The veterans who told their stories before the video camera were all able to construct coherent and powerful accounts of their Vietnam experiences, and, at the same time, they continue to suffer. Telling one's story is not a cure; it should be seen, however, as a significant step on the path to recovery. Obviously, narrativization of traumatic memories must include some form of significant linking to at least one other, the listener/witness, and, most powerfully, also to one's community, beginning with one's group of fellow veterans.

Flashbacks, nightmares, intrusive thoughts—these are the disturbing reiterations of traumatic experiences that *protrude* (to use the image of J. Glenn Gray (1970), the World War II veteran and author of the classic *The Warriors*). The related effects run virtually the entire gamut, from distortions in personality structure to ruptures in relationship and an inability to tolerate intimacy of any kind, to hypervigilence, to paranoia, even to a kind of addiction to the rush that danger brings: reenactments, risk taking of all kinds. Then, especially, the survivor used street drugs and alcohol to control the inner turmoil, something treaters and veterans alike call self-medication (medicated forgetting would do as well). Just as the nation had turned away, treaters for years would by and large ignore the profound clinical implications of war trauma. It is no wonder that Vietnam veterans were frequently misdiagnosed and treated as hopelessly neurotic or psychotic or characterologically disordered. Many have stories to tell of being locked in psychiatric wards and placed on Thorazine and similar antipsychotic medications, or, more commonly, treated briefly with no acknowledgment of their trauma histories and then sent on their way. It is not that war trauma's profound effect on the person is anything new. In World War II the term used most commonly was *battle fatigue*, in World War I *shell shock*. It was thought that the concussions from shells exploding did damage to the neurological system, an early attempt to come to a bio-

logical understanding of psychological trauma. War trauma, whatever it is called, is, rather, a human universal, something that Shay
(1994) demonstrates in *Achilles in Vietnam*, where he juxtaposes
quotations from the spoken recollections of Vietnam veterans with
passages from the *Iliad*. The battle experiences of Homer's warriors,
in this context, cast in a universal light the combat experiences of
the U. S. foot soldiers, the grunts, who continue to live a double
life, one foot in the present, the other stuck in the mud and grime
of Vietnam.

It is an understatement to say that the experience of the veterans as very young men has shaped their lives since, that they have
lived as aliens in their own land for over two decades, that they
have sought treatment for years. Only in the last ten years have
they been able to anticipate understanding and help from treaters—
and usually only from those with specific training in treatment of
post-traumatic conditions. By reason of their trauma and, more so,
by way of the misapprehension and outright hostility with which
returning warriors were greeted, leading to marginalization and isolation, Vietnam veterans have lived in another world, not The World
that they anticipated returning to. One of Michael Herr's (1991)
grunts remarks, "Far's I'm concerned, this one's over the day I get
home" (p. 250). Nothing could have been further from the truth for
the overwhelming majority. Home but not really home, living in a
psychic landscape of one's own, driven to try to maintain its boundaries by the hypervigilance that comprises one of the core effects of
overwhelming trauma, perhaps enacting the feeling of dangerous isolation by literal escape for years into the woods, the Vietnam veteran was left to dwell within his own isolated world.

The narratives here tell of jungle warfare, unimaginable violence,
and prolonged overwhelming trauma. In the telling, the dim horizons of a firebase or the ominous clearings of Vietnamese villages
come vividly to mind for the participants. These are alien horizons,
yet the veterans manage to convey much of their experience both in

6

what they relate and, especially, in how they relate it. In some cases, the formative power of this kind of storytelling is especially apparent. In a few cases, the veteran came into the exercise with a specific narrative goal (confession, closure, political purpose). At the same time, the veterans saw themselves as entering into something larger than their own story, as contributing to a permanent, collective historical record. It seems that the very opportunity to speak out had an enhancing effect on treatment and contributed to the individual's sense of belonging to a healing community. Taken together, the narratives do clearly converge to widen the scope of the Vietnam veteran's story. On the other hand, it is possible to see the way narrative norms work to constrain and distort. This is particularly so insofar as the Vietnam veteran also suffers from the collective amnesia of the country as a whole regarding the war.

The question of historical documentation was raised with the participants, but they were asked only to speak about their own experiences, what they themselves went through. By listening to their stories much may be learned about the rendering of a recollected reality by persons profoundly affected by the trauma of war and the ways in which they make use of culturally available, multiple narrative conventions to improvise, as it were, a life story for the moment. This last point is critical. People tell versions of this and that depending on the given context. This is not to say that they are telling untruth; rather, the telling of a tale is always a telling to and for and with someone. This, then, would bring the experiences of the individual participants into closer alignment with the wider community, providing a somewhat greater field for reconciliation and healing. That reconciliation and healing can take place through narrative may seem a bold claim. On the other hand, telling one's story or listening to another's story are complex and commonplace activities that hold out the promise of change for the better for the teller and the listener—and for society. Thich Nhat Hanh (1993), the Vietnamese Buddhist monk and spiritual leader, was a participant as a peace activist and as someone who suffered along with all who were there in the decade of America's intense involvement. He reminds us that we all share responsibility, and so everyone who remembers has a story that must be told. This book, by gathering together the stories of a number of Vietnam veterans, comes to constitute one of the narratives about a war that is still to be integrated into the collective memory. Veterans of all kinds, American, Vietnamese, civilian participants, and those of us on the anguished sidelines all have a part of the story to contribute.

■ ■ ■

A word about the title: one of the veterans told a story of love and trauma. The events that make up this tale were overwhelmingly painful, given its tragic outcome. Still in the combat zone, he decided that he would put off dealing with these memories, and, since they were so devastating and impossible to manage at the time, he elected to lock them up in a memory chamber for twenty-five years, where they remained until, exactly twenty-five years later, the door sprang open. So, of all the many people, named and unnamed, who have influenced and inspired the present work, I must thank Alan S. first of all, for his wisdom bought at too high a price, his wit, his creativity, and for his gift of the perfect title.

2

■ ■ ■ ■ ■ ■ ■ ■ ■ ■ ■ ■ ■

GROWING UP IN ANOTHER TIME

■ It took me till later to figure—they aren't really memories, they're like mental glimpses, little pictures that I can still kind of recall. And it took me till I was older to put those pictures into where they made sense to me, y'know, how I got to be how I got to be.

Phil B., *The Chambers of Memory*

■ I confess that in my adolescence and early manhood, before World War II, I longed for one more war, in which I might participate.

J. Glenn Gray, *The Warriors*

■ I remember going out after the school bell rang and I went home that night. And it seems like I woke up the next morning and I could smell diesel fuel and hear sounds of war. And I was someplace far, far away from home. And I was scared and I was lonely and I was— I was terrified of the fact that something was going to happen to me. And I was in Vietnam.

Arthur S., *The Chambers of Memory*

PRELUDE

Memory of childhood and growing up is especially selective, its narratives especially subject to the structuring effects of fantasy, family lore, and the culture's mythology. As we scan back to the remotest part of our histories, we naturally look for what is meaningful to later chapters in our stories. We seek motivation in the ongoing improvisation of our self-narratives. Motivation implies explanation, rationale, congruence of some kind. Motivation also denotes something formal, that which drives the plot or generates structure. In fiction, this can be as obvious and determinative as a character's name: Squire Allworthy, Raskolnikov, Nurse Ratched. Something as direct may well be operative in the construal of the early phases of the stories we tell of ourselves. If you grew up in the country, you might structure or motivate your narrative by way of down-to-earth country values or the principles of native pragmatism. Or you might strive to differentiate yourself from a humbler background and for decades maintain, quite contrary to the facts, that your formative years really began when you entered the university. Looking back to childhood and adolescence from the vantage point of a quarter of a century is a recreative and reconstructive task for anyone. The material from which one's life narrative is fashioned have been reworked time and again as the life course flows and as the view from the present is constantly affected by the shifting perspectives that aging alone introduces. Reappraisal of one's past is part of the work of assimilating today's developmental tasks. This stage-related perspectivism can be discerned in the stories people tell about themselves, of course. Less obvious but equally true, the perspective of this particular time of life is being generated by the reworking of the life story. In other words, the past interacts dynamically with the present to produce the narrative shape that memory takes.

When traumatic experiences loom large in the past, their effect can hardly be ignored in the retelling of earlier times. Vietnam veterans today are in midlife, around the ages of forty-three or -four to fifty, definitely a natural period of reappraisal and assimilation of the hard facts of aging, if nothing else. In anyone's story now there is quite probably less time remaining than lived through so far. For the Vietnam veteran there is the lingering taint of trauma memory and the difficult task of attempting to come to terms with the profound, and still ongoing, effects of combat experienced as a late adolescent. There is also a forbidding sense of little time remaining. Two decades of struggling with the effects of wartime experiences have taken their toll on everyone. Many comrades have succumbed; Vietnam veterans are often attending, or avoiding attending, funerals these days. Thus, there is a further shift in perspective, a radical one, as the foreshortened future means that, now in middle age, the end could come quickly. As in Vietnam, it could come at any moment. This has the effect of rendering the distant past even further away. The time before the war, the first seventeen or eighteen years of life, appear in the veterans' accounts as a brief, long-lost prelude, the merest preface to the larger and vastly more painful time at war, which for most was limited to one year that seemed to never end. "What did I get myself into?" is something more than one young soldier thought as he stepped off the plane into the stifling heat and disorienting chaos of Vietnam. Something like family tradition might have been critical in the fateful decision to go down the path leading up to that moment.

A version of a family myth often lies at the heart of the account of a life; one is fulfilling a certain familial destiny or carrying on, or diverging from, a family tradition. Many veterans, in fact, mention especially that their fathers or uncles or men in the neighborhood were combat veterans of World War II, heroic figures with stories to tell. John Wayne is another figure regularly cited as influential in shaping expectations of military service. In the narrative tradition in which the contributors and their comrades grew up and attained adolescence in the late 1950s and early 1960s, stories fathers told and World War II movie heroics were blended into one fictionalized representation taken, with youthful enthusiasm, as truth, the way it really was. In addition, the veterans often allude to the heated rhetoric of public pronouncements emanating from the White House and elsewhere and establishing the simplistic public mindset of the

11

time on both domestic and international events. Although no one here mentions it specifically, this was also a time when the words of a young President, recently assassinated, could still resonate in youthful hearts. Ask not what your country can do for you but what you can do for your country is one thing; the myth of America as the bastion and defender of freedom lurks behind it all. This was the simple story of danger to the Land of the Free as mortally threatened by what a later, aged President would call the Evil Empire.

THE STORY BEGINS

The veterans' stories begin, in all cases, with some reference back to family life and high school days, some attempt at alignment of what went before with what came after. Most, however, exhibit at least some indication of the significant disruption to memory that accompanies prolonged terror and violence in the alien region of the combat zone. Looking back to the beginning, these narrators must deal with the transition between beginning (childhood and growing up) and the middle (Vietnam and after) as rupture, as a violent shift in perspective. Most take explicit note of the jarring contrast between their life before and their first exposure to what was to become the long middle phases of their stories, their tour in Vietnam with its sense of lying outside time, followed by the prolonged years of suffering since. Many recollect their early days to have been halcyon and carefree; a few others refer to traumatic childhoods. One or two condense their accounts to the point where they seem to have had only the briefest life before the military and Vietnam. It must seem this way to them. Arthur S.'s account of life before is brief but rich in detail, including references to childhood abuse. It moves from before to *being there* with breathtaking deftness. No matter how extended the transition is, however, in all the stories there comes a moment when the 18- or 19-year-old soldier, so recently a fun-loving kid, high school athlete, misfit, or dropout is face to face with the harsh realities of combat. Virtually all the narratives share this feature: that moment of the terrifying realization of the blatant reality of life and death in the battle zone. Thus, the accounts given of "life before Vietnam" actually end structurally with the veteran in Vietnam and suddenly in possession of a new vision of what his life is to be about for what now must look like an eternity, a time in hell to be terminated by death, a terrible wounding, or, at long last, the flight back home to The World.

Wayne W.

Wayne W.'s style of speech is eliptical in the extreme, which has the effect of heightening the tendency in the veterans' stories to condense the account of growing up before going to war.

> My life started back in Western New York, a small dairy farming community called Cuba. I spent sixteen years of my life there. Moved to Connecticut. Finished high school. Got a bad draft number. Enlisted in the U. S. Navy 'cause I didn't want to go to Vietnam and get my ass shot off.

This is about as terse an account of a life to age 18 as we are going to get. What about the family, siblings? What was it like there in that tiny town with the exotic name? Why go to Connecticut? Certainly it was a family thing, but we are not to know any of that. Judging by Wayne's numerous anecdotes about his time in Vietnam—he ended up there after all, of course—he was an athletic and fun-loving teenager. We're going to be left to speculate, however; Vietnam looms so large in memory that what one hopes and assumes were good times earlier are lost to this story, just as, we have to assume, they are fundamentally lost for Wayne. Not that this little introduction lacks narrative integrity. Its first few sketchy images capture in a quick, almost cinematographic style a typical kid in a typical family growing up in a typical farming community, a dairy-farming community, actually. That's important. (It must be to have made its way into Wayne's spare beginning.) Then comes a disjuncture, the move to Connecticut with its chilling event, getting a bad draft number. Now Wayne begins to specify and to fill in the details and to supply affect-laden language, just at the point that Vietnam enters the frame.

Things don't work out according to his quite reasonable plan, as we learn from a few more of Wayne's clipped phases. He becomes a Seabee (i.e., a naval engineer), member of an organization he describes with some pride as "basically a construction company—but we shoot back." He "laid a lot of asphalt" in other venues, until military life started going sour for him (though, typical of Wayne's account, we do not learn why).

> Right about then, me and the military weren't getting along too good, we had a difference of opinion. And that's when they said that we need volunteers to go to Vietnam and if you'll volunteer to go to Vietnam, we'll let you out a year early. Yeah, that sounds like a good deal. Well, guess what!

The Navy's good deal turns out, of course, to be a matter of twelve months of terror with the military's construction company, punctuated by a few good moments drinking and smoking pot back at base camp and even some fun out on the road. By volunteering in exchange for getting out of the military a year early, Wayne was blindly choosing random violence and daily terror. His handling of the prelude to this period in his life, the shadow of which will darken his life in future, is in its unconscious structuring and its sparseness as right as the opening moves of an Updike short story. The sense of a life divided and times lost is especially apparent. Vietnam splits life in two, with the days before collapsed into just a few moments, some basic details, and life after stretching out over two decades that also seem but moments in retrospect. Again and again, the veterans recognize this collapsing together of a vast stretch of time: Where did that quarter of a century go?

Alan J.

The more typical accounts of early life supply a picture of happier times marked by a naive hopefulness about the future. Alan J., an African-American, remembers growing up in New Haven fondly, a time he recalls as one of opportunity and free of prejudice.

Childhood days were good, 'cause we had a middle-class family, owned a house. We came from New York, moved to Connecticut, and lived in the projects maybe until I was 3 years old. Then, we moved to our house in New Haven, and I'm still living in that house at 47, so that's how long I've been living in this house. My family—my mother didn't work. My father, he was the boss of the house, he didn't want her to work because he was old-fashioned. He was a mailman. I didn't see him that often, because he had to work from Monday to Saturday. My uncle Bubba was the guy who took us fishing, to baseball games, etc. I loved my family. We didn't get beat; we did get scolded, we had to stay in the house. Kids would come and knock on the door and say, "Come out." But I'd say, "I can't." I gave my parents that much respect; I wouldn't sneak behind them. Ah, now as I got older, I did a lot of fishing, bike riding, skating. I was good with my hands—I'm a carpenter today—so I used to build go-carts. . . . I used to do all that, race go-carts, when I was younger. Then I turned 16 and got a driver's license. Everything changed—girls!

Nothing could sound more ordinary or more untouched by tragedy or even by discrimination. Nothing in Alan's later life, after Vietnam, is untouched, however, by the horrific disorientation deriving from twelve months of jungle warfare. So, like all the stories told here, his, too, is shot through with irony: look how good life started for me and see how badly it has ended. Alan goes on to recall how he got his first car (his father rarely let him have the family car), about being a track star ("the 100 in 9.8, 9.9"), about going out with girls, then unexpectedly getting a draft notice. His plan to attend college on an athletic scholarship goes by the board. He has no thought of not responding to his country's call, at least he reports nothing of the kind. His story, then, employs an idyllic picture of early years that contrasts completely with later suffering, which is a tendency evident in virtually all of the veterans' stories.

Jim D.

For a very few of the contributors, childhood and especially adolescence seem to spring to mind vividly and to exercise sufficient allure in the moment to result in a fuller representation, a narrative richer in detail. Jim D.'s introductory account is a case in point. His native enthusiasm comes through clearly, as if the very process of recollecting carries him away. The good times have not faded to memory's dark chambers of oblivion; recalling them can still evoke a spirited narrative. Jim ranges freely, albeit briefly, over his earlier years, speaking of friends and family, in particular of his grandfather, who would take him hunting and who gave him a shotgun when he was 7 or 8. Flying was something his father inspired in him by the time Jim was 13 or 14. His father had been an aviator during World War II.

And he was taking flying lessons himself at this time. He was a waist gunner in 17s himself during World War II, in the bombing of Germany and Europe, the infrastructure of the Third Reich. He had a lot of pictures that he showed me, growing up . . . of him and his squadron and so on. I guess this was an influence on me, at least as far as my flying went. And I could actually fly an airplane, a Piper Cub, long before I could drive a car, like three or four years before I could drive a car. In fact, I did pretty well in high school, but I cut a lot of classes. And in the afternoons when I had the money or I'd have the other guys kick in—I couldn't take passengers, but I'd get a guy who was older—the airport was about ten, fifteen miles away—and he'd drive down there, and they'd park down the road. And I'd go rent the airplane and taxi back up—it was out of sight of the operations building. And they'd climb in and we'd go for a joy ride in an airplane—used to buzz the high school in fact. Never got caught! But I guess it was in my senior year in high school that the Army was coming through and telling us there were opportunities—most of the services were, I guess. I remember the army, and they caught my attention whereas they had a flying program.

The year was 1966. Jim was aware that the Vietnam War was going on at that time, but, as he says, "it was fifth or sixth page—it wasn't on people's minds; at least it wasn't on mine!" Jim continues to tell of the good times before the service, when he was already committed to flight training with the U. S. Army but still out enjoying his youth to the fullest. As his story progresses, the fun never really stops. Vietnam, too, could be a place where a determined young aviator could have a good time. That the young are full of enthusiasm and ready for adventure is as apparent in Jim's narrative as is their naïveté. It was not until he reached flight school that he realized he would be flying helicopters, not airplanes. And, as his story unfolds, with high jinks and fun predominating right through training and shipping out to Vietnam, we nowhere detect any of the second thoughts and trepidations that are frequently expressed in others' accounts at this point. Instead, we sense the enthusiasm of the kid who learned to fly before he could get a driver's license. Rather than going directly out of flight school to Vietnam with most of his classmates, Jim was assigned to a new unit forming up. He was a kid still, a recent high-school graduate.

That's where I started to specialize. I got into the gun platoon, and I really enjoyed that. I really liked the fire missions. We used to go out and fire inert rounds, rockets; there were no inert machine gun rounds, but we had miniguns. I loved those things, I loved the rate of fire, I loved to watch just the red tracers. They were capable of firing six thousand rounds a minute, but we fired at about two thousand because of the vibration and the amount of ammo . . . which was sufficient, I guarantee ya.

I loved to hear the sound of them going off, it sounded like an electric discharge, I can't really describe it. But it was not like pop-pop-pop or bang-bang-bang. All you saw was a line of red; every fifth round was a tracer, and that's all you saw, a red line like a laser line touching the ground.

Such is the mystique of the military, with all its hardware, for young men. In Jim's discourse we can read unmistakably the way in which the fiery energy of adolescence meshes perfectly with the aggressive design of the equipment of war—and its power. This matching of delight in mechanical extravagance to wildly destructive force continues to inform Jim's narrative; it is also characteristic of something known about all war. As Gray (1970) expresses it in *The Warriors*, there's a "beauty in destruction" (p. 36). And there is a price to pay. Although Jim is never hurt, in spite of being shot down, crashing, and experiencing numerous close calls, he sees and experiences enough death. (A co-pilot of his is shot from below, the bullet piercing his head from underneath, and a crew member has to support the body to keep it from falling onto the controls while Jim flies home.) It seems that the thrill of flight and the exhilaration of commanding such firepower at the touch of a button never really fades. In fact, Jim returned for a second tour in Vietnam, this time flying the heavy Chinook cargo helicopter, spending much less time under fire and even more time than before in what he often refers to as "partying."

Jim D. is obviously someone with tremendous reserves of energy and enthusiasm still, rendering his whole account more of a piece with his lively testimony to the pleasures of his youth. Thus, it seems that temperament may overcome the distortions of trauma memory, at least to this degree: one may still remain more in possession of the story of one's years before traumatic events changed life irrevocably. This has the effect of providing a sense of more narrative wholeness and coherence. One gets the feeling that he takes the violence that he encountered in abundance in Vietnam and the suffering that ensued by way of addictions, broken relationships, and the dampening of commitment as just something that happened thanks to bad timing. He joined the service to fly; the fact that there was a war going on did not have any impact on that fateful decision. The fact that the war caught up with him quickly while in training, where everyone could count on going to Vietnam sooner or later, is presented as if it were just another factor, just another chance convergence of circumstances. At least, Jim seems to take it this way, which may help to account for his being, to all appearances, less haunted by his Vietnam experiences than many of the other narrators here. In addition, his narrative memory may be more intact; in any event, his story of early years is more detailed and more directly related to what comes after. It is indicative that Jim gives no hint of memory loss, something many of the veterans mention in their stories as happening to them.

OTHER STORIES, OTHER BEGINNINGS

That traumatic memories may be dissociated is a commonplace; that trauma affects one's very perception of self before the trauma and one's ability to tell the story of life before is something demonstrated again and again in the veterans' stories. When childhood and adolescence were in reality distressed, either because of abuse or some family circumstance, then the narrator is faced with the task of dealing with this aspect of his or her life in the course of telling the life story. Looking back, then, one's past may seem to be doubly cursed, first by the sufferings of the child, then by the distortions of combat experiences endured in late adolescence. This is not to mention the burden of life haunted for twenty-five years by the disorienting images of trauma memory. Making narrative sense of all this is a daunting task but one that the several narrators who recount events in an abusive or distressed childhood take in stride.

Mark A.

Mark A. supplies a coherent and thematically decisive account of his life before Vietnam; everything is explained and motivated. He speaks of his large family and its trials. His father was and, he emphasizes, remains an alcoholic; his mother died when Mark was 6. His father then remarried quickly, within a year. He gives several revealing instances of his father's caring "only for himself" and of his stepmother's devotion to the family.

> He cared only about himself, basically. He made it extremely difficult for her. No matter what she tried to do, he threw her down. She was out working—he wanted his share of the money so he could buy his booze and do what he wanted to do. More times than once she threatened and did leave for short periods—it was just too much for her—but then returned for us. I give her, I can't say enough for her. Because she did come back and think more about us than she did about herself, which took a heavy toll on her, physically. My father kept threatening to break us up as we grew up, give us to different families, different aunts and uncles. My uncle stepped in and said, "You're not going to do this."

In Mark's retelling, he always tried to do the right thing, and his stepmother tried her best to encourage and nurture him. This young man clearly adopted his stepmother as a model, striving always, as she did, to do what's right. Mark pushed to finish high school early, squeaking by in math and excelling in physics, in order to enter the military at the first possible opportunity. For one thing, Mark wanted to preclude a brother with a pregnant wife from having to go to war. (There was a policy that prohibited someone from being sent to Vietnam if his brother was already serving there.) His motivation was not unambiguous, altruism blending with animosity toward his father.

> I was able to get out of high school halfway through my senior year. Basically, I graduated in January instead of June. The reason for my pushing in high school—I'd say the eleventh and twelfth years where I

20

really started pushing—because I wanted to go in the service. Vietnam was going on and I saw things on TV that upset me, and I wanted to do my part in Vietnam. I wanted to get over there and help do what I could. A particular incident would be Khe Sanh; I was watching things go on there. And here I am sitting at home, there were meals on the table. Yet there were guys that needed help over there. My father was still drinking, making things hard for us at home. Another reason I acted to go to Vietnam was to try to give him something to worry about. Instead of pushing on my mother and everybody else, let him start worrying about me possibly getting killed over there.

His father, however, was hardly nonplussed by his departure for the combat zone.

As Mark speaks he does not take note of the emptiness of his altruistic sentiments, but from his later account it is perfectly clear that he now has a deep and quite personal grasp of the futile nature of the war. He is not at pains to take anything like a political perspective here; his story is told from the point of view of a decent and caring man whose life has been tainted by combat experiences that reduced his idealism to the common denominator that binds all foot soldiers together. As he says, "It just overtook us—kill or be killed." The fundamental disjuncture between the cold realities of the war, its futility, its brutality, its negation of ordinary morality (all of which Mark recognizes implicitly in his later account) and his youthful idealism are givens of the narrative strategy that he adopts. So here is a childhood and adolescence remembered in a moment in time over twenty-five years later, after a year of traumatic wartime experiences and the long aftermath. The story of this distant time functions perfectly to motivate both the young marine's participation in the war and the young man's struggles afterward: do the right thing, help others, put the family before all else. Mark's childhood and growing up certainly comprised more than his striving to follow the righteous path of his stepmother and his religious upbringing, which he mentions only briefly. We are told nothing of any adolescent rebellion, any conflict, any acting out. This would have constituted another version of his story. This narrator goes intuitively to the central theme of his story, early and late: a fateful striving to *do the right thing.*

Jim E.

Jim is one of the veterans who makes explicit, although not detailed, reference to a severely abusive childhood. His strength of character is evident in his account. As he begins his story, he speaks briefly about his large family and mentions his religious upbringing and how the Catholic Church was a refuge for him.

> I found that for me it was a safe place. My father was an alcoholic—he drank an awful lot—and as a young fellow I was physically abused, quite badly. I never forgave him for that. I remember the pain and fear and the anxiety I felt sometimes when he came home drunk. I was frightened to death, and my way of handling that was to go to the church and be with the nuns. My mother . . . was an RN—my older sister was handicapped with cerebral palsy, and that left her at home most of the time caring for my sister. For me it was a life alone on the street. I had to learn about everything by myself. I had nobody there to point me in the right direction or [show me] how to handle difficult situations or people. It was like this for most of my young age, up until I was 10 or 11. . . . So there was a lot to growing up in a dysfunctional family. It was very difficult for me to understand why things were and why they were happening to me, why I had to go through all this.

Jim goes on to review his schooling quickly and to tell about transferring from Catholic school to public school, all the while getting good grades, getting along well with people and remaining with the Church. He played sports as a youth, both for his church and for his school. With the greater independence of high school years, things changed for the better.

Academically, I was a real good student, and I found my high school years rather pleasant. I had a steady girlfriend, and the fun we had was plain and simple. There was never any substance abuse involved because I was never, ever drawn to wanting to drink or to drug because I was actively involved in sports. In the middle of high school, things began to change; I began to hear Vietnam mentioned, sporadically, every now and then. And not knowing what it was, I just ignored it. By the time I was in my senior year in high school, I knew that there was a conflict going on in Vietnam, and I also knew that I had to spend some time in the military. Both my mother and my father were veterans of World War II. My father was a pilot, and my mother was a flight nurse. We were taught to serve our country honorably and faithfully, to fight Communism. So by the time I got down to the draft board I believed I was going to fight Communism—Communists—that I was there to serve my country when they called me. One of the other reasons I got involved in the military was because I had a younger brother. His name was Jack; he was three years younger than me, and I figured if I went to Vietnam there was a good possibility he wouldn't go. And so that's what I did. I enlisted in the U. S. Army and asked for special training as an infantryman and a paratrooper.

Here, as in Mark's story, a young man grows up in a distressed environment; he attempts valiantly to withstand environmental stress and, like Mark A., to do the right thing, even to the point of volunteering for combat duty in the military to protect a brother from having to go to war. (A third veteran among the contributors, Roosevelt H., tells of a similar motivation for volunteering.)

Doing the right thing and serving one's country are of a piece; they go together like loyalty to one's school and to one's family. Jim is also, like many veterans, following in his parents' footsteps. The moral, societal, and familial imperatives of youth come together to compel the young into the most serious of commitments. That this irresistible impulse to serve leaves young men with no alternatives is obvious, not thoughtful young men like Mark and Jim. As will quickly become apparent in Jim's story, the idealism of youth with its unambiguous treatment of right and wrong is quickly replaced by the stark reality of the combat zone with its ambiguous—and utterly alien—choices. Jim does not lament the very real trials and traumas of his childhood and adolescence, but he emerges as a passionate champion of the exploited and the underprivileged. As he looks back on the day he stepped forward and took the oath of allegiance, his perspective is clear and his tone unambiguously condemnatory.

> I can remember going to New York, the guys getting on the buses. . . . They were all young fellows who were poor. They came out of the ghettos, they came out of the South. They were all young men who lived in poverty and whose families could not afford to keep them out of the service at that time. Most of the guys that were wealthy or were in school were able to avoid the draft. And so this is the way it was—it was just a group of young men, very young, because essentially they had no other recourse.

Jim speaks here, as he does throughout his story, in a somber and somewhat dispassionate tone. With great weariness he tells of his life that is so burdened with the memory of the horrors of the twelve months he spent in Vietnam.

Willis W.

Jim identifies one large group, the vast majority, of youths off to war who came from lower-middle class and working-class families. They were heavily represented in the combat zone. All but two or three of the veterans here fit this broad profile. A large subgroup is constituted by the six African-Americans who shared their stories. Especially in the early and middle years of massive build-up of troops in Vietnam, African-American soldiers and young men of Hispanic descent were overrepresented in combat units. The stories African-

American veterans tell here are as varied and rich as any others, while at the same time sharing a certain theme of early hopefulness and expectation, in particular the expectation that the military would be a route to advancement for young black men growing up in a racist society in transition. Willis W.'s story, for instance, speaks of a struggle against the inequalities endemic to a racist society. He tells us he is a twin and speaks of the family having the resources to send only one of the two boys to college.

> We weren't a poor family, but by my having a twin brother we finished high school at the same time. My family couldn't afford to send both of us to college, so we decided that the one with the highest SAT score would pursue education. So at this time, I was a little leery and I wanted to leave the South. That was the time of demonstrations, the early sixties, latter part of the sixties. I had finished an all-black high school, and I really didn't know any other people, so to speak. And there was a lot of prejudice and things of that nature that we had to deal with. So I was 18 years old, my brother was going off to college so I decided to join the Marine Corps and see the world and possibly get the G. I. Bill. We made a contract, the Marine Corps and myself—I was to go into the Marine Corps Band and play the trombone, I was to go to the school of music in Norfolk, Virginia. But to no avail. After boot camp, the Vietnam War was in full blossom and the Marine Corps had different plans. They made me an 0341—mortarman, infantry.

Willis ends up with an assault force based aboard ship and sees a tremendous amount of action in the field. His story of life after Nam is testimony to the struggles of African-Americans to make a life, as well as to the depredations and suffering of Vietnam veterans traumatized in the War. Bobby R., Tom T., Willie W., and Roosevelt H. also exemplify in their stories the generation of young African-Americans who came of age in the turbulent time of the civil rights struggle—with its hopes for the future. All too often, members of this generation found themselves walking point with an M-16. One of them, Bobby R., moved constantly from unit to unit throughout his tour; he reports that wherever he went the majority of the troops he saw in the field were black.

Bobby R.

Bobby was ambitious as a youth and, judging by his account, militant as a young soldier just back from Vietnam. He begins his story with the seventh grade, describing himself as studious, athletic; he read a lot. Then, quickly, he shifts to high school, where again he excels (a word that obviously has significance for Bobby). He says he was "always politically inclined," which, looking to the future in politics, was his rationale for entering the military.

> I wanted to expand my knowledge. I came from a small town . . . a population of 1,500–2,000 people, so everybody knew everybody. And in that town—I excelled. I was pushed by family and members of the community because I was a sort of bright light of that town. So I sort of had the limelight at a very early age. I graduated high school in 1966, and I volunteered for the draft—I and several of my friends. Because we wanted some adventure; we'd heard about Vietnam. There were a lot of political issues going on at the time. There was Martin Luther King, there was Malcolm X, there were a lot of political issues. And to get a head start on what I wanted to become would be to have a military career. So I volunteered for the draft. . . . I went to basic training, and I excelled in basic training—I was in the top ten.

Things did not work out for Bobby as he had planned. They might have; he went from basic training to missile school, a skilled job that would have kept him out of Vietnam, until it was discovered that he was colorblind. (The wiring to a missile is color-coded, as he explains.) He is designated a cook, but that doesn't work either since he can't tolerate the heat and turns out to be allergic to grease. So Bobby, would-be first black mayor of his home town, moved about from unit

26

to unit in Vietnam, at first performing the function of back-up grunt, duty soldier, in one dangerous assignment after another. Here is a young black man of the sixties, from the South, with high ideals and political ambition and obvious potential, a born leader.

Bruce W.

Bruce's account of life before Vietnam is rich in detail and vivid illustration of deriving meaningful history. For him, growing up had its good times and its bad times. He mentions his extended family several times; his account of his early years tells of his having a wide circle of friends, of doing well academically through the eighth grade in a parochial school. He also speaks about his father, who was a salesman and often away from home, as an alcoholic and a gambler. The family moved often, apparently sometimes leaving behind unpaid bills. Financial problems meant Bruce had to enter public high school, which marked the end of his taking his education at all seriously. He dropped out at age 16 and, in order to have peace with his father over that, promised that he would work hard, stop staying out late and, when he turned 17, join the army and "be responsible." Then, one summer day his seventeenth birthday comes along:

Of course, I did exactly what I said I wasn't going to do. I wasn't working my job anymore, I stayed out late. And it was summertime and everything; I was just having a good time. My father woke me up and took me down to the recruiter and I had no say in the matter. My mother came to my bedroom and told me it was my birthday and she didn't want a big fight going on in the house—just to get up and go with him. I didn't even know where we were going. And so he took me down to the recruiter, and in 1967 you didn't have to be too smart to get into the service. You didn't even have to sign to get in; you could put your mark on the piece of paper and have somebody witness it and you could get in. It all happened rather quickly—almost like it wasn't really happening—

all of a sudden I was down in Fort Leonard Wood, Missouri, in basic training. . . . That was my first real separation from my family, my immediate family.

So, as in a dream, as if it wasn't really happening, childhood and adolescence come to an end. At this time, Bruce was only vaguely aware that there was a war going on in Vietnam. The Army did make some difference for Bruce, for a time at least. He began to take some pride in being in the service. His sisters told him he looked good in his uniform, and his girlfriend was impressed, too.

Sent first to Germany, Bruce began to become disaffected. He was not given work for which he was trained (as a cook); he started getting drunk regularly. He was, as he says, "still kind of feeling my way through things." Things reached a point where he could have taken a discharge on the basis of being unfit for the service, but he persevered, not wanting to dishonor his family. Then the entire unit was returned to the U. S. to be readied to ship out to Vietnam. It was a critical time for the country and a critical time in the war.

Spring of 1968, and television was full of things about Vietnam. The Democratic National Convention was getting ready to come up. It seemed like the whole country was in turmoil. I really didn't know how I felt about things at that time. Had a lot of mixed emotions. . . . We felt that we were going to go to Vietnam as a unit and that was quite fearful. I was really scared at that point, thinking about the war.

To add to the mixed emotions this 17-year-old soldier was having, his unit was given riot control training; the country was, indeed, in turmoil. Stationed quite near home, Bruce, always keenly aware of his place in the relational matrix, began to picture himself breaking up riots—with people he knew on the other side. He packed civilian clothes in with his military gear, thinking that, if called upon to deal with rioters, he might just join them. He continued to be confused about his feelings, the country, what he was going to do. He stresses that he did not have much information about the war to guide him. The soldiers coming back were no help.

> The guys that were coming back from Vietnam, they weren't saying a whole lot. They were just putting their time in and, kind of like me when I came back, they were able to tell you some of the good things, the good times they had had there. A lot of them weren't able to express what they had been through.

Bruce is one of the few veterans here to express some confusion about the reasons for going to war. In addition, he depicts himself throughout as someone who had a hard time tolerating authority in general. The most meaningful dimension of his life is relationship. Again and again, he mentions family, family members, friends, recalling the names of fallen comrades. Relational life was really what he valued, that which he took as giving meaning. It didn't take long for radical thinking to come to the young combatants in the field. Ideas like "kill or be killed" or simply "survival" are radical, in the sense of being fundamental to a radical situation.

In a state of confusion and fed up with life at his duty station, Bruce volunteered for the only place open at the time—Vietnam. This decision, based on so little by way of insight and made under duress, led him to a critical moment, a pivotal juncture that is both dense with feeling and structurally apt.

> Next thing I knew I was getting my jungle training and going home on a thirty-day leave. I had just had my eighteenth birthday, and I went home on a thirty-day leave. And I remember having a family reunion. . . . It was in a city park there, where the swimming pool was. And I remember walking away—having a few beers socially with family members, my cousin. He was an Airborne Ranger, kind of a role model for me, almost went to Cuba in the early sixties. I remember seeing pictures of him with his uniform on, always really looked up to him. We talked a little bit. Then I found myself wandering away from my family

and standing at a fence surrounding the swimming pool; they had a huge swimming pool, which was closed at that time. I can remember thinking that that might be the last time that I'd ever see that spot again. It was a really, really special spot at that time. I thought about all my childhood days, about being in the pool and being down in the park, and my relatives. It was just like, even though the pool was closed, it was like it was full of people, full of life again, looking through the fence. And it dawned on me that that might be the last time I'd ever see that place and these people.

Like many veterans, Bruce speaks about his years before Vietnam, which clearly had their ups and downs, as preamble to what follows. Much of his account is devoted to the early part of his military service leading up to Vietnam. Indeed, it must seem to the veteran telling his story that childhood and adolescence end all too soon and all too abruptly with the jarring shift from home to the alien environment of Vietnam. This momentous disjuncture in the life course is one of the meanings that Bruce's critical moment at the town swimming pool conveys. What Bruce did not know then, of course, is that although he will survive Vietnam, he will never truly come home again, thanks to the traumatic events he will encounter there.

FASHIONING A BEGINNING

If one major concern in crafting an opening section of any story is to fashion motivation for what follows, nowhere is this more apparent in the contributors' stories than in the narrator's use of a symbolic event or critical moment, such as the one in Bruce W.'s story. His is as skillful a use of the critical turning point as any to be found in narrative literature. It gathers together human emotion, relationality, the social context, and structural features (especially the plot) in a fashion that is perhaps unconscious while remaining constructed, indeed, "literary," nevertheless.

Roosevelt H.

Roosevelt provides an example of another version of literariness: the fateful prediction of the future course of events. The device that he employs constitutes the center of his brief account of his early years, an amazing instance of prescience. This is decidedly in contrast to any psychodynamic perspective, as we shall see. Like Mark A. and Jim E., Roosevelt enlists in an effort (successful) to preclude a married brother from having to go to war. He starts his story directly with Vietnam, the first fleeting thoughts he has about going into the military, which pass until his brother, whose wife is already pregnant, gets a draft notice. As Roosevelt recounts his first period in service, basic and advanced training, he appears deep in thought. He looks off into the distance, as if gazing past the nearly thirty years since, at a 17-year-old kid who left high school with a semester remaining and joined the army for love of a brother. He provides all the dates of his service precisely; his memory of those times seems fresh, as if it had all been last year. As he begins the central passage that follows, he immediately becomes more animated; he continues fluently without a break as the narrative flow carries him forward.

I came home for leave from Fort Campbell, Kentucky, for a week, and I met this lady, I met this lady. She wanted to see me—my sister told me that she wanted to see me. I didn't know the lady and about that time it really didn't bother me about knowing anyone or not, y'know. I mean I was me, I was wild, and it didn't bother me whether I met the lady or not. But then my sister told me that she had something important to tell me. And I said, "What was it?" My sister said, "I don't know. She told me to tell you that when you came home on leave to make sure you didn't leave for Vietnam until you saw her." . . . She was an evangelist. She knew I was coming to her house before I got there. She told me to sit down, she told me not to worry. She said not to be afraid. She said she could feel it in me that I was scared to go to Vietnam. I said, "I sure am." And she said, "Well, don't be." She said, "God told me to tell you

this: you're going to get wounded but you're not going to die in Vietnam. You're going to be in Vietnam nine months and you're going to
come back home. You're going to stay in the hospital for two-and-a-half,
three months, then you're going to come back to the states. You're going
to be all right, so don't worry about it." I didn't know how to take that
at first because as far as believing was concerned, y'know, I believed in
me. At that time I knew there was a God, but I believed in me.

With that, Roosevelt's story of the evangelist's assurances is at an
end, and for a long few moments he pauses and sighs deeply as, it
would seem, he again gazes across the decades and sees himself as a
young soldier, 18 now and leaving for the battlefield, where he will
soon see and experience more violence and bravery, cowardice and
stupidity than he could ever have imagined. He will also be quickly
promoted to platoon sergeant, lose his entire platoon in one battle,
finally be wounded after nine months, then recuperate in a hospital
in Japan for two or three months and come back home, just as God
had told the evangelist. What was not told was the toll all this takes
on this young man, who, by the time he is 19, is back in the states
with a burden to carry forward in life, right up until the time of the
taping and surely beyond until the end. In fact, in Roosevelt's narrative, as with all the veterans' stories, there is a bitter irony. He
reports the words of the evangelist, with whom, by the way, we learn
he is still in contact, as reassuring: now don't worry, you won't die
in Vietnam, you'll be wounded but you'll be okay. No mention is made
of the subtext of Roosevelt's story, which is his sense that his life
ended in some fundamental way in Vietnam. The overwhelming
emotion felt throughout his story can be read on his face and in his
tears, shed and unshed.

Ray C.

Ray uses another version of the determinative moment, and quite
consciously; his narrative style is thoughtful and considered. He is

at pains to remain in control of his story and to lay it out in a reasoned and convincing fashion. Ray begins with a brief review of his background, mentioning in particular the fact that his parents immigrated from Canada and that they themselves had very little education. His father sees to it that Ray gets the best education available. In fact, before entering the service, he spent a year after high school at a seminary.

> One of the things that, I think, might be relevant for my upbringing—I remember watching TV replays, I guess, of the Nuremburg trials. And maybe because of my Catholic background and maybe because as an individual the things I was taught about morality and ethics were specifically important to me. I took them to heart. I believed in God, in caring about people, I believed in loving your fellow man, turning the other cheek, and all the things that organized religion, Christianity, Judaism, whatever, all the things that they teach their people. I wanted to be in the seminary. But anyway, before I get off the Nuremburg trials, I wanted to specifically point out that all those people on trial—they all said they just followed orders. It was an important part of their defense; it was the only part of their defense. And they were all tried and convicted, and many of them were executed because—well, the lesson for me at that point was: even if you're following orders in time of war you're accountable for your actions. These men were held accountable and executed because they committed war crimes. And that always stuck with me because society was telling us at that point you're responsible for your actions. . . . You have to follow your own conscience. At least that's the way I took it in, which fit in with my philosophy anyway.

Later, Ray, a helicopter mechanic in Vietnam, will be enraged at the wantonness of the slaughter and, in particular, at one commanding officer who ordered senseless raids in which men died, all for his own reasons and for the sake of his own speedy rise in the upper ranks of the officer corps. Indeed, problems with authority come to constitute the core of Ray's post-traumatic condition. There can be no clearer example of the way in which the contributors—all of them—consciously or unconsciously shape their stories, harmonizing what goes before with Vietnam experiences and with what comes after. Given what comes after—a time of unmitigated violence—it is no wonder that almost all of the veterans make special mention of leave-taking.

LEAVING HOME

Leave-taking is a critical juncture in any life story, an obligatory developmental move. One of the most extraordinary accounts of leaving home is provided by Willie W., whose story up to this point in his narrative is brief but explicitly referenced to family and family relationships. Here is a migrant worker's son, now in the New Haven area where the family had moved, no doubt looking for a better life. Here is how an African-American high school graduate with a great deal of motivation to move ahead, even to go to college, was introduced to the realities of the service and, as a foretaste, the inhumanity of the Vietnam war with its insatiable hunger for ever more troops in the field.

I got drafted in 1966. It was directly after I graduated from high school. I graduated in June of '66; I was inducted in October of '66. What had happened, they sent me a letter to show up at the induction center, myself and a bunch of other guys. When we got there, they locked all the doors and they gave us tests. I must have passed the test pretty high because I ended up in the military police. But the way they did it, after we took the tests they herded us out the back like cattle. They put us in a bus, took us down to the New Haven train station. There, they loaded us into boxcars, cars similar to boxcars. I think they had about five, six boxcars loaded with guys that were leaving. Some of the guys that they had in there, they had gone to the jails and got them out of jail. They could either serve their time in the service or serve their time in jail. A lot of them chose to go into the service. So after they loaded the boxcars—I think they had about five or six, something like that—we went to Bridgeport. They had about four, five more cars they linked on. From there, we went to New York, about six, seven cars they added on from New York, same thing—boxcar type. Then we went to New Jersey, they had cars they linked on. Then we went to Philadelphia, that was the last stop they linked on the cars. The longest train I've seen in my life, full of guys. After we left Philly, they opened up all the boxcars. And they had guards between each boxcar to make sure the guys wouldn't get off. And they let everybody mingle, some afraid, some guys scared. We didn't know what was going on, really. All young, high school, 18, 19. We finally ended up in Fort Jackson, South Carolina. They backed the train in, and guys started coming in with uniforms on, hitting us, beating us, talking about get into line, fall out, get in formation. Bunch of kids, scared, afraid. Finally, we got situated down there, and I did something like six, eight weeks down at Fort Jackson. It was rough, it was a struggle. My family didn't even know where I was for those weeks of basic training—we weren't allowed to call out.

In the following section, we will follow the veterans' stories into the combat zone. The descent into this inferno brings with it another shock of recognition that could hardly have been part of any teenager's world view.

3

■ ■ ■ ■ ■ ■ ■ ■ ■ ■ ■ ■ ■

IN COUNTRY

■ Can the foot soldier teach anything important about war, merely for having been there? I think not. He can tell war stories.

Tim O'Brien, *If I Die in a Combat Zone*

■ Patrol went up the mountain. One man came back. He died before he could tell us what happened.

A grunt, *Dispatches*

■ Vietnam was a brutal Neverneverland, outside time and space, where little boys didn't have to grow up. They just grew old before their time.

Mark Baker, *Nam*

■ Oh, you know, it was just a firefight, we killed some of them and they killed some of us.

A grunt, *Dispatches*

■ Time's got to come when war's got to get outlawed, or something. There's never been a weapon made by man that wasn't used on man. Now they have weapons that can blow this place up. And that scares me. And the people who decide on wars—there's an old Latin saying that I love. It says, "War is sweet to those who've never tasted it." I love that statement.

Mike V., *The Chambers of Memory*

VIETNAM—THE PLACE

There is consistently an echoing of themes as well as a symmetry in the representation of recollected events in the veterans' stories of their experiences in Vietnam. Parallel accounts and virtually identical representational language abound. Of course, the experiences of the veterans are of a piece, and at the same time the combat zone was, naturally, different for everyone. There is another force at work shaping these stories. Warfare, whether seen as a collection of discrete actions, campaigns, or indeed, an entire war, has its inherent narrative structure. Military men come naturally by their stories. To combat there is a prelude, an opening; a central action with its players and their parts; and a culmination of the issue, a postlude. In Vietnam, however, the story line was hardly so neat, hardly made up of elegant little chapters. Often in the field, nothing much happened, or the central episode was just some soldier tripping a booby trap and dying.

Vietnam was a place most of the combatants had never heard of before their senior year in high school. Late adolescent fantasy shaped the mental image that accompanied them there. Lewis (1985), Barker (1981), Herr (1991), and others have noted that the U. S. soldier went to war in Vietnam with a picture of what it would be like fashioned from the lore of World War II, in particular with a vision of John Wayne in their heads. As Barker writes, "The war billed on the marquee as a John Wayne shoot-'em-up test of manhood turns out to be a warped version of Peter Pan" (p. 49). One grunt warns the combat journalist Michael Herr (1991), "This ain't the fucking movies over here, you know" (p. 22). Lewis (1985) goes so far as to suggest that John Wayne may well be "responsible for more combat casualties in Vietnam than any other American, civilian or military" (p. 41). This is an overstatement, surely, and Vietnam was no Peter Pan Neverneverland either. It was an eerie, unearthly place for the American teenagers who arrived there with their preconceptions and their fathers' war stories in their heads.

. . . .

Their narratives all take account of the harsh divergence between expectation and reality. Their version of the shapeless monster of a narrative that was Vietnam for America, from the late 1950s until the fall of South Vietnam in the spring of 1975, diverges radically from the official one of the day with its special rhetoric and optimistic outlook. For the generation that fought the war, this all begins with John F. Kennedy, who, according to whichever writer you're attending to, would have or would not have gotten us out of Vietnam had he lived. It was Kennedy who said, "Now we have a problem in making our power credible, and Vietnam is the place" (quoted by Karnow in his study of Vietnam and American involvement, *Vietnam, A History*, 1991). It is Kennedy whose rhetoric is, after all, full of cold-war bluster. It was the Johnson administration, however, that undertook to pursue victory, come what may. The policy of "guns and butter," meant fighting a foreign war without imposing rationing upon the populace, in fact, without inconveniencing most people at all. As Jim E. wrily notes, especially protected from discomfort was the great majority of middle class citizens, as well as those higher on the social scale. Their sons would be granted deferments from service in order to attend college, or they could go to Canada. The war was, therefore, fought—especially in its earlier years—by kids who did not or could not go to college, high school dropouts, and especially African-American and Hispanic young men, something reflected in a number of the stories here.

Of course, the military is traditionally at pains to tell its own story, to write its own history. The military in Vietnam had its own figurative language, its own rhetoric, in construing its versions of reality. Operations were given fanciful names like Rolling Thunder (bombing attacks on North Vietnam), Ranch Hand (spraying South Vietnam with herbicides, including Agent Orange), and, in deference to Nixon's penchant for the sports metaphor, Linebacker I and Linebacker II (air strikes in support of South Vietnamese forces late in the period of America's combat role in the war). Pacification, strategic hamlets, rural reconstruction were all renderings of various ultimately failed policies to win the hearts and minds of the people. (Hearts and minds is a phrase Johnson borrowed from John Adams speaking of the American Revolution.) General withdrawal from extensive direct involvement in combat on the ground could be called Vietnamization, defeat, peace with honor. In Saigon, there were the daily press briefings, called "The Five O'Clock Follies" by the journalists whose job it was to be audience to the official version of the events of the day. If events in the field turned out to be not to the liking of officialdom, there was always a way of twisting the plot, decontextualizing, emphasizing the bright side, or just plain lying about things. One of the most egregious rhetorical distortions was the body count. Nightly, the day's images from Vietnam were run on the evening news. Weekly, the total body count was announced, as if it were a summation of the week's football events: American dead, always a much smaller number, and enemy dead, a vastly greater number. Common sense would tell anyone that the second, much larger number included both military casualties of America's much greater firepower and all too many dead bodies of people who could hardly be construed as combatants: villagers of all kinds, old men, women, children. Daily distortion had a way of becoming institutionalized in Vietnam, making it much easier to tell massively distorted versions of events, that is, to cover up events that otherwise would be damaging in the extreme, as Bilton and Sim (1992) document in their book, *Four Hours in My Lai*.

The very falsity, the very corruption, of narrative integrity was part of the profound corruption of the war itself. "Search and destroy" became the order of the day, along with "free fire zones." In practice, this meant: go out and kill and destroy anything you find. Where the killing happens will be dictated administratively, and the labeling of an area as hostile will make it so. Here is how Caputo, in his (1977) *A Rumor of War*, formulates this policy, strictly from the point of view of a young lieutenant in the field:

In the patriotic fervor of the Kennedy years, we had asked, "What can we do for our country?" and our country answered, "Kill VC." That was the strategy, the best our best military minds could come up with: organized butchery. But organized or not, butchery was butchery, so who was to speak of rules and ethics in a war that had none? [p. 218]

The language and the narrative strategies of the veterans are radically at odds with the official jargon and the official construal of the war. This gives the veterans' own personal experience historical place and importance. Their experience is unassailable. This is what they suffered in their own skins; here are the scars, both physical and psychic. And these are the stories they tell about all this, beginning with eye-opening first impressions.

THEIR STORIES

Arrival

Again and again, there is a registration of the sudden realization that something was going to happen, something deadly, in the veterans' accounts of their first moments in country. This was a critical point for everyone. (The veterans' stories seem to cluster around parallel critical moments like this one.) Vietnam was another world for the grunt; everyone seems to have had this feeling. Elsewhere was The World. For Jim M., the memory of the moment of arrival is marked by the faces of a somber welcoming party as he stepped off the commercial airliner that had brought him and other marines into Da Nang. As he and the others filed down the stairs into the withering heat of Vietnam, they passed a line of troops getting ready to leave for The World, finished with their tours. He was transfixed by their "thousand-yard stare," the vacant look of 19-year-old kids who had seen and experienced more terror and death than anyone should be asked to endure.

We landed in Da Nang on a commerical airliner. As we unloaded off the airplane another group of people were leaving—they were also marines. It was roughly the same number of people getting back on the airplane, roughly 100–120 people. We spoke to 'em, just normal courtesy, as people do. These men were all dirty and filthy. We had spit-shined shoes and our clothes perfectly creased. These people looked just terrible, unshaven, but they had—they had a different look in their eyes. I'd never— I never saw people look that way. They looked as if they could look right through you, and their eyes were kind of glazed. They looked as if they were in a total state of shock. We didn't think much about that. We lined up in these different lines, and these trucks came.

As Jim speaks about his first impressions here, he pauses from time to time, his voice not hesitant but studied, as if he is seeing these men again in his mind's eye, now aware of all that their stony gaze portended for him and the others in the coming months. He goes on to describe, briefly, his group's immediate departure, then ends this section with a laconic repetition of, "We didn't think much of it." Arriving in a war zone as a new combatant is one of the critical moments that the contributors use to build their accounts. It is to be followed by others, in particular that moment when death becomes a stark reality and a very real possibility.

First Brush with Death

For one veteran (not a contributor to the Vietnam tapes), it was during his first week in country on a fairly secure base from which helicopters operated. He had arrived trained as a helicopter mechanic, thinking that surely he would have weekends off. He had yet to fly his first combat mission, never thought he'd be involved directly in combat; he was trained as a helicopter mechanic, after all. It was nearly Christmas. Early one morning he peered out of his bunker to see, fifty yards away, bodies being loaded onto a truck, the men tossing the body bags on as if they were sacks of grain. "That was it," he said. "There wasn't any U. S., no Christmas—just this place. I thought, What am I doing here?" Most propitious of all, in the early days, is a young soldier's first direct experience of death. For Alan J., the high school track star, this moment came early, in fact during his first time in the field. Actually, for him, things started happening even during the brief in-country training period that some of the veterans mention.

> The first day, we got mortared, and I don't know what the devil to do. This is really happening. So, boom, and I see flashes and everything. So I just, y'know, like a kid getting chased by a cop, I'm just running. And I ran and jumped in this hole with the rest of the guys. And I'm in this hole saying, Boy is this what I have to go through the whole year? Like, scared like this? Oh, I got over that—that was nothing.

Indeed, that was nothing. Apparently no one was hurt. It was just a little mortar attack, like hundreds of others every night of the year in Vietnam. Soon in-country training is finished, and Alan finds himself on day one in the field.

> Okay, here we go again. First day. Nobody showed me anything. The Sergeant, he just said, "Okay, Mr. Jones get on that APC [armored personnel carrier] with the rest of the guys." So I got on the APC with the rest of the guys. And we rode out into the bush, first day! I say, well, this is okay, no action, nothing happening. We saw a couple of guys and the sergeant shot the 50-caliber at them. The day was beautiful. On the way back, they started racing the APC's. We were the first, the point track, so the other one pulled ahead, and he went down the road and hit a mine. Okay, the first day in the field, the combat field. So I jump out. We all put up a position. And they pulled this guy out. I thought he was a black man. I was about—not too far—I'd say, four feet, five or six feet, when I saw them pull him out. I said, Oh, there's the first black man I saw killed. But I found out later on that night that it was a white man. And so my whole mind of Vietnam at that time, first day out, seeing

somebody killed like that and thinking he was a black man, made me really shook up. That shook me up for a little while.

Your first day could be worse than that. Soldiers could and did die on their first day. Tommy T., whose elliptic style is as effective as Wayne W.'s in conveying his story, provides an almost cryptic account of the brief preliminary period of training in-country that usually preceeded actually going into combat. They were told, "Stay away from kids and don't kick cans." First day out in the field, and a few of the new troops can't resist mixing with the kids. A little girl pulls the pin on one of the young men's belt, then disappears (an episode paralleled in Alan J.'s story).

First time we saw medevac come in, first time we saw a body bag. One was put in a body bag. The two weren't hurt bad, they were treated and returned in a month or so, one in two weeks, one about a month. But one was dead. We went out, set up that night. Strange, soon as it got dark they airlifted some mortars in, 81 mortars—that was bad news. Soon as it got—they'd checked them in the daytime, they worked good. Soon as the night came they tried 'em—dud rounds. They went straight up in the air and came straight back down, landed on the perimeter. Killed all three people in the bunker. So the first day was a bad day— four dead and two wounded in the same day, the first day. I was ready to come back home.

Others waited, as they reconstruct it in their narratives, for their transforming moment right up to their first firefight, or, as with Mark A., his first look at raw death, in the torn form of a young combatant with an AK-47 whom he had killed in the dark the night before. Another milestone is reached.

Killing Becomes a Personal Thing

Mark's narrative of this event is preceded by an account of his time up to that moment, which is structured along the lines of death's getting closer and closer. This begins as he gets off the plane in Da Nang (where the marines usually landed when arriving in country by air). "Getting off the plane there were these flag-draped boxes, and right away I knew I was here—I was in Vietnam. And there was a choking smell that made me, y'know—you're in deep shit. You're in trouble." Many weeks in the field follow, with the patrols and especially the ambushes at night. Along with the others Mark fires his M-16, of which he had thought as he loaded it the first time out, "I might kill somebody with this." He goes on. "The first few weeks weren't bad at all." He'd see an occasional dead VC. He was on a lot of ambushes, with a lot of shooting and a lot of enemy killed. But this was all prelude; so far it was just a matter of firing ahead with all the others. "I didn't know if I was killing anybody or—everybody was shooting and everybody was getting hits." Then it happens.

One particular night, we were out on an ambush—it was about three or four months in country, I guess, I can't remember exactly, and everybody was racking up kills, whatever. And we were out on an ambush, and I'm very low to the ground. And I'd just been awarded the radio to carry. I became the radio operator. I was very low around this—when the Vietnamese bury their dead they bury in circles, so they were perfect little forts, it seemed, perfect little area for ambushes. And we were down below the little berm of this graveyard. I kept looking, and we kept seeing movement in front of us. I didn't use my radio; I didn't want the static or anything. And all of a sudden my squad leader yelled, "Open fire." And everybody opened up. So everybody was firing, then it got quiet. And I looked up and there was this VC hanging over me. He'd just thrown a grenade inside our little area, and a friend of mine jumped on the grenade. And it didn't go off—it was a dud. So when I saw that I looked up and he looked down at me. And I opened fire on him. And I dropped him. And all through the period of the night, I could hear him moaning and groaning. And I—jeez, I just dropped this guy. Now the squad leader says, "Finish him off, finish him off." And people were saying, "No, you take him as a prisoner." So I said, "No, finish him off." So we opened fire and literally disintegrated his head. Brain mass was all over us, in fact; he was so close to us. But the unfortunate thing was this was my first kill that I could register, the first person that I shot. And that morning when we went out to see what had happened, how many we got, it was quite a shock to see that the one I had killed was around 12 years old.

Mark recounts how he was at first excited—a kill, after all. Then other thoughts occur to him: this was a kid, after all. The impersonal work of the soldier, killing the enemy, becomes in Mark's mind a personal matter.

I said, "No, the kid was only 12 years old. Kids at home that age are playing, out playing." But this kid was carrying a weapon, carrying grenades, and trying to kill us. But that just seemed to have been not on my mind. The fact was I had just killed a 12-year-older, and somebody's son is dead because of me.

This thought, extraordinary in the combat zone, for the family of the dead young enemy soldier is indicative of this veteran's story, with its preoccupation with his own family and self-sacrifice, early and late. Throughout the taping of his story, Mark's tone seems somewhat casual; he smiles frequently and in general appears to be striving for a light, somewhat ironic tone. Perhaps this is because his wife was there for the taping and he was trying to avoid distressing her as much as possible? This would, it seems, be in keeping with his character, always thinking of others. Was this also Mark's response to the potent, ritualized atmosphere of the video testimony? In any event, his narrative is coherent and fluid; it is also lucid and insightful.

Thomas T. is especially effective in rendering the stark contrast between shooting off into the distance and one-to-one killing. He speaks a kind of staccato, repetitious description of the "rule" about everyone firing at once.

If one person shoots a gun, everybody shoots. It doesn't matter what 'cause you know what's out there. If this man shoots, you shoot, just spray the area hoping you hit somebody and they're dead. That's the rule. If one shoots everybody shoots. That way you never know who killed who. If one shoots, everybody shoots, that's your policy. You might not see anything—they might be there—shoot anyway. That's the rule. You know, people always say, "How you know who killed who?" Most of the time you don't 'cause when one person shoots, everybody shoots. Y'know, you're spraying the area. How you know who's going to hit who? Because you fired first and the man was there doesn't mean—that's the good part about it. Keeps you not knowing. You can say, I didn't kill him. You don't know who killed him. So you can say you did or you didn't. But then, y'know, when you come to an individual thing, like, you're on point or something.

Thomas then goes on to the episode he has been concerned to highlight, the time when it gets all too personal. A B-52 strike had been called in earlier, and the enemy had booby-trapped an unexploded two-hundred-fifty-pound bomb. As Thomas's platoon sergeant walks by, it goes off and he is blown apart. His squad leader had been killed that same day, and he is given the job. They say to him, "You're going to prove yourself. Your sqaud stays here, we're going that way, you're going to set up an ambush back here." So they do.

All of a sudden, just about dark, we hear some noise, me and Smitty sitting there, y'know. Rodriguez, he was gone to take him a bowel movement. Here, we hear this noise, these two, three Vietnamese soldiers, two have bayonets fixed. They've got the sergeant's arm—blown off from here to there—sticking it, throwing it up in the air, laughing, coming down this trail. We already had the ambush set up. So now we see the arm fall in front of us. Before, we couldn't see because they were in some hedges, but we could see when they got in a certain distance and they came in that distance. The arm falls in front of us. Now here comes another one, he wants to stick the bayonet in it and raise it up. Me and

Smitty fired on him. The other two are over here and I open fire on these two. Well we only killed two right there. Smitty killed this one, I killed that one. . . . I was still 18, y'know, I said, "Damn, I killed somebody— 18 years old." Before it was always everybody shooting. This time we know exactly who killed who. That's bad. I'm ready to go home now.

Hardly a Perfect War

Other, even darker moments lay ahead for the new arrival, as the green soldier was plunged into the harsh realities of this place where he had landed and for which he was so ill prepared. The veterans' tapes are marked with the mileposts on the way to complete immersion, to going berserk, a traditional term from the Icelandic sagas that Shay (1994) uses to describe the warrior who is totally caught up in combat. It was usually a mixture of terror and rage that brought the soldier to that boundary, judging by the veterans' accounts. Killing also brought with it a rush, to use a word the veterans often employ. Becoming a "blood-crazed killer" and becoming "kill crazy" are phrases used by two of the contributors to describe this terminal state. Having arrived in an alien world, where all the old ways, the old rules even teenagers live by, were suspended, the young American soldier responded to the traumatic environment of combat as soldiers have done everywhere and in every age—he adapted. The psychic price of this adaptation, however, was high and to be paid out over years on the installment plan. In fact, for the veterans who contributed their stories and for their peers in and out of treatment everywhere, there is no final payment, no fine day when you burn the mortgage. Thoughts of suicide are apparently universal among veterans afflicted with severe and chronic post-traumatic conditions; the continuing burden is heavy. War always constitutes an alien environment for the young soldier. The war in Vietnam was alien in ways peculiar to the country, the people, the political situation, and to the conduct of this brutal struggle on both sides.

Children, their mothers, grandfathers, and their grandmothers—
clearly noncombatants—were often victims of American firepower,
especially firepower coming from the air or from artillery located
far away. Routinely, they became part of the body count. For Jim
M., his most traumatic memories are of going into villages that had
been bombarded. It bothers him most that it was he who, as RTO
(radiotelephone operator), often had the job of calling in the artillery or the air strikes. As he explains, his unit would typically encounter enemy fire coming from a village in the distance. Assault
would have resulted in unacceptable American casualties; this was
in the Mekong Delta, the rich rice-producing area of South Vietnam
with its open paddies. The entire area of South Vietnam was subject
to artillery and air attacks of devastating intensity. A village brought
under full bombardment simply ceased to exist as a spot on the face
of the earth. Jim relates that his unit would go into a village after an
attack to discover dead bodies, to be sure—of civilians. Often, no dead
combatants would be found. "They always had their escape route."
Earlier Jim has explained that because of his deep, resonant voice
he was made to carry the radio, making him—something he doesn't
mention—a desirable target for the enemy.

My memory of what happened isn't all too clear. I remember bits and
pieces of it. But I remember my first time calling in an air strike. We
were pinned down in a rice paddy. The whole platoon was pinned down.
We were about 200 yards from the village. And we were receiving automatic weapons fire, and the lieutenant was about thirty yards in front
of me, because on patrols we walked with about thirty yards between
people so that one artillery round, one booby trap wouldn't hopefully
hurt but one person. He was about thirty yards away. I couldn't get to
him, I had the radio. He told me to call in air strikes, and I called in for
air strikes. I had to look up the grid coordinates—where we were located,
where the enemy was located—and give 'em to a pilot who was still sitting on the runway in Da Nang. And after I gave him the grid coordi-

nates, he said his time of arrival would be something like three minutes, and we were thirty miles south. I knew what direction he was coming from, it was just one Phantom; he was just above treetop level. The trees in Vietnam were normally smaller than the trees in the United States, normally about thirty feet high, so he was flying about forty feet off the ground. The only reason that you knew he was there, because I knew the direction he was coming. He knew about where we were and about where the village was, but we directed fire on the village so he could follow the tracer rounds right into the village. He was outrunning sound, so most of the marines didn't even know he was there till he had already dropped his first bomb and he was pulling up. They pull up sideways, banked either right or left. He dropped 500-pound bombs, I think; it was a couple bombs he dropped. He made three passes all together; one was a napalm strike. Because we were only 200 yards out, you could feel the heat from the napalm; you turned your back on it. The fragments from the bombs were hitting the water in the paddy, twenty, thirty yards in front of us. You could see shock waves traveling up in the air. It looked like heat coming up off a hot highway in the summer. After it was all over, we started into the village again. We didn't receive any fire at all this time. We went on into the village. We were ordered to find all the bodies and make a body count. We didn't find any North Vietnamese soldiers. They either had a tunnel and got out of the village by tunnel or knew that we were calling in either artillery or air strikes and left beforehand. If we hit any of the NVA soldiers, their habit was to drag the wounded soldier off and cover up the blood trails and let us find nothing but civilians that we had killed in that village. It was one of their little mind games. There were times in different artillery strikes and air strikes we found NVA, but this time we didn't. We found about fifteen or maybe twenty—I don't know—people that had been killed in the air strike. The enemy knew that we were going to call artillery or air strikes, one, before they fired on us. They knew that the villagers in that village stood at great risk of becoming casualties, yet, I guess, it didn't seem to matter to them. There were old people, women and children. The ground inside that village—being a farm boy—it looked like a plowed-up field, all of it fresh dirt, smoke still rising from it. I stepped on—I felt something soft under my feet. I uncovered it, and blood came up through the dirt, so I uncovered the dirt. It was an old lady.

Here, Jim pauses for a long, long time. As so often in all the tapings, this veteran here appears weary and distant, as if seeing the events he has just recounted happening all over again. "It's a hard thing to tell," one of the listeners says, perhaps trying to relieve the distress. Jim goes on, as if he hadn't heard—maybe he did not.

Well, anyway, that was one village. There were so many different villages and air strikes and artillery strikes. We did kill a lot of the enemy, too—a lot of innocent people were killed at the same time. It would be nice if wars were perfect, the two enemies would be the only people hurt; but that's not true, a lot of innocent people are caught up in it, too. Each time that we called in artillery or I called in an air strike we were in a very dangerous situation, and myself or other marines were likely to become casualties if I didn't do my job and call air strikes and artillery in. Even if I knew there were civilians in the area, I had no choice but to call in air strikes or artillery. At times since then, being brought up very religious, I felt maybe that I might have traded my soul to stay alive.

Trading your soul to stay alive must have been the experience of many of the young American soldiers in Vietnam. Staying alive until the end of your tour, just surviving, became the understandable goal of most of the troops, judging by the Vietnam literature and by the testimony of many a veteran.

Dead Buddies

Among the critical moments that, it seems, all the combat veterans of Vietnam recall vividly is the loss of buddies. Intense friendships spring into being quickly in the combat zone—how could it be otherwise? When a friend is killed it comes suddenly, unexpectedly, and one is powerless to prevent it. The loss is traumatic; it engenders rage and, often, an irresistible thirst for revenge. Such was the motivation for Sid L. as he focused his hostile feelings on the Vietnamese populace. His MOS (military occupational specialty) called for him to operate mobile search lights mounted on a sort of tug. When the call came for someone to go down and perform the same duties aboard river boats, he and his friend Alfie tossed a coin to see who would go.

> Anyway, he went down there, and I went to another firebase for, I don't know what period of time, then I found out that Alfie got killed down there. So I got really upset and volunteered to go down to the river, y'know, to avenge his death or whatever, y'know—it sucked. He wasn't down there a couple of weeks when they blew the boat up. And the boats consisted of four sailors and three marines, and every time a boat blew, seven people were dead. We never had any survivors. So I went down there.

In his story, Sid makes many references to friends of all kinds. He was apparently someone with a gift for making connections; this admirable trait led to his being consumed by a thirst for revenge, as one after another friend perished. In a change from river duty, Sid tells how he once went back out in the field for a short time. He recalls his friend, Eddie, who was medevacked out with burns all over his body from a rocket that came out of nowhere.

> And third degree burns instantly. And I pulled some of his clothes off; they were still smoldering. And a corpsman came over and gave him a shot of morphine, and he was still crying. And I was holding his hand, more or less, what was left of it, and the corpsman gave him another shot till he passed out or died, I don't know. And it took the chopper quite a while to get there; like I said this place was in the middle of nowhere. And they came and picked him up. . . . So I went back down to

the river. I don't know what happened to Eddie, he was a good guy. He was from Kentucky. His mother used to send him, ah, Avon. He was a good guy, and to this day I don't know whether he's alive or dead. I went back to the river.

Remembering this buddy and his mother sending him Avon, Sid laughs, and then, as he finishes talking about Eddie, tears come to his eyes. The sorrow that is hidden, that is always so fiercely contained, comes through here in the telling for the camera. Now things go from bad to worse. Soon after, a boat is destroyed and, together with the four sailors and two other marines, Sid's friend Winston dies. They find his body two days later. The thirst for revenge begins to consume Sid L. He begins to see all Vietnamese not only as potential enemies but as responsible.

It might not be true, but I trained myself to think these people were responsible for all these people's deaths, especially my friends Winston and McCarthy. And I got extremely vicious, nasty. I mean I used to—anything short of actually shooting them. One time I put this rifle right in this woman's mouth. She said something I didn't like for an answer. Her husband just looked at me with hate in his eyes. I said, yelled, I don't know, "Just do something. I'll shoot your fucking brains out." And they couldn't do anything. . . . And the kids, they were screaming, and I used to put the bayonet right up to little kids, babies. But the worst thing I ever did to civilians, one time on land patrol, we went in this village into this house, this hooch or whatever it was. And this little baby was screaming, so one of the other marines picked the kid up and said, "Here, Sid, catch." And I had a fixed bayonet. And the mother was screaming and trying to grab the kid, and he was throwing the little baby up in the air, and I thought he was going to throw him over to me. And I don't know if I would have actually just skewered the kid on the bayonet. I don't know. I'm glad he didn't throw the kid to find out. I can tell you this, if it had happened after Winston's death I would have done it. I would have hoped he'd have thrown the little kid, and I would have made sure I stabbed the little bastard. I know I would have. And I'm glad it didn't happen, because I'd really regret that now, but at the time after his death, it was really—I was at the breaking point.

Sid appears to be an ordinarily reserved and detached man. His passionate attachment for friends drove him to act cruelly toward civilians, some of whom might have been allied with the enemy, most of whom probably weren't. He goes on to reflect, with great insight, on the meaning of his actions to the victims.

> Nowadays, I put it together like this: if somebody came into my home and did the things to my family I did to them, I'd go after the bastard and kill him. So I can understand the hatred these people had toward us for the way we treated them and their families. And at the time, you don't care—you're full of hatred anyway.

Hatred like that never leaves you, as Sid will confirm later as he speaks of his life since Vietnam. The veterans make numerous references to the loss of buddies and its effects on the soldier in the field, but Sid speaks more openly than others of seeking vengeance and ties this most explicitly to the losses. Thoughts about lost friends evoke a feeling common among Vietnam combat veterans—a desire to have died in Nam. Sid says, "I think of my friends all the time. I think about Eddie, I think about Winston in a body bag. I think about the guy—I can't remember his name—I borrowed a T-shirt from. I just, you know, it sucks. You try to keep busy; it creeps up on you."

Stuffing Emotion

Another effect mentioned again and again by the veterans is the choking off of feelings for others in the combat zone, consciously avoiding becoming attached. This is another thing you bring home with you, this numbing of fellow feelings. The two medics among the contributors, Steve B. and Arthur S., had to disassociate feelings, not for buddies but, if they were to do their jobs, about their day-to-day exposure to the carnage of war. Of course, all combatants are exposed to the dead and to all the grotesquery that modern weapons can inflict on the body. The medic deals with nothing but. Arthur talks about his first exposure in a field hospital; it was just a matter of drawing blood. He really didn't want to do that; he thought of the pain he would be causing the patient. A number of officers come over, however, and persuade him to try, and a few men volunteer to be guinea pigs. Arthur even likens them to "victims" and himself to the "perpetrator." When he was drafted into the service, Arthur had, in fact, wanted to be a combatant. He wanted revenge for Charlie, his friend who had gone to Vietnam a year earlier and had come back terribly wounded and permanently disabled. Revenge, however, was not something the war would provide him with. The army would use him to the fullest as a medical corpsman. Drawing blood was nothing, Arthur goes on; soon enough the unit got busy.

The next week we had mass casualties come in; that was the first time I'd ever seen mass casualties come in. I helped with getting them in and disbursing the people on litters into, like, an emergency room, what we called a pre-op. And at that time we were asked to take care of bleeders or people that were bleeding and try to pack the wounds and try to keep them alive until a doctor could get to them. So thinking that I—I was very, very nervous about doing this, so the first thing I did, I went looking for the easiest person to work on. And I saw a fellow sitting there. And he had one hand up on his chest, and lying back. And I said, This is my man. So I went over to him and I grabbed his hand and it felt weird. I'm saying, "My name's Arthur and I'm going to be working with you." And all of a sudden his arm fell off the litter and onto the floor. It wasn't attached to him. And so that was my introduction into, into—and from there I—I, I just, I guess it was just—I don't know how, but, ah, something changed then, instantly, that this is no longer a game, that this is incredibly, ah, an incredible awakening. And I proceeded to pack the arm and deal with this guy. And most of my tour was like that. I just did what I had to do.

Arthur's demeanor throughout his story is calm and collected, his voice steady, his tone controlled. It is, however, the disrupted flow of speech here that signifies the emotion, that registers just how powerful still the traumatic memory of this experience is. This was the first of endless days of working on young men's torn and broken bodies. Arthur continues, quickly and with great narrative authority, accounting for the inexorable process of disconnecting from feeling and, finally, confronting face to face his own death with indifference.

> As time went on I just got better at what I did. I made rank fast, I became much more confident. And I found as time went on I didn't really look at faces anymore, and I didn't really pay attention to names. And I didn't feel pain anymore. I started feeling I was becoming a cold person, but I couldn't control that. It was just—I had no way of being emotionally attached to people. And I missed home all the time, I just wanted to go home. And it seemed like through the whole tour, after dealing with so many people who were dead or dying or just even sick, that I'd never leave Vietnam. I was certain after a couple of months here that I'm going to die here. I saw no way out of it. And then even that went away. There was just nothing.

Something happens here that is often happening in the veterans' stories: the present tense slips in and adverbial positioning shifts from there to here. Grammar tells us dramatically about the feelings associated with the events in the story as the image of them comes vividly to mind, even with someone as naturally in control of himself as Arthur is, at least as he was during most of the taping.

Arthur is later transferred to Chu Lai and another hospital unit, but, already a sergeant, he now has the job of driving an ambulance. This mostly meant, in the inverted world of Vietnam, driving dead bodies and body parts to Graves Registration, the military's organization for processing the dead for the trip back home in a box. He says there were many incidents, many terrible events.

The one that comes to mind. This man was a flagman on the landing strip. And a landing gear collapsed on a jet plane. And the jet hit him. And after picking up body parts for four hundred yards on the runway, they got this man and they put him on a big silver plate in the emergency room. And they were doing a count, checking to see what was missing and what-have-you. And I was on duty that night, and I remember walking into the ER. And there it was just a great big pile of meat on top of this tray. And at first, I don't think it even hit me what I was seeing, and as I sat there a couple of seconds it dawned on me what I was witnessing here. And this was the first time I'd seen a body in such one-inch pieces. I had already accepted bodies as meat; I considered people to be just meat. But this more or less verified it—people are just meat, and don't get too attached. After the body parts count they brought him out to me at the ambulance, and I remember carrying him into Graves Registration. And it was in a bag, a body bag, and I could feel it swishing as I was carrying him on my shoulder. And I could feel somebody behind me. The body was still warm, but it wasn't warm from him, it was warm from being in the, in the—just exposed to the heat. And I could feel that warm body just trying to wrap around me as I was carrying the bag. And then we got him loaded into there and then I had to drive him to Graves. And again when I had to get him out of there and I was sliding him over my legs—it was a feeling I'd never had before, a sensation I'd never had before. And I think what frightened me the most was I didn't give a fuck, I just didn't give a fuck. There was no name to him, there was no nothing. There was no sense of feeling for this guy. Other than I just, I was just tired, just drained, when these things happened, when I had to deal with carrying a foot or somebody's shoulder. It took—it drained me to do it. And I didn't know what that was about.

Yet Arthur tells us that he did have relationships in Chu Lai, with the men of whom he was in charge and a dog he found under his bed that just wouldn't go away. After a few days, Arthur gives him a name. He also goes on to describe seeing men perform small heroic actions selflessly, giving him a feeling of solidarity with his fellow soldiers. Fellow feelings die of necessity in the war zone; fellow feelings spring up spontaneously for your comrades in the war zone. It is confusing, but at least your fellow soldiers understand.

Arthur builds his story around an account of arrival in country and of the few days in the first transitional phase prior to taking up his duties in the field. He goes on to detail his first experience of what his life will be like in Nam, the difficulty he had with drawing blood that first day out. This is immediately followed by the two episodes of dealing with the reality of the war, the first real casualty he worked on and an event selected to exemplify the sort of extraordinary—and traumatic—experiences he encountered in abundance. He ends the Vietnam part of his narrative, "Chapter Two," saying how he could speak of many, many traumatic events. The story has been told, however, and most effectively. Arthur's narrative instinct tells him to let it rest there. He goes on to speak about leaving the country and about life after Vietnam, "Chapter Three."

Finally, Nothing but Death

For those troops in the thick of the fighting, a time could come, and did for many, when they felt engulfed by death. For Mike V. this came after his most traumatic experience. He was pinned down in an exposed position during a firefight that lasted some two hours. Just ahead was his best friend, also pinned down, even more exposed. Mike's friend, who had been walking point, was carrying an M-79, a sort of shotgun that fired grenade rounds. It was, Mike explains, useless in the circumstances, and his friend called back, begging Mike to toss him his M-16. This Mike cannot do; a soldier is conditioned to guard his rifle with his life, not to mention being in one of the most traumatic combat situations: pinned down with no means of escape. Mike's friend dies; he survives.

I just looked around. There was nothing on that hill but death and destruction. It was nothing to fight for. I just wanted it to end. I didn't care if I lived or died, it didn't matter anymore. I just wanted the madness to end.

Death, as Mike reminds us, is not something reserved only for humans. He provides the following account of the killing of an innocent creature his platoon encountered by accident, possibly beyond the border of Vietnam.

We also had to kill an elephant over there. We were in—it's nothing I can prove, but I say we were in Cambodia, near the Laotian border. We came across an elephant that was chained to a stake. We called in and we were ordered to destroy it. My squad had to do it, and we were firing into it with 16s, the M-16, which aren't really geared for taking an elephant out. It screamed, it broke—it tried to break away from the chains. And it cried like a baby, which was the most horrible thing. It felt like you were shooting a baby after a while. And you kept on firing because you wanted to end the noise. It's something that—it's a brutal feeling. I went hunting once after I came home and I winged a pheasant. It started crying, too, and I bashed its head in with this one shot with the rifle, just to shut it up. I couldn't eat it or anything. I've never been hunting since.

Such is the death of innocence.

JIM E.'S STORY

Jim's life narrative, as he improvised it for the camera over two sessions and a total of over three hours, is a powerful and deeply affecting account of a hard life lived under the burdens of trauma in childhood, in war, and after. Jim died in the fall of 1994, victim of many years without treatment, struggling on his own. He used a lot of alcohol over the decades to ease the pain, and he utilized to the fullest treatment when it became available to him, as to many Vietnam veterans, too late. Jim's story of his tour provides a prototypical account of the Vietnam experience, from first impressions to rude awakening, to being overcome by the traumatic violence of it all, and finally being swept away—going berserk. This was a thoughtful man, a brave man, a man loyal to his family, and a good, supportive friend to his fellow veterans. As Jim speaks, he uses his retelling to try to make some sense of all that happened to him. It is also clear that he has gone over this in his mind, again and again. Yet, ultimately, there is no answer, no way to understand fully the incredible things he survived. He does, as we shall see, take a forceful stand on the war. Jim's story is in ways incredible; he was also an honest man. All that happened to him—and more that he does not relate in this version of his story—is true. This is the truth of the war in Vietnam as one veteran lived it, and as he recollects it for the camera.

We've already seen how, looking back on himself and the others as teenage draftees, Jim perceived the injustice of it all, the fact that the vast majority of the troops had no choice but to respond to their country's call, while other more fortunate youths went off to college or to Canada. He went to war with a greater sense of justice and fairness than most adolescents, perhaps in response to the unfairness of his abusive home and, as he emphasizes, from his close association with the Church. The Church and the nuns who were his teachers provided him with refuge and a steady, guiding hand. As he turns to the Vietnam section of his history, his face, already somber, takes on an even graver look, and his voice, already darkly studied, deepens and his words come more slowly. (In fact, after the taping Jim remarked on his losing track of time as he spoke; he was, apparently, in a mild trance throughout.) As we shall see, here is someone with a burden of traumatic memories that is exceptional even for a Vietnam veteran. Through the vicissitudes of fate, mere chance, and bad timing, Jim experienced all the violence and horror that the war had to offer. It was more than even he could tolerate. His recollection of arrival is of a piece with most of the other veterans' accounts, although, typical of Jim's approach, he is more reflective than most. He is more clearly seeking a meaning to experience tainted with the inherent meaninglessness of random violence.

> The reality of the whole situation hadn't sunk in yet. I knew I was going, I knew what it was about. But in my own mind and my own thinking, I never knew what was actually going to take place. So landing in Vietnam I still felt just like a normal American boy who'd gone through some training. I had no idea what I was getting into.

When the plane landed, the young man stepped off to be greeted by his first sight of what was in store, although the reality of the war was only partly apparent to him.

> The minute we got out that door, you could see the heat rising over the ground—it was intense, well over 100 degrees. And around the area you could see different things, helicopters, planes, cargo planes. I saw body bags, I saw silver coffins stacked up. And the whole thing hadn't really struck me yet. The smell. And the first glimpse of Vietnamese was intriguing.

The new arrivals all head off in different directions, to different units. Jim is still open to the newness of it all and, as he recalls his first few days in country, he pictures himself as still curious about all the new sights. In-country training is next, sometimes involving quite unexpected duties.

> We were all given a detailed course in how to burn—how should I put it?—how to burn shit. A lot of diesel fuel and a big strong stick to stir it all with. These were things we never planned on; nobody ever thought he'd be caught doing anything like that. And the funny thing about it was we were still so far away from the actual war. And yet, these things— flares at night, ground troops around us—were attracting.

Looking at the veterans' stories in detail, it is fascinating to see them using with such subtlety all the devices of literature. Here, for instance, Jim crafts a rendering of himself as a young man intrigued by the strange attraction of the war as he approaches it, stage by stage, from a distance, from that first moment off the plane onward. Finally, he gets orders to report to a unit in the field. He is issued gear, including an M-16, and told to go down to a hooch (a shack) and get ready. The men return from an operation, and the first of the many extraordinary events that await Jim occurs.

While I was in my hooch, the company came in from an operation. I was really anxious to get to see these guys and what things were all about, and I had a really friendly attitude. But when they came in their attitude wasn't friendly at all. You could see the strain that they'd been under, the mud all over them, the worn-out jungle boots, the solitude that they lived in. It all showed in their face, the anger, the excitement, everything. I just sat there and watched them. I didn't know what to do. I tried to talk to a couple of guys, but they didn't acknowledge me at all because I was a new guy. And while everybody was in there, some went to the front of the hooch and started a card game, smoking marijuana. And others sat on their bunks and relaxed and took it easy and put everything off until they got some rest. And while I was sitting there I watched a white ground soldier, a grunt, get up, take off his .45 automatic and started cleaning it. Not being nosy or anything, I just happened to be watching what he was doing. And after a while watching him, I couldn't figure out why he was standing up holding the .45 automatic. I got more curious, and as I watch the .45 automatic went off and shot a black GI lying next to him. Right through the head, killing him. So my first impression there was, I didn't know who I could trust. I didn't know who was—all I knew was life really didn't mean much here and that I was on my own. I couldn't depend on anybody and I'd be darned if I could trust anyone. And my personal feeling at that moment was that this man did not like black GIs, and he proved it. And nothing ever happened to this fellow. The guy's body was just taken away, and nothing was ever done about it.

This moment, sobering as it is, just marks one step closer to the combat zone for Jim. The next day, he goes out with the others, trusting no one, getting help from no one. It was a typical day in Nam, as Jim recounts it. On the one hand it was all new to him: the anxiety about getting hit by rockets out of nowhere, the firefight that breaks out, getting pinned down, dustoffs (helicopter medevacs) to take out the wounded and the dead. Then the guns fall silent. The men regroup and head back to their base. Another day in Vietnam. For Jim it is all new and arousing.

> I walked into the hooch. After all this I couldn't stop talking. I was so, I was so exhilarated from everything that took place I couldn't stop talking about it. The funny thing was, nobody was listening. Nobody was paying any attention. I don't even know why I was talking like that. But somehow I knew I was aroused, the whole thing had been a real shock to me. And I knew there was a lot more to this whole thing than I ever thought of.

Jim recalls that after this first firefight, his sergeant said to him, "Move on, soldier." He gets a certain satisfaction from that, the first recognition that he has had since arriving in country. There follows a series of search-and-destroy missions, then some dangerous work blowing up tree lines in the Delta, with its more open terrain. Back at their base camp in the evening, the troops all turned to drugs and alcohol. Not Jim.

> I never participated in any of that. I knew from my training that you had to be aware 100 percent all the time. You had to have a clear mind and be ready to think and make decisions in a second. That to be under the influence of any alcohol or any pot or anything like that limited your ability and the likelihood of your living. So I never got involved, I never got involved in anything like that.

By now, Jim has started to feel more accepted in the unit; he begins to feel accepted as a grunt, a ground soldier. He starts forming "small relationships with a few of the guys." The search-and-destroy missions continue. One day, the thing happens that moves Jim beyond a line that had not yet been crossed. From now on, he is beyond that boundary, his life divided—all that had gone before and all that will come after.

And we started to go out on search-and-destroy missions. Basically they were exactly what they said they were: search and destroy. We'd be flown into villages in places where civilians, women, children, and the enemy had been reported and basically just destroy and kill everything that's there—everything. I had a top sergeant with me one day who ordered me to pick up an M-60 machine gun and kill all the women and children. I told him I didn't want to do that; I said no. He put a .45 automatic to my head and said, "Fire or I'll kill you." And that's what I did. That's only one example of something like that happening to me when I was over there. When I first did that something changed inside of me. I was not the same person anymore. Having been close to the Church spiritually, having some foundation about what's right and wrong, what I believed in, I felt used and I felt horrible that I had to do something like that because someone had threatened my life if I didn't. And I knew that I was in a place where nobody could stop anybody from doing anything.

Given the power of this account and the impact the telling clearly has on the teller, it may seem all too academic to point out the parallelism that underlies the narrative structure here: the black GI apparently assassinated early in Jim's tour, the 45-automatic put to Jim's head here. Jim is the one veteran among the contributors to speak at length about the search-and-destroy missions. As he tells his story, he seems intent upon documenting all the inhumanity that he experienced, that he witnessed, and that he participated in. He conveys this horror by mixing passages of summary with accounts of specific events. Wearily, he continues.

This went on for a long time, a real long time. . . . Village after village we would strike unexpected and leave with nothing, just pure devastation. A lot of times guys would be killed going in, and that just seemed to provoke everyone even more. Even to the point they were shooting the pigs and the chickens and the kids, the kids. And the women. They had what they call the double veteran. A double veteran is a guy in Vietnam who has raped and killed his victim at the same time. That's what a double veteran is—there was a lot of that.

Throughout, Jim reflects on the meaning of his experiences to him, the devastating impact participating in the war had on him as a person. We see someone who struggled at the time to make sense of what was happening, someone who continued with that struggle, which ultimately could have no clear outcome. Death becomes a fact for Jim, the death of a part of himself.

A lot of search-and-destroy missions, a lot of death, a lot of horrendous scenes that didn't make much sense to me because I really didn't see them as the enemy. I saw them as women and kids that lived a very, very hard life, poverty, a war-stricken life. It didn't make any sense to me to have to kill them and not the enemy. So I had a difficult time trying to figure that out in my own mind, in my own heart. But I was not the same person anymore—part of me died and is still dead to this day. The guilt lingers and it just doesn't go away, it just doesn't go away.

From here Jim mentions untold days and weeks of fighting. It was the late fall of 1967, and the unit was encountering more and more of the enemy as the buildup to the Tet offensive of 1968 was underway, not that Jim and the others were made aware of the facts. Casualties began to mount, comrades dying or getting wounded and flown away for good. You wonder when it'll be your turn. You began to change again, deadening even the affection for comrades that had been at least somewhat sustaining before.

People you get to know a little die, so you learn not to get close anymore, you shut it off. There's no more relationships, no more feeling or anything, you're just numb, you're dead—and you're mad. You wish there was something you could do, but you can't. You just wait for the next time it happens and hope that you don't go down like everybody else. Nighttime is especially frightening, the shadows, the thoughts about being home, what it would be like if you were home and at the same time realizing where you are. It's a very, very lonesome feeling. There's very little pleasure in it, very little pleasure.

The fighting continues. We begin to get a feeling for how useful information about their immediate situation was denied the troops in the field. Meanwhile, Jim himself has become a leader. He was by now an old-timer in the field, skilled at walking point and leading "killer teams" on patrol. Again and again the unit struck villages. As Jim puts it, "But for some reason or other, going out on search-and-destroy missions was a steady thing. We did it all the time to different villages for two or three months. And always men were getting killed and horribly maimed." Along the way, Jim has a few good words to say about the enemy. "Their weapons were better than ours, especially the AK-47; they were trained jungle fighters." And Jim always comes back to the losses, the bitterness and the hatred.

Another of the themes of Jim's story—the incompetence and corruption of the leadership in the field—comes into focus at this point.

We didn't have an understanding of what was going on, and the leadership we had was very poor. You'd depend upon the person who had the most time in the field and the most experience. The second lieutenants were almost useless. They were educated, but that's all they were, they had no practical experience. So, consequently, they would give orders that people would follow, and they'd end up getting somebody killed. Basically, what would happen then is they would get fragged, somebody would kill them, one of those accidental killings. Because a guy like that, out of control, can hurt—can make a mistake that can be quite costly to a lot of people. So he was kept on a leash just to make sure that he didn't pull anything crazy and get half a dozen to fifty men killed at one shot.

Jim's bitterness about the leadership is deep, and, one cannot help feeling, quite justified. He recounts a period during which the unit was overrun, one of the most terrifying combat experiences. How this plays out only heightens the feeling of alienation from the leadership, and no wonder.

The word was we were going to be overrun by a large enemy force. I can remember them putting up concertina wire three rolls high out in front of us, along with claymores. And all around the whole perimeter there were howitzers, 105 howitzers, set in between each three or four positions, with beehive rounds designed to take out large groups of enemy at one time. All the way around the perimeter. I also remember placing quad-40s, 40 millimeter dusters that shoot 40 mm rounds, around the perimeter for firepower. Along with that, I can remember them putting three strands of concertina wire behind us on the line so nobody could go backwards. And that was, ah, pressure that was unbelievable, not knowing any second what was going to happen, knowing you couldn't go anywhere. It was a life-and-death situation. But it brought about the feeling of not really mattering to anybody, that our lives were, were just nothing, y'know. Nobody cared whether we lived or died—they just put us out there because that's all they had. And for what—we didn't know why. What was their reasoning—nobody told us anything. But we were overrun a couple of times. And there was a lot of dead, a lot of enemy dead. At that particular time the assault lasted for two days. And at the end of it, there were four hundred dead enemy and there were almost two hundred dead on our side. We won't even consider the wounded. It was bad—right through the wire, flares, fighting, knives. A lot of the enemy were drugged up—they were just fanatical. They wouldn't stop, some got through the wire, some had to be taken out with bayonets, others were shot with 45-caliber pistols. And what seemed funny about the whole thing, all of our leaders were in the middle of the base camp all by themselves, with men surrounding them so they wouldn't get hurt. So I guess we weren't very important, or our lives weren't important.

But this kind of thing happened all the time. And I took it really personal. I didn't like what I was seeing—I knew somebody was lying to me. And the damage had already been done; I'd already killed many, many times. And that's something you can't take back. I lost a lot of people I knew over there that I'd hoped would live through it but didn't, and as far as the leadership was concerned it wasn't worth a damn at all. They didn't care for anything but the glory. We had officers who were putting themselves in for Silver Stars and Bronze Stars, making a mockery of the whole thing. The real foot soldier didn't care about that stuff—he did his job because he had to. A medal didn't mean a thing. Pride in being a good foot soldier, a good infantry soldier is in how well you do your job. And the ultimate honor is to give your life to save somebody else's. But apparently our leadership and our officers weren't interested in how we felt and who we are—or who we were—as men, young men, who had to grow up very quickly.

This is a poignant account from a foot soldier who managed to be proud of his accomplishment while destroyed morally for all that he had been required to do, all that he had been induced into doing. Jim goes on to tell the story of his whole company being ambushed. A skilled, intuitive soldier by then, he was walking point for the entire company, with what would have been many dozens of men strung out behind him. He smelled the trap; his captain didn't want to believe him. Again, many, many men are killed or wounded, as Jim sees it, for nothing, "For what? Some company commander wants to be a hero."

This brings Jim's story up to January 31, 1968, the eve of the Tet offensive, which most students of the period take to be a watershed, with public opinion turning more and more against the war after the heavy loses and the assaults on the cities during Tet. Jim was in the thick of the fighting in and around Saigon. "The stress of the whole thing—whether you were going to live, or without one eye or a leg, torn up. We were losing our minds anyway. It just never stopped. It went on and on and on. There was one tragic thing after the other. Everything that moved was the enemy." Jim tells us that he does not remember much about the Tet offensive: "It was so insane. It was just crazy. . . . It just became so overwhelming . . . I have a very hard time remembering." This continues taking its toll. Jim's final weeks in Vietnam are a jumble in his mind, something common if not universal among the veterans who were pushed to cross the line of no return, to descend into the depths of war—to becoming berserkers.

It just became so overwhelming, you couldn't understand anything. I have a very hard time remembering all that. So for the most part we stayed in this area throughout the whole Tet. It was during this period that I started taking out more and more patrols, more and more killler teams. I had changed. There was something about it that intrigued me, and there was something about it that lured me into doing the things I did. I became reckless. I became mentally involved in the whole situation to the point to where I got to liking it. And it was very, very bad for me because I continued taking out these patrols, springing ambushes. I lost men that I had known for seven, eight months—shot between the eyes in a little village. Burned bodies, burned beyond recognition from napalm, having to go out and pick them up and bring 'em back so the bodies could go to the United States, having to notify their parents. An awful lot of guilt, an awful lot of rage, and a lot of bitterness. For what? They lied about it through the whole thing. They lied about who was winning the war. They lied about body counts. They lied so they could be big-shot generals and politicians. And at the bottom of the totem pole, there were guys getting blown away, cut in half, maimed—for no reason at all. Go out one day and lose a dozen men, pull back. And go back to the same place the next day and lose a dozen more, over and over. It made no sense at all. Bitter. Everything that I had seen—the loss of life was tremendous—had taken its toll on me internally. I felt nothing anymore, I felt no compassion. I felt nothing for no one, for anything. I was dead, to the point where I wanted to die. I became very reckless, I took chances nobody would take, I did things nobody would do, hoping I could die. All the time. It got so bad that they put me on medication in combat to calm me down, but that didn't work. I just kept on going out and going out, hoping, because I had no reason to live anymore. The damage was done, and I became a brutal, cold-blooded killer, something totally against everything I was raised to believe in. For this country. And I'll tell you, like I've told a lot of other guys, that I think it's the biggest, the single most, worst war guys of young age have ever experienced.

Then the ending comes. Still alive, if spiritually wounded unto death, the day comes and they take you out.

So with that I was still out in the jungle when my orders came down. They sent a chopper out for me in the bush, because they couldn't keep you any longer out there once your orders came down. And I was flown out, taken back to base camp, where I was processed out the same way I was processed in, and eventually just left Vietnam. I was a whole different human being. I was not the same guy that went there. I had no faith in this country whatsoever. I really didn't think much of myself, either, for all I had participated in. All I could think about was death, combat, death, over and over. It never went away. I remember talking about guys who were getting hit, killed, just before they got on the jet because they had sporadic mortar attacks and things like that. I picture the babies, the women, the torn-up bodies, the hate that had developed from the whole thing, the terror of it all. It was with me, it just overpowered me; it overtook my whole being. And I left Vietnam to come home.

There is much more to Jim's story: his arrival home, the silence that enveloped him, as it did all the other Vietnam veterans. In addition, Jim experienced extraordinary and traumatic events while still in the service in Germany. As Jim tells his story, he frequently moves from traumatic moment to the present, as if using these mo-

mentary shifts in time to anchor the story as he shapes the narrative
to render as truthfully as he knows how all that he remembers.

IN, THEN OUT,
THEN HOME FROM THE WAR

Having experienced all the violence that warfare has to offer in a
concentrated twelve or thirteen months (the marines going the army
one better and adding another month to the standard tour), the U. S.
soldier returned to no hero's welcome. In fact, although he may have
traveled to Vietnam with his unit (or at least with members of his
unit), he rarely remained with comrades from his days of training.
Planeloads of fresh soldiers landed in Vietnam and were assigned
as individuals to replenish units in need of replacements, hence the
phenomenon of the FNG ("fucking new guy"). A replacement would
arrive in the field to his new unit and typically be shunned by the
old-timers, at least not welcomed in and tutored in the ways of survival. (There were many exceptions to this, of course.) This dynamic
had nothing to do with any hostility to the new member of the unit.
Two things were coming together to produce the coldness with which
the FNG was greeted. A new, raw replacement could be a burden
and a danger because of his inexperience. In addition, and more
importantly, a new guy could get himself killed, and often did, quite
quickly, so it would be better to have as little as possible connection
with him. Old-timers, which is to say anyone in the field for two or
three months, had had bitter experiences losing friends to whom they
had become closely attached. Limiting one's connections, then, became a way of limiting the pain of loss when men were killed.

When it was time to leave the field and return home, the combatant was considered a short-timer. Often, during the last few weeks
of his tour, the soldier was given some respite, for instance, sent to
a more secure area or not sent out on risky duty. In other cases, the
situation would not permit that, and men had the bizarre experience

of going directly from a battle zone to the rear and, within days or sometimes hours, boarding the "freedom bird" that would take them back to The World. In everyone's experience there came a moment when the immediacy of battle was past, and it was time to think of going home. Willis W. tells of an unusual version of that moment. He was very short, but still in the field.

> So it was my time to leave, and all these things were in my mind, all the things that happened, the deaths that I saw. I was thinking about the NVA that—we were on the back of an amtrack. My rifle was pointed at him. He pointed his rifle. I didn't pull my trigger and he didn't pull his trigger. And it seemed like it was a rite of passage. And I often think about that today. I had the enemy in my sights and I didn't pull the trigger. And he had me in his sights and he didn't pull the trigger. He dropped his weapon and I dropped my weapon. Down to his side. And it seemed that was a rite of passage. And I never will forget that. So from that day on—it was about twelve and a half months in Vietnam—I didn't kill anymore. I didn't shoot at anyone. I had two weeks left.

If the generally wrenching experience of leaving for home was not bad enough, the return home was a traumatic experience in itself for almost everyone. The veterans of the Vietnam tapes all have a story about the shock and the trauma of homecoming. The U. S. combatants came home, one at a time, alone, with no debriefing, certainly with no treatment for the post-traumatic stress that they were already experiencing. Aggressive instincts that were conditioned—and life-saving—for the soldier and his fellows and destructive for the enemy were often triggered in young veterans just out of the jungles and rice paddies, firebases, and urban squalor of Vietnam. The stories of returning veterans being spat upon and called baby killers are true, as attested by the contributors to the Vietnam tapes. There certainly were no parades; nobody wanted to hear their stories.

4

■　■　■　■　■　■　■　■　■　■　■　■　■

OTHER STORIES,
OTHER GENRES

■ I have fond memories of brave deeds by young men.

Tim W., The Chambers of Memory

■ In the thousand chances of warfare, nearly every combat soldier has failed to support his comrades at a critical moment; through sins of omission or commission, he has been responsible for the death of those he did not intend to kill. . . . Add to this the unnumbered acts of injustice so omnipresent in war, which may not result in death but inevitably bring pain and grief, and the impartial observer may wonder how the participants in such deeds could ever smile again and be free of care.

J. Glenn Gray, The Warriors

■ Insofar as Eros is physical passion and sensual impulse, war has been from of old its true mate and bedfellow, as the ancient myth makes clear. And erotic love of the fuller sort can find a dwelling place in the violence of war that forever astounds us and remains inexplicable. Here Ares and Aphrodite meet as opposites who have a powerful attraction for each other.

J. Glenn Gray, The Warriors

■ ■ ■ ■ ■ ■ ■ ■ ■ ■ ■ ■ ■ ■ ■ ■ ■ ■

STORIES OF WAR, OF GUILT, AND OF LOVE

In their accounts, all but a few veterans turned to the template for telling one's story that naturally comes to mind: call it the life story genre. Life stories, however, can be told to other patterns. Even while maintaining the overall design, significant parts can be told in ways different from the norm. Several of the veterans, in fact, used other fundamental genres in major sections of their narratives. One of these alternative forms may be called the Warrior's Tale, and two of the veterans told of their war experiences using this format. One of the veterans devoted his story primarily to confession, and it may be seen as belonging to the confessional tradition. One contributor told a love story in a quite legendary vein, and I am calling this the Warrior's Romance. (There are literary traditions to which these alternative genres refer.) A number of the veterans employed elements of the Warrior's Tale without, however, conveying a sense of themselves as ultimately determined by this self-concept. These were citizen soldiers, like Jim E., Mike V., Alan S., and Willis W., whose narratives were partly fashioned from warriors' lore. Jim E. speaks here and there with the pride of the foot soldier, to use a term he employs—a traditional one that could refer to a professional warrior from any historical epoch, from the seige of Troy on. Wolf T-E comes close to rendering his story in this form, while qualifying it significantly as he comes to see that for Vietnam "there was no glory in it." Many of the veterans clearly saw themselves as ultimately damaged by their war experiences, which involved what they perceive as unforgiveable transgressions. This is a common theme in the contributors' stories. Features of the confessional genre are present in most of the stories.

THE WARRIORS

Combat has a profound effect on any human being, in any time or place. Making war may be the second oldest profession, yet it seems so very unnatural to those of us not part of a military tradition. To see this as one's personal destiny may come through family tradition, as with Lewis B. Puller, Jr. (son of the legendary Marine Corps warrior General "Chesty" Puller, and author of the autobiograhy, *Fortunate Son* [1991]). Warriors' tales have been told, time out of mind, around the campfire, in the men's lodgehouse, in medieval castles, in the local VFW lodge. The young men listen eagerly, knowing that they, too, might someday be called upon to go to war; the old men, with their own memories, listen solemnly. This telling of the trauma story was always structured by the ritual aspects of the setting: the special place and time, the listeners—the witnesses—the unspoken knowledge that what was being told was both modeled after a tradition and would become a part of that tradition (thereby altering it). The form of the story, therefore, is ready to hand for the teller. Certain themes will be in order, including themes of valor, honor, and suffering. Comrades lost in battle will be remembered with great feeling, along with their deeds. The enemy will be characterized according to the tradition as well, valorized or vilified, according to their conduct. Victory will be celebrated; defeat will be acknowledged. In either case, loss, suffering, and wounding will be recognized and a compassionate response will be assured among the witnesses. We will see in the two warriors' tales below all of the features of the genre. Their stories will be presented at length and in some detail; they are worthy of our attention in their own right. They are also both concerned coincidentally with the great seige of the American base called Khe Sanh and, as such, represent significant contributions to the history of the war and of the Marine Corps.

Joel's Story

Joel D.'s contribution to the project was a masterful performance. Joel is the consummate marine, athough a post-traumatic condition eventually precluded his being a career soldier. His account of life before Vietnam is devoted mainly to his family background, which he is at pains to present as aristocratic and traditional. He begins by specifying that the family's holdings go back to a land grant from 1670. He depicts the family as stern and solid: no drinking, no drugs, no divorce, no cancer; people on both sides "typically live into their high 90's." The only thing divergent is a reference to uncles on both sides of the family who were in the Marine Corps during World War II. Joel describes them as "rounders," and adds, "Let's say that they knew how to have fun." His father, however, is someone whom Joel presents as all business. He is still, Joel tells us, a well-known banker with powerful political connections. Part of family tradition was observance of the religious tradition. Nightly, they would have "family altar," reading scriptures and praying together. It was expected that sons and grandsons would go into the banking business, which Joel found stultifying, boring, and poorly paid. So in 1963 he joined the Marine Corps without informing his family. When he revealed this, they were "greatly disappointed." Vietnam, at the time, was a "far-away thing," something people were assuming would be "a short-lived thing."

Joel's aristocratic, Southern background would influence his life in the Marine Corps and his war experiences significantly. They said to him, "You're from the South, you probably like dogs." Joel did not know what he was getting into when he agreed. Dog handlers in Vietnam walked point; that's what the dogs were for. Walking point meant being alert in the extreme, as only situations like combat can induce, for hours at a time, day after day. Walking point meant that you were first in line to contact the enemy, that you were first in line where just putting your foot down could mean the end for you or the loss of your foot. Troopers who were good at walking point consititued an elite, people with a sixth sense, a nose—you could sometimes literally smell trouble ahead. Walking point successfully put one in an uncanny world, something like the legendary Indian trackers of popular lore; walking point unsuccessfully got you—and probably a lot of other people—killed. The emotional toll of walking point was heavy. As Olson (1987) puts it:

The need to be constantly alert to every detail of the environment, to any aberration in the nature of the terrain or vegetation, to smells in the air, to any changes in the noise of the jungle—to a sudden quiet or the sound of startled animals or birds—had a grinding and exhausting effect on the men who stalked the jungles. All of their senses were finely honed so that reaction came instinctively. But such a high level of alert consumed enormous amounts of nervous energy. [p. 478]

Joel's work as a dog handler meant that he frequently traveled from unit to unit, which he just mentions. This would mean that he would never have been with any particular outfit long enough to form really close connections. But it was almost always a matter of walking point: "So, everywhere we went you *knew* the shit was going to hit the fan— it was not going to be a walk in the park."

There is a structural integrity, a seamless quality to this warrior's tale. It may be the long tradition of ritualized telling of the war story that ultimately shapes this narrative. Or it may well be that Joel is simply a great teller of tales, a talented narrator. In any event, consider the skill with which Joel introduces the story of his Vietnam experiences. He tells us just enough of his family background as we need to appreciate the great divergence from his father's plan for his life and career. Joel also looks ahead in his introduction to two significant events from life after Nam, which tell us much about the years struggling with the aftermath. He speaks briefly about abandoning his business and family one day in 1979, quite out of the blue and for no apparent reason—things were going well. This marriage and two others fell apart, we learn, and one son dies of a rare form of cancer. His wife at the time, a nurse, attributes this to Joel's exposure to Agent Orange and says, "You killled him as surely as if you shot him." For Joel at his son's side as he died, there were no feelings. He was there and prayed with his son at the end, but it was just "a business type thing—matter of fact." So he both sets things in motion for the story he, the warrior, wants to tell and hints at what is to come living later with a warrior's memories.

Joel begins his story proper by first mentioning a colonel whom he admired and with whom he served early in his tour. This is the Corps' "Bull" Fisher, described by Joel as a ferocious warrior and "a fine gentleman."

> He had been at Iwo Jima and Guadalcanal and those places and he had no patience with the enemy, and his idea of fighting a war was killing everybody in sight who was enemy—no quarter, no rhyme or reason. There was just no slack given to the NVA and VC in the area. When we found 'em, he'd run 'em till they dropped.

With this vignette of Bull Fisher, which links Joel directly to Marine Corps lore, he is ready to speak about some of the first experiences he had, how he reacted to them, and how they affected him. His opening move, in this, is to recount his reaction to his first exposure to the day-to-day violence of the war. He arrives, well trained but unseasoned, to take up his role in combat. Some of Bull Fisher's troops are relaxing after what must have been a prolonged battle.

> They had loads of VC and NVA soldiers they had killed. They had them stacked up on the beach like cordwood, and they were playing cards on their bodies like they were tables. That freaked me out, but I was determined that I would not show any reaction to it. So I didn't. I began to walk point.

Joel goes on:

> We'd make contact, kill as many as we could, and pursue the rest of them no matter where they went. He would pursue them to hell if he could. What I did admire about Bull Fisher is he was there, too; he was not back in the rear—he was out there with us. He was a good colonel; he was a good man, but he darned near scared me to death.

Joel gets over that; in fact, he and his dog began to enter into it. "The dog became very good at it. I was beginning to feel very comfortable and good at it. Actually, what I felt was immortal. I didn't

■ ■ ■ ■ ■ ■ ■ ■ ■ ■ ■ ■ ■ ■ ■ ■ ■ ■ ■

feel like they could get me." So we have a three-step process of entering in, of becoming a warrior: the first is a brutal and macabre look at death; the second is falling in with and tolerating Bull Fisher's style; and the third is that feeling of immortality. Along the way, Joel contributes a bit of Marine Corps history, how "The Walking Dead" got their name.

> I continued to work with the 9th Marines. 1966, they inherited the name The Walking Dead, Delta Company, 19. I was sent somewhere up north and there were no Marine Corps choppers available. I was on a U.S. Army chopper, and this chopper had something to do with an army intelligence unit, 'cause they had lots of radios [on board]. As we rolled towards 19 in the mountains—it was still the rainy season—the army warrant officer aboard said, "The unit we're taking you to is under fire now, you're not going to be able to get in unless we can slip you in somehow." As we rolled over the mountain top, I looked down and thought that I saw marines standing up and they were in a headlong frontal assault being directed by this captain, and he was with them. The radio operator in the chopper radioed them and said, "If you will run left and right we'll do what we can to get 'em off of you until you can regroup." The captain said, "Fuck you—you fly your helicopter, I'll run this assault!" What I was looking at was forty marines or approximately forty marines who were dead, but they were in the mud up to their knees so they could not fall. So that's where their name came from. He continued the assault while we circled, and it was obvious that I was not going to get in.

This, too, is what makes one a marine, loyalty to the legends, the tradition, of the Corps. For Joel's narrative, clearly, the fact that such élan was wasteful of lives does not enter into it. He was also present at one of the Corps' most difficult times in Vietnam, the Battle of Khe Sanh, which ran from late 1967 into March of 1968. This was really a seige insofar as the strategic base, located in the northwest corner of Vietnam, was never assaulted head on. In point of fact, the whole affair was staged by the NVA as a diversion, while the assault on major cities known as the Tet Offensive of 1968 was being set up and executed. General Westmoreland was taken in, President Johnson backed him up, and a decision to hold the base was made, though sounder minds considered abandoning it to be the wiser thing. Six thousand marines were ordered to defend the base, while a huge number of air and artillery bombardments were expended on what was assumed to be as many as 40,000 NVA troops in the area. Ultimately, 100,000 tons of explosives were expended on a five-square-mile area around the base. The seige lasted for a total of seventy-five days. Joel's account is concerned with action outside the perimeter of the base on Hill 861. (Hills, or mountains, were designated by numbers corresponding to their elevation in meters.) This is where Joel and a small group of fellow marines encountered all of the violence, suffering, and exaltation that ground combat has to offer. (Tim W.'s story also gives a central place to Hill 861—and the same action—and will be reviewed below.) Joel begins his account:

> The latter part of 1967, I did something I hadn't done before, I wrote my mother a letter and said, "I'm in a place called Khe Sanh. It's a beautiful place, it's very quiet, there's nothing going on—tea plantations, mountains." On or about January 2nd, 1968, as I was patrolling, I would notice the sign and the dog was picking up a lot of signals that there were a lot of people in the area other than us. And I began to report it. Unbeknownst to me, the recon teams were also reporting it, but nobody was believing them, like they didn't believe it. And we had had some sporadic exchanges, hit-and-run things, but they wouldn't close with us. They'd shoot and run, and we'd have to chase them and they would vanish. As the month of January progressed, things got a little more tense. From the actual line of Khe Sanh, I was sent to one of the surrounding hills and was running patrols off Hill 861 with Kilo Company, 326th. Over the night of January 20th, 1968, the company commander passed the word for nobody to be in the bunkers because intelligence said we were going to get hit. But we

did not pay a lot of attention to it, but we did what we were told. The proverbial story: they're coming, they're coming. Before many times before then—I'm well into my third tour and I've heard many times, "They're coming, they're coming " and it didn't develop. I had very little faith in the intelligence operation over there, very, very little.

I knew the place could be bad because September the 10th of 1967, operating with the 26th Marines and being attached to Lima, we were several clicks [kilometers] behind Mike Company, when Mike Company walked into a regimental-size ambush. And we were on the high ground and they were on the low ground, and they did not have a dog with them. I was with the other company, trailing, when the NVA hit them with artillery, and then moved in a wave across them. A lot of marines were shot trying to get down. Subsequently, there were four hundred and some-odd people killed and wounded, U.S., that day. I later found out I was wrong—there were about 300 and some odd killed and about 150 wounded. It was a hell of a day.

Now, back to Khe Sanh—this is '68. I felt like I could do anything in Vietnam, I was not really—by that time I had sort of outgrown or put fear away. I was walking point for Kilo Company off 861 North, and there were only three approaches. There was the Khe Sanh side that went down; the other two approaches left that hill toward Laos, which we could see. Before this started, we left one morning, we went off the high side of the 2nd Platoon. And we were not very far when we made contact, but they wouldn't shoot and we wouldn't shoot. I knew they were there, and they knew that we knew it, and everybody knew that everybody understood they were there. It gave me an eerie feeling, and I reported it. I said, "They're there, they're definitely there." And the Colonel says, "Well, everybody else says they're there too, but we're not making contact—I need some bodies, I need prisoners or I need bodies, we've got to have some evidence." I was not able to get the evidence, I was not able to get to them. I could not get a point where I could set the dog on one to hold him to where we jumped on him. Subsequently, the evidence never materialized.

But the night of the 20th of January, the company commander passed the word that none of us would be in the bunkers. At about 9:30, all hell broke loose. We took a really intense artillery barrage that did not lift as usual. It wasn't two or three rounds, it was 18 or 20, maybe 30 rounds. All the officers were killed immediately, all the staff, the head corpsman was killed. They had the bunkers plotted. See, we were put in a position we weren't trained for anyway. Marines are not trained to hold defensive positions. There's no training for that. And the shit hit the fan. Just a very few minutes later, a North Vietnamese major stood up down the hill, fired a red flare. And they came up the hill on line in a dead run. The squad between me and Cecil Y. were killed, they all died. That's about 30 yards between me and Cecil Y., there was nothing left. Cecil was on the right about 30 yards, and they kept coming—I couldn't shoot fast enough. And they finally jumped the trench, they were down in the trench with us, on top of the hill with us. About two in the morning, I looked up the hill under illumination, and a guy named Chavez who was by himself, he had run out of ammunition, and he had a pistol. And he fought them off until he ran out of ammunition, and they bayonetted him and killed him. And we couldn't get to him, they were all over him. And I knew Cecil was still alive, because I could hear his squad—they were kicking ass on that side. They kicked a lot of ass. After he stopped them from running over that side, 'cause if they got on that side they'd kill us all.

And it went on all night long, and it was in close. People were getting killed with two-by-fours, knives, shot. I must have thrown a case of grenades, and I shot that shotgun [M-79] until I just couldn't hold it anymore hardly. It was bad. When the morning came, there was about twelve of us left, and there were a lot of dead NVA everywhere. Cecil Y. had the major's body that fired the flare, he had the flare gun, and he was dead. We took eleven prisoners, NVA soldiers. And sometime after sunrise, I had the gun team to my left, and Cecil was in charge, and he said, "You guys need to get your ass down in that parapet. If you don't you're going to get your ass killed." And they said okay, but they didn't do it, and a few minutes later an RPG landed on them and killed them all. And this kid Panelli was killed—it just blew his head off. So he took the POWs down in the trench and we shot 'em and cut their heads off, all of them. There were six POWs. About eleven o'clock they called on the radio and said, "You need to go to Lima Company's lines. Because they're getting probed and they need a dog down there." So I went toward the LZ (landing zone), and they lit the LZ up on me, I couldn't get there—they waved the chopper off. And they came again about 11:30, and I tried to get on the chopper with my gear and my dog, and they lit the LZ up again—I couldn't get on. The third try was, I think, around almost twelve. And we went down the hill quick, the pilot kept it low—he actually dove off the hill above the trees. He flew into Lima Company and said, "Now, when I hit the dirt you get off this goddamned thing because shit's flying." And I did. I went to the trench and found the company commander to find out what he wanted me to do. And he said, "Put your dog out because I'm afraid of the dog, I need to talk to you about what I want you to do." So I took my dog and put him in a bunker and tied him to the main member of the bunker, a dog I'd had for three years and worked with him. So I went toward where the company commander was, and we took a lot of incoming. And I got up and looked back, we took a lot of incoming, so I'm still in the trench and I'm trying to get down where he is, but artillery's flying and shit's flying everywhere. Very intense artillery barrage. So a little time passed. When I got up again, I looked back to—the bunker's smoking, so I ran back there. And the dog was just chewed up, he was burned, he was mangled, but he was alive. I couldn't find the corpsman and I didn't have any morphine, and I had to kill him. And when I went down towards the trench again, not thinking what I was doing, I got it. So now I'm down and the dog's dead. So they medevacked me, and we're going out to Phu Bai, but we can't get in 'cause they're under attack and we can't get down. So they fly me way south.

This extraordinary account was told just as it is transcribed here, in a stream, a flow of images and details. The rhythm of the narrator's speech is measured and certain. At the same time, the emotion behind all this comes strongly to the surface from time to time. This is especially apparent as Joel is speaking about his comrade, Chavez, whom they could not help, whom they had to watch die at the hands of the enemy—and beyond, as Joel recollects that night of hand-to-hand combat and all the deaths, particularly the death of the soldier named Panelli. Feeling is withdrawn to just under the surface of the narrative flow when Joel turns to speak of the vengence taken on the six captives. This seems to reestablish the distance he wanted, as narrator, from the intensity of emotion associated with the story. Even as he speaks of the death of his dog he remains outwardly stoic.

After recovering from his wound, Joel continues walking point here and there, including a time under a company commander who was obsessed with capturing a certain NVA officer. This episode in itself, material enough for a whole chapter, is only sketched in by Joel. For him the war was winding down. By comparison with earlier years, he says, 1970 was basically "uneventful." He is nearing the end of his account. At Phu Bai, Joel is training troops in the art of firing the .50-caliber machine gun. Then the unit is hit, and "an intense little firefight" breaks out. The gun Joel is using blows up, and he's back in the hospital. The platoon sergeant says to him, "You've been here four years—you've got to go home, buddy." Instead, he is assigned to spend his last two and a half months in country with a bunch of misfits Joel calls "maggots," draftees into the Marine Corps. Later, back in the states, Joel tries to get orders back to Vietnam, but no one will sign off on them. Thus, he ends his warrior's account anticlimactically, as he experienced it. The only war we had, and he cannot return to it. After he has finished his story, as usually happened in the tapings, a conversation ensued. When Joel was asked if he had any regrets, he answered, "My only regret is that there's no war going on now for me to join." Everything after years in Vietnam was anticlimactic, and everything was muddled.

Tim's Story

Joel's experience is paralleled by that of another true warrior, Tim
W. Tim's personal style is radically different from Joel's; their experiences are amazingly close, at least insofar as they were both
present during the seige of Khe Sanh, in fact both spending the critical time up on Hill 861. Tim's style of narration, however, differs
radically. His native manic energy translates into staccato rhythms,
sentences started and then, restarted, ellipses, a jumpy movement
from topic to topic and back again, though there was nothing confusing or unclear about his story as he told it. It was lucid, forceful,
and highly organized (not unlike all thirty-one stories here). Rarely,
if ever, was there any sense of emotion welling up to spill over into
the narrative flow. It was a brilliant performance.

Tim begins with only the briefest outline of his life before joining
the service. He speaks of getting swimming scholarships, first to prep
school in Greenwich, Connecticut, then to college. During summer
break after his freshman year, a friend asks Tim to drive him down
to the recruiters so he can sign up for the Marine Corps. On a whim,
as he describes it, Tim joins up, too. "By the time, we left I'd signed
my ass up, too. I don't know why—there was no John Wayne men-
tality, there was no—didn't want to go kill the yellow menace or
anything. It was a whim." Tim had not the slightest idea of what he
was in for. Stepping off the bus at Parris Island, the Marine Corps
basic training camp, was a bit of a shock, he tells us; however, after
devoting but a sentence or two to basic and advanced training, Tim
shifts directly into his warrior's narrative. Curiously, he speaks of
shipping out, not to Vietnam, but to "Asia." His war was the little
one—monumental for him—that took place in the period, roughly,
from November, 1967, to March, 1968, in a quiet and remote northwest corner of the country. We will learn that he disdains veterans
who slept on cots once in a while and, in particular, those who did
not live by the code of honor of the warrior. Tim's timing is exquis-

itely right—or wrong, depending on how you view it. He arrived at Khe Sanh just before the beginning of the seige, after which he had his first "baptism by fire." He was on a listening post outside the perimeter. He was terrified, we later learn, and he vowed never to be again.

They subsequently probed the lines and all hell broke loose up there and the rounds were flying over our heads from the base. And that was my first baptism of fire—though I never got to fire at anybody. I pretty much got the idea what this thing was all about—I guess it dawned on me, y'know. Because I'd pretty much been tiptoeing along, y'know. I really had no idea that this was pretty serious. I was still tripping along.

Tim began to witness the daily carnage of combat. He provides this little vignette with his usual élan, seemingly without giving in to the feelings that must be associated with it.

A guy in my squad got killed when we started taking incoming. He ran down into the bunker, had his helmet off, 'cause you run faster with your helmet off. And underneath the sand bags, you've got a detonating layer—you put any kind of crap you can, 'cause they penetrate and detonate, so you try to put a detonation layer and then more sandbags, then you use runway [material], corrugated metal. He ran full force [into the end of a metal plank], stuck him there, right in his head—he was hanging there. Right in his head. People were getting killed left and fucking right.

In due course, Tim's platoon, part of Alpha Company, 126th Marines, is sent up to Hill 861. It was January 16th, he recalls. The NVA was massing on the hills around the base. He begins this, the main part of his narrative, as the fighting starts in earnest here, a few days later at exactly 9:30 in the evening, just as Joel remembers it.

Nine-thirty at night, the first red flare went up, and that's the night we got overrun. It went on till 10 o'clock the next morning. They'd been spotting their mortars for the last month. The first two seconds they knocked out the machine gun nest, the mortar nest, and this whole end of the trench line. And the shit really started hitting the fan—they were coming, whistles blowing, screaming. I thought, I thought, y'know, they'd sneak up and try to slit your throat. They do it like we do, whistles, fire-team rushes, four-man, four-man. And they come. They'd blow the wire—they're coming like hell. And, like I said, they'd taken out the machine gun—three of us ran to reinforce that. Then they broke through at the other end, and I ran down the other end. And it got down to hand-to-hand combat. I took a Chaicom, that little fucker threw a grenade— a Chaicom, on the end of a stick, you bang 'em and throw 'em. They took a piece about that big out of my ass. And, ah, it was about six hours we were going at it. They were in the trench line, they were behind us firing back at us. They were still coming up the fucking hill. The next morning we had 83 confirmed kills in front of our position. But by the time I got back up to where my position was, two of my friends had been bayonetted and shot, lying there, dead. I can still see my friend's helmet with the picture of his 3-year-old daughter lying there. He was all fucked up. His name was Wally T., from West Virginia. He'd signed a special release to be allowed in the country because his brother was there—you weren't allowed to have two brothers—but he wanted to go, all gung-ho. They totally fucked him up. And another guy, Earl C., from Maryland. They'd been bayonetted about twenty times. I always had this feeling, if I'd have stayed up there something would have come out different. So as I say, it went on and on till ten o'clock the next morning. They were all over, still in the command bunker. Y'know, they were all over the fucking place. And [we] finally resecured the area. They brought the rest of my company up.

You see, there were two hills. There was 861 Alpha and there was 861, and there was a ridge that went between them. Well, that's where they all were. Prior, you could hear them chopping down trees and bullshitting and building bunkers—from the trench line, you could hear them. So you knew it was coming. They came right over this ridge line and swept down this way, 'cause the wire went around this way. They broke through here and they just got between the wire and the trench line, and they were coming through like a throughway, like I-95 out here. So eventually the rest of my company came up and took a position on 861 Alpha. And I was over here. I went down to the base, got my ass stitched up. They told me, "Leave the metal—do more damage taking it out." I was down there six or seven days. Incoming. Then, I went back up on the hill, figured it'd be safer. And generally survived a hundred and three days up there. On one-half a canteen of water a day, one meal a day. When I came home I was a hundred and twenty-three pounds. And I'm six foot one. The trench line when I got up there was about three feet deep, shoulder width. When I left, it was seven feet deep. So all we did was dig, go out, clear a field of fire. And they slowly picked us off with mortars every day. When I left, there was twenty-three guys left from the seventy-six I went up with. Wounded, I mean, rat bites—I mean, one night I became M-79 man. I got called down to the trench line—there was movement down between two hills—there was a small stream. And the lieutenant woke me up because we were on 100 percent alert at dusk, and then you had two hours off, two hours on, one hour off, one hour on, two hours off, two hours on, then 100 percent. You got five hours of sleep a night. And I got woke up, brought down, and told to fire a round down there. And you could hear a tiger or some shit roaring.

We were way up north and to the east [west, actually]. We were the farthest base to the east. The staturation bombing. I remember sitting on the hill and the B-52's, chunks of metal this big flying by your head, when the B-52's came through. Getting sprayed. No resupply at all. Mostly, I remember people getting picked off one at a time, every day, y'know. Picking up body parts. I can tell you, after we got overrun—it's a funny story. We had to go out on body count. And we got a little ambitious—we were posing 'em in certain positions. And then we started taking illumination granades and burning their faces off—we were just fucking with them. That night the wind shifted. And I don't think any-

one in that whole trench line wasn't puking—stink! Jesus, that stink.
So that just about cured burning people up after you'd killed them—it
was nasty. So we had to drag 'em up on the landing zone—they had a
small LZ—and there was a Chinese officer—six-four, a hundred and
eighty-five pounds. That son-of-a-bitch was as big as I was. So these
guys wore khaki—none of this black pajama wishy-washy shit. They had
canteens and belts with whistles—just like we did, y'know. Yeah.

So I stayed there till March 18th, day after St. Patrick's Day. I was
going out on a listening post. I had Rap Brown—actually, his name was
Ronald, Ronald Brown, from Newark, New Jersey, and we called him
Rap Brown—the activist. And he always hated going with me, because
I used to sleep in a body bag. We were so high in the air, clouds would
actually come through and it was always wet. So I picked one of them
up, and I'd get in the son-of-a-bitch and zip it up. He'd say, "Get out of
that bag, man, don't get in that bag." Well, we went out this night, we
went down on the listening post. I had the radio. There was a guy named
Morey, he was from Tennessee, and I'm trying to remember who the
other guy was. And we went through the gates, and we set up a listening post. We'd key in—you don't call them, they call you and say, "This
is Bulldog." And I was Snap, and there was Crackle, then Pop all around
the hill. And key your handset four times if you're secure. So the code
was two less, so you'd key it twice. In case they picked it up, and if you
keyed it four they'd know you'd bought the big one. So about an hour
later, we started hearing chatter, talk. And I could actually see the little
fucker smoking a cigarette. So I took Ronald Brown, and we were going
to go down and get 'em. Well, they were waiting for us. I mean, him and
I went down there and they had booby-trapped it with a mortar. So it
blew me, Jesus, about eight feet in the air and back off about fifteen.
Thank God, the radio took most of it. It broke both my legs, I got a piece
of metal in my eye. It broke a few fingers, a hip—generally just fucked
me up all over. I've got scrap metal all over me. And I don't know what
happened to Brown. I don't know whether he died or not. He didn't get
medevacked with me. When I got medevacked off that hill—usually, if

you were wounded you went, if you were dead you stayed for a few days. Because every time a helicopter came in—what they'd do is send the Phantoms through first, then gun ships, then when the helicopter comes the little bastards would pop up and start shooting. They didn't want us, they wanted the helicopter. He wasn't on the helicopter with me. So— this eye was burned. I didn't wear glasses before. This eye's now 275 and zero in this eye. So I couldn't see, I was all taped up. They hit me with morphine all the time. And he wasn't on the helicopter with me, so I assume he died. From there I went to the hospital ship *Repose*, where they operated on my eye.

It is, at first, difficult to read the emotion in the story. Tim's style was manic; he often spoke in fragmentary sentences, and his exuberant gesturing helped carry a greater portion of the meaning than usual. He never really gave way to the feelings that one would assume are associated with these events. He did speak of his emotional experience of events, in a negative way, as if feeling something other than hatred, and the berserker's rush was a weakness. In particular, he tells of a dead friend's helmet with the picture of his 3-year-old daughter inside. Tim's view is that he should never have listened to this young father talking about his child. The man's name should never have meant anything to him. In fact, he says that it was not until sometime in the year before the taping, his first year of sobriety since Vietnam, that Tim began to remember comrades' names at all.

In this warrior's story, the account of life after his brief "time in the sun" (as he puts it) is filled with references to the war, with regrets that *that* was the best of times and the worst of times and that everything after is just that—after. Tim seems only to look back, while wondering what he is to do with the rest of his life. As he says, "Keep breathing—and hope that some divine sign hits me in the forehead to find out what I'm supposed to do with the rest of my life." This waiting for a sign is associated with his belief that his destiny was to be there in Khe Sanh at that fateful time. "So I sit and wait."

I wait for my calling, so to speak. I honestly believe my life was, I'd say, plucked and switched, and my purpose in life was to be there in '67 and '68. And I was spared. And now I roam, unfulfilled. You know, I was needed and I was plucked. . . . My life was just [upended]. . . . [I've got] no aspirations to write the great American novel. Like Patton said, "Nobody every did any good dying for his country—you make the other fellow die for his." And I was good at it. I was so good, I was one of the youngest sergeants in the Marine Corps. And since then, I've been hanging around, trying to keep some sense of honor and right and wrong. But I don't see any purpose for me anymore.

It is as if divine providence made a mistake; he was supposed to die there. We learn that he has mixed feelings about the Corps. They treated him badly later; they did not really want Vietnam veterans around, he feels. That the country ignored, marginalized, and reviled the veterans is something that Tim does not go into. His Marine Corps was supposed to honor and take care of him, as he had been taught that honoring the Corps first and the country second would be what was expected of him. What is right—like killing as many of the enemy as possible with as few comrades as possible lost—is something Tim refers to again and again; that is what he takes pride in. He refers equally to the purity of all this, the distillation of existence down to basics—one-half a canteen of water a day, one cold meal and, every day, life and death in combat.

That camaraderie, that trust; the object and the mission was so fucking important. It was life and death. And anybody who survived and kept their honor and their pride, y'know, didn't act cowardly. It was something to be proud of; you didn't need a medal, you didn't need a ribbon, you didn't need recognition. You were in a situation where you were taking fire, and you're pinned down. And you give an order for on-line assault *on my command*. What that means is that on my command everybody is going to stand up and start firing back. The object is, if we can put out more firepower than they do, they'll put their heads down.

■ ■ ■ ■ ■ ■ ■ ■ ■ ■ ■ ■ ■ ■ ■ ■ ■ ■ ■ ■

And then we walk forward, standing up, and assault their trench line. Now, you got eight guys to your right and three to your left, and there's bullets flying. And you know that somebody, a couple of them, are going to get killed. But if you stay there you're all going to fucking die. You give that command and everybody stands up.

This is the kind of situation you plan. It's not a matter of going to the boss and telling him he's working you too hard. This is not the same thing. This is an on-line assault. If you stay there they're going to bring in mortars and they're going to pick you off. You can't just get up and run. You're from here to, to the elevator, and you can see their eyes. The only thing you can do is put their heads down, so you got to get up and go towards them. And if one puts his gun up and starts firing, you buy the farm. And that's when guys listen, don't question, and you say do it. And you look around and try to call in medevac for whoever's wounded. And there's almost like a complete collapse afterwards, y'know. After everything calms down. And you almost feel like hugging and sobbing together, but you can't because you're marines. But there's a certain, there's a certain—at that moment, you are alive. Before you die. There's a nanosecond there where you are completely alive. And, I mean, you've tested yourself, you've tested your mettle, you've faced the enemy. And nothing—there's got to be something in your life. There's got to be something that compares, but everything after that is a big letdown. So ever since I was 19 years old, life has no meaning, it's not worthwhile, y'know.

This was Tim's Vietnam. He is exceptionally disdainful of the war he knew nothing of, the beer and pizza at the end of the day, the women, the rapes, the drugs. He is particularly incensed about actions he considers dishonorable.

I never saw fragging. I mean, this is a phenomenon that I find fucking hard to believe. Y'know, right off the top of my head, I mean morally. I don't see how anybody could frag one of their own men. This shit never went on in my Marine Corps—blacks, whites, we had a Mexican. We were all marines. And there was a certain honor among, y'know, killers. We took great pride in what we did.

As far as Tim is concerned, he won his war. Indeed, how could anything measure up to his experiences as he speaks of them in this warrior's narrative? Nothing could compare.

I look back now—I'm 45 years old— I look back, that was the one proud time of my life. [It] was that short—I was only there from November to March. I got wounded twice. All hell broke loose. I had guys following me up the hill with bullets whizzing around and listening to what order I had given. We kicked their fucking ass for them. There are a lot of guys out there walking around because they were with me. I mean it was the proud moment of my life, and I've never been able to come close to that, that sense of duty, the sense of honor. Even moral—I mean, there was a righteousness to what we were doing, yeah. I feel strong about that.

Small wonder that life has been all aftermath since then: a lot of drinking, pointless fights, three marriages, three divorces, innumerable girlfriends, and, especially, innumerable jobs—over sixty jobs in twenty-five years. We learn that for fifteen years Tim did not even bother to file an income tax return: "It didn't apply to me." He goes on, "If I couldn't have my old Marine Corps, I didn't want anything else." Yet between the lines we can discern a glimmer of hope for change. Tim spoke highly of his therapist at the V. A. Hospital and how the latter was urging him to enter the advanced inpatient program there. He was, of course, ambivalent at best.

THE CONFESSION

When an unburdening is at the heart of the motivation for telling one's story, the overall narrative structure may look like that of the life story; the intent, or motivation, however, is different. If the generic form of the life story is the usual vehicle for a developmental history, the confessional form of the life story covers the same territory while promoting an entirely different purpose. As usual there is a generally recognized tradition, going back at least to St. Augustine, whose *Confessions* was written in A.D. 400, that governs the shape of the narrative. Religious practice dictates regular, ritualized confession of sins, and popular culture tells us to "get it off your chest" and "make a clean breast of it." In this way a purging is sought; you will, it is assumed, no longer be burdened by the deed you have confessed. You will be forgiven. Seeking forgiveness is something Vietnam veterans with combat trauma frequently do, mostly believing that they will not find it, knowing that they cannot forgive themselves.

The quest for relief from the suffering of a moral burden is predicated upon facing what really happened. In fact, when telling your story you are always implicitly accepting the condition that you will tell the truth. Even under circumstances that encourage embellishment, for example, the story of your recent fishing trip, you have the sense that the listener is anticipating hearing something about what really happened. There is a sort of implicit contract between teller and listener that obtains. When your story is one that will have you unburdening yourself of shameful events, guilt, even criminal acts, then you either do not undertake to tell it or you undertake to tell the truth. Anything else would be false confession; the contract would be broken, both you and your listener engaging in a futile exercise.

Bob's Story

For Bob L., the main function of telling his story was to confess in the search for forgiveness. Bob is one of the seekers looking for a way to wipe out the taint of what he views as unforgivable actions in Vietnam, to purge himself of traumatic memories of transgressions

94

that haunt him. His confession is carefully situated in his whole story; clearly, for him, the context is important. Context, however, does not explain or justify; we get, instead, a sense of the extent to which transgression came with no significant link to the distant past, and of what a toxic influence it had on the future. Bob's family situation was unusual. His father was an engineer and worked on the development of the atomic bomb. During Bob's childhood and adolescence, therefore, the family lived in a cloistered "atomic community" in New Mexico. His father is described as somewhat stern and standoffish, but Bob speaks of having close friends and plenty of educational opportunities. In fact, he had an athletic scholarship to the University of New Mexico for the swim team. It was 1966, and Bob says, "I didn't feel I was ready for college." He goes on, "I wasn't going to evade the draft . . . I knew it would be against all my father's wishes" (i. e., joining would delay his education and therefore would be frowned on). He went down and, following in the footsteps of a friend, Eddie, Bob joined the Marine Corps. "I never got to grow up as a rough-tough person in high school. . . . If you join the Marine Corps you'll become a man . . . and that was in my mind . . . around women and all of that. . . . It wasn't until the very last possible moment that I told my father I'd joined the Marine Corps."

With a typical teenage desire to distinguish himself from his father—go against his wishes—impress the girls, and become a man, Bob was off to Parris Island and the traumatic experiences of Marine Corps basic training. (If not traumatic, certainly basic training during the Vietnam war came as a shock to everyone.) Bob emphasizes that he tried to resist what he describes as "military brainwashing." Probably because of his academic promise, Bob was trained and designated a munitions specialist, a handler of all the various types of ammunition and explosives. As he speaks about his first experiences in Vietnam, it is clear that Bob is anything but a warrior. He was a reluctant citizen-soldier in spite of being a volunteer. Things start happening from the beginning, of course; it could not be otherwise in Vietnam. First assigned to the main ammunition dump at Da Nang, where the 122 rockets fell regularly, Bob spent most of his tour on a base at An Wah, which was under fire from the outset. It is especially significant for any understanding of Bob's story to note that he speaks frequently of losing friends. "I didn't have a lot of close friends, but they were starting not to come home."

On the eve of the Tet Offensive, 1968, during an attack on the base, Bob sees a friend go down.

> January 30th, things were intensifying and we were on red alert. . . . This was just prior to the Tet Offensive. . . . The grunt units we had there went out in the field. This was the first time I'd lost a very good friend of mine. His death was considered accidental, although I saw exactly what happened.

From his bunker, Bob sees his friend, Ziggy, fall as a mortar round hits close to him. He panics, there's no way to get to him with the attack going on. Twenty minutes pass, a time that must have been agonizing for Bob, then the mortars fall silent. Bob gets on a "mule," a kind of motorized sled for moving goods. He goes over to his friend to find that he had been knocked down by the concussion and, as he fell, his rifle went off inflicting a mortal wound.

> He died in my arms. There wasn't a lot that I could do. I could look at him, but I couldn't help him. I knew he was going at that time, and I just had to let him go. I didn't know what to tell him. He couldn't talk or anything, but it's just the look, like what's happening, a kind of blank in his eyes. That's kind of a funny feeling—they just keep looking at you. He died with his eyes open.

At this point Bob has mentioned, with feeling, several friends by name. He was obviously a young man with the ability to form close and important links with peers. Loss of buddies is the most common force driving men mad in combat; it is certainly the primary factor in generating the thirst for revenge. What follows may be at least partially explained thereby. It was difficult for Bob to speak of his friend's death. It becomes even more so as he turns now to the two incidents that he cannot forget, for which he cannot find forgiveness.

Bob is careful to describe the area in which his base was located, beyond Da Nang and near or in the A Shah Valley. Next door to the base are two villages, one to the southwest, the other to the southeast. Both will play a role in Bob's confession. Every night the base takes a few mortar rounds from the village to the southwest, ostensibly a friendly village, at least by day. "By the time we'd called it in and it went through the normal channels, nothing else was going on and we got into a political thing, with it being a friendly village." Authorization from higher up would not be forthcoming to fire back. A friend gets wounded during one of these routine attacks, then Ziggy is killed. Things begin to build up in Bob. The base is on the verge of Tet, the major offensive beginning January 31st, 1968. By this time, the base, which blocks the approach to Da Nang, a major objective, is under attack. Most of the combat troops assigned to the base are out in the field, some of them pinned down in the A Shah Valley.

We began receiving mortars from the south—I've got to get my directions right—from the village to the southwest, over the village. Then we began receiving heavy small-arms fire from a village to the other side of the base. Up until that point we hadn't been receiving much air support because of the monsoon. And I started having a real fear of hand-to-hand combat. I don't know what it is—I'm not afraid of fighting, I'm afraid of taking someone's life in front of my eyes—I don't know what it is, I don't have that numbing, blank feeling to do it. I began to have this fear of hand-to-hand combat. I couldn't convince myself that I could take a human life. It went against my upbringing as a Catholic. I believe strongly in the fifth commandment. And being that my dad was such a logical person—statistics and logic—war became insanity to me, I couldn't justify it. Granted that it had to be, because it was going on,

97

but I couldn't rationalize it. And I had this fear that we'd become involved in hand-to-hand combat. When we started receiving heavy small-arms fire, that's an indication that you're going to get overrun. I took an M-60 machine gun with five other marines. We went over to the other side of the perimeter because we thought that we'd be overrun at that point. The small arms fire was intensifying. . . . As the M-60 was being set up we had an F-4 Phantom air strike come in, strike a tree line with napalm right to the outside of the perimeter, and just lit everything up. But we were still receiving rounds from the tree line. There was a lot of confusion. The rounds that were coming in were—the village was being attacked by the NVA from the other side—the rounds were the NVA rounds going through the village. They weren't coming from the village.

As the napalm subsided, I was in a prone position. I had my M-14. The M-60 was being set up at that point. I sighted in on a woman and child, a woman carrying a child, coming out of the tree line that was still burning. She wasn't on fire, but she was running. I knew she was unarmed, and I followed her in my sight for a while. It seemed like a long time. And it seemed like I was the only one sighted in on her—I don't know. But it got up close enough to where I could see her. And obviously she was holding a child and I—I don't know what it was—I pulled the trigger. And she went down. And what was happening, the civilians were trying to get out of the village that was being attacked from their side, go through the tree line that was burning up, and get to our base. You might say that my overreaction by shooting her and the child—I didn't shoot the child separate—she was holding the child in front of her and the rounds just went through there. So more women and a couple of papa-sans—they started opening fire. What happened to me at that time—I stopped firing. I knew what I'd done was wrong. And I jumped up and yelled at them to cease fire, and they started making these horrible sounds. Anyway . . . just like—I can't explain the sounds, gurgling, like, growling sounds. And I yelled at them to cease fire, and this one turned to me and looked at me and just stared with this look on his face. I didn't say anything to him, and I thought for sure he was going to shoot me because I seemed to be spoiling the fun. They were joking about why I wasn't in on the shooting duck gallery. I looked at him, and I was frozen. And he just turned back and continued firing. And I dove to the ground again, and all I can remember doing, I just put my hands over my head, and I was just hoping that nothing would happen to me. Anyway, that incident happened. We did suppress the assault.

Bob, who has struggled to tell this story, seems far away at this moment. As if in response to his listeners' unexpressed perplexity, Bob goes on to say:

I don't know. My first reaction would be, I guess, I—people have said, a lot of people I've talked to have said a lot of different things: This was going on and this was going on, and you didn't know this and you didn't know that. But it boils down to the few seconds that I sighted in on her, and I try to tell myself that maybe I was insane and that I wasn't—I can still remember seeing her and who I sighted in on. I know, I mean, you know how to fire rifles—I know what I was looking at. I can't answer what—I know I was confused, I didn't know what was going to happen. I had a lot of fear, I had a fear of being overrun. After she came out, I knew that the people coming out of the tree line were civilians, and I tried to stop it. But it didn't stop. So thirteen women and children, eleven women and children and two papa-sans were killed right there. They were killed quite—I mean they killed—I guess you could say bullet-riddled.

This central episode in Bob's story does not quite end here; there were repercussions. The others conspired to say nothing and warned Bob that he was to do the same. The Marine Corps ends up saying it was an accident. Still, the others remain suspicious of Bob, and when they get drunk he hides, fearing for his life. He had already seen one fragging, a friend of his.

Then, just after Tet, Bob's very best friend dies. His girlfriend was pregnant at the time but had refused to marry him. This buddy, who actually committed suicide, made it look like an accident so she could collect his death benefits. Bob states, "This is how I started becoming insane, started losing my sanity." He goes on to detail how he contrived to burn out the other village, the one from which nightly mortar attacks continued. He altered some illumination rounds that a mortar squad was using so they fell directly on the village and started multiple fires. As he watched this hated hamlet go up in flames, Bob recalls, he laughed insanely. Amazingly, it was only during his stay at the V. A. Hospital in West Haven, where the taping of his story took place, that he learned that after his departure a commando (or sapper) on a suicide mission had blown the base's ammo dump, with American casualties resulting. Bob assumes that this was in retaliation for his burning of the "friendly" village. "You burn us out, we'll burn you out—they won," he says.

Bob's story of life after Vietnam is of a piece with most of the veterans' accounts: three marriages; alcohol and drugs, especially alcohol; at least two suicide attempts. When the story of the My Lai massacre broke, Bob "just snapped." Speaking of Lieutenant Calley, Bob says, "If I was different, I couldn't see it." He spoke to his parents, told them what had happened, and tried to talk to someone at the local V. A. hospital. No one understood; no one wanted to believe. Subsequently, Bob tried hypnosis in an effort to erase the memories. In the last section of his story, Bob is asked if the experience of the taping was in any way a healing thing. His response left the question unanswered. He said, "The reason for me volunteering for this . . . rage and anger . . . and the other is guilt and shame. . . . Most people come in to deal with rage and anger . . . but the guilt and shame is something very few . . . will come in here and admit to." So it seems that, at the moment anyway, Bob felt no great lifting of the burden for having told his story. He does mention that he felt "lightened a little" after performing a ritual letting-go while a participant in an advanced V. A. program for Vietnam veterans. As part of this ceremony designed to allow the veteran to release dead buddies harbored as trauma memory for over two decades, Bob had included the woman and child he killed in his public statement of those he wished to remember and let go. He goes on to admit to being "still very paranoid" and to having sought punishment. In addition, he intimates that he feels undeserving of anything good, in particular, undeserving of being a father to his four children. Bob L. was not the only veteran to use the taping as a vehicle for confession; several did.

Others: Joe D., Wolf T-E, Roosevelt H.

How does one tell a story like this, one filled with so much guilt, shame, regret, and self-hatred? The motivation must be great, the story is so painful to tell. Of all the veterans who told their stories for the project, the great majority were combat veterans. Only Steve B., Arthur S., and Joe D. were not, and Joe D. is one of the veterans who wished most to confess. All but Steve, Arthur, and Roland L. spoke confessionally of things they considered shameful. This is not to say that any of the participants acted in any way for which we should condemn them. It is just that the business of war so often brings with it a burden of shame and guilt. Joe D. was the veteran who appeared most visibly shaken by the pain of telling his story. At many junctures he became tearful and was on the verge of being overcome. Yet he continued, forcing himself onward through the story. In fact, he required two sessions and over three hours to tell everything that he needed to tell. It did not seem at all a matter of wanting to tell—he needed to. Joe explained that this was what he must do to help himself; the burden he has carried for so long has been great. He feels himself to have committed murder in Vietnam. Joe was essentially a noncombatant. He was a sergeant in the Air Force when he arrived in Vietnam in July of 1966. He was intending to make the military a career and had been in the service for nearly six years at the time. He recalls the pride he felt in helping to deal with the devastation of a typhoon on Guam, where he had been stationed. He was filled with pride when he got his orders to Vietnam. He felt he'd be taking part in "stopping communism in its tracks—and in this way America would be safe." Then he found himself in an Air Force transport plane circling at night above Tan San Nhut Air Base outside Saigon, looking down at the war. "I looked down and I said, Holy shit. . . . People were down there dying—it looked like the Fourth of July. The reality! I felt a terrible fear." Fear continued, as Joe tells his story, to plague him throughout. Indeed, Joe often makes mention of gaps in memory. For instance, he overhears two men talking about fragging a sergeant; he protests. Thereafter, his memory fails him, only fragments come back, like being upbraided by a master sergeant, but he doesn't know why. "It haunts the hell out of me to this day, I don't know whether the sergeant got killed or not."

He was most overcome by fear on one night walking back to his base from Pleiku. Interestingly enough, his memory seems quite intact for this event. The town was off limits later in the evening, but he and two others stay behind, hitting the bars, then finding it necessary to walk the fifteen miles back to their base. This walk in the dark turns into a nightmare. There are firefights going on nearby. Joe becomes disoriented and terrified. "I'm scared . . . and I've never been so scared in my life." First one, then another miniature taxi, a sort of motorized pedicab, goes by but will not stop. When the next one approaches, Joe grabs a stone and, when the driver speeds up, throws it through the front window. The cab careens into the ditch. Joe runs over and pulls the driver out, kicking him in the head. The three of them make it back in the hijacked scooterbus. This is a terrible scene for Joe to describe. He says, "I don't know if I killed him or not." In the morning, back on his base, it all seems like a bad dream—except his boots have blood on them. "That's when I cried. 'Cause I don't know who or what I killed. I'm thinking now that I did kill him." Later, this seems to be confirmed.

An Air Force man, newly in-country, is touring around Pleiku and he is stoned, "bricked to death," in retaliation, Joe assumes by other scooterbus drivers. Like Bob L., Joe tries to confess, but nobody had heard of any driver found dead in a ditch. No one will believe his story, and nothing is ever said by the other two air force men either. Joe mentions that his nightmares about this event started in 1969. Through the years, he often sat up for hours at night, rocking and smoking, trying to shake the guilt and to make some sense of it all. Then it would be time to go to work. The nightmares continue, he tells us, until today; they are even more vivid since getting into treatment. Joe recounts several other incidents at length, but none is so starkly confessional as this. One wonders how this memory can be tolerated; Joe's suffering is so great, seemingly unmitigated. Forgiveness, that is, self-forgiveness, seems remote, perhaps unobtainable.

Others spoke of transgressions equally severe, but seemingly with greater ease than Joe. Is their suffering any less therefore? Probably not. There is, after all, no scale for comparing the painful effects of past trauma. Joe D. seems to suffer directly, that is, his suffering is the direct result of the memories that burden him. Others may translate the affliction of traumatic memory into a whole array of symptoms, especially drug and alcohol abuse. Be that as it may, the veterans who told their stories did not appear to be holding anything back. For instance, Wolf T-E., whose narrative fits partly into the mold of the warrior's tale, was also intent upon telling of events that he certainly experiences as transgressions. And he now sees his role in the war as toxic to life since then, in particular because of his complete immersion in bloodletting. He is one of the "berserkers," hence a certain kind of warrior. As a helicopter crew chief, his killing station would have been at the open door of the aircraft; his weapon, the M-60 machine gun. Here, he embeds an account of what was certainly a transgression in a general account of life on the other side of the line.

To this day, I don't know how many kills I have because I quit counting. I got to where I enjoyed it. I got a rush out of it every time I killed somebody, just like that family I killed one day. Papa-san came running out of the hooch one day . . . and shot a few rounds at us, so by the time we got turned around his wife was out there and his little girl. I killed all three of them. I ain't proud of it, it was just—it was war. I got kill crazy. I didn't feel any remorse over it till after I came back to the country, stateside. And then it ate on me for years and years.

Wolf's story is extraordinary; his experiences in Vietnam seem to range through the entire spectrum of horror and trauma in the combat zone. His openness in characterizing himself as "kill crazy" is reminiscent of several of the veterans who described being swept up in the rush that combat delivers. Some transgressions are accidents, however. Wolf recounts how he fired on a sampan one night in what must have been a free-fire zone. Finally, radio silence was broken by an agonized call from the boat below, manned by Americans, actually Green Berets in Vietnamese attire on some sort of secret mission. According to Wolf, he killed thirteen of them. For Wolf, as with all of the veterans, when they come to a confessional moment in their stories, the emotions well up.

Roosevelt H. was overcome by emotion, momentarily, at several points; he apparently did not really know how far he would go in telling his story. He indicates, in the course of a brief conversation after he has finished his story, that the taping had elicited "more than anybody else." Of those things he relates, several prey on his mind in particular, in fact he builds his whole account on these incidents. One involves what can be seen as fatal mistakes while in command; he was made a platoon sergeant within months of arrival in country. Another was one of those split-second impulses driven by rage over losses. The first incident occurred early in his tour with his company on a search-and-destroy mission, a deadly routine affair.

This time it was a little bit different, a little bit different. We came through one village and we were like a short distance from another one.

We searched [the first village] and destroyed what was there and killed what was living and burnt it. We got between the two villages after we had gotten through the first one. And midway to the next one we were fired upon with automatic weapons fire. And we were pinned down for about eight hours and a half. At the time, I had—for some reason or another, I don't know why, they did it, I didn't see anything great that I had done, but I was made a platoon sergeant. So I was a squad leader first, then I was made platoon sergeant. I didn't actually hold rank as a platoon sergeant, but they had put in orders for me to become a sergeant. And I was the highest ranking E-4 in the unit, so I was made platoon sergeant. And this particular—about two o'clock in the afternoon, we were fired upon, automatic weapons fire. And doing what came naturally we all hit the ground. I felt that hitting the ground was what we all did on our own to maintain cover and safety. But six and a half, seven hours later I found out that, that, ah, well my whole platoon was killed except for me. And, and, and, ah—

Roosevelt cannot go on, momentarily. He cries softly, then describes how air strikes are called in and the enemy is subdued. Twenty-seven men, his whole platoon, have perished, including his best friend, and Roosevelt appears to feel the burden of responsibility as powerfully at this moment as he ever has. He helps to bring out the dead, who are placed in a refrigerated container of some kind. He speaks of spending an hour inside with his friend and the others. Then he insists on going out again into the field, in spite of his commanding officer's wish that he stay behind. In his account, time contracts and expands to accommodate the key events, those traumatic experiences that make up the Vietnam that lives on inside his skin and that we see and experience as witnesses to his story. He mentions another major firefight, in which seventeen or more men are lost. The company is reinforced, with green troops as usual. They move on without respite, a total of three straight months in the field. At some point, they encounter a company of NVA soldiers.

There we were again, and this time it got a little worse than it was the last time for the simple reason more of our leaders were killed—the first sergeant, the first lieutenant, Lt. Waters—he was the XO. And my first sergeant was killed. Ah, an old lady and a baby—we had gone up into this village after a firefight that we had. But after we got inside the village we realized that it was just a trap. They fled just like they were defeated, but they weren't really defeated. They had booby-trapped old women and babies. They had shot their own men and given them weapons because they knew the Americans were soft-hearted to old people, babies, and if they saw somebody lying on the ground dying they would try to comfort them before they died. And my first sergeant walked up on this old lady. This old lady, she blew his brains out, and I was maybe ten feet away. And, and, when I realized what had happened, I shot the woman and I shot the baby. And I, and I didn't feel good about it. I didn't feel good about that, and they, they talk about the Vietnam war and what they called the guys that came from Vietnam—baby-killers and shit. But we had a job to do, and if we didn't do it, we'd still be called shit. I guess it's why I feel so, so worn out now.

The emotion associated with Roosevelt's account is everywhere present; this is a man with obvious depth of feeling and someone overcome with remorse for what he must see as unforgivable transgression. He remains in control of his narrative, nevertheless, pausing, wiping his eyes away, powerfully affected throughout. Roosevelt is relentless in speaking of traumatic and, for him, shameful events. That his rationale is weak—we had a job to do—is beside the point. He doesn't believe that, just as we do not. What he may have been trying to say, which he conveys with his whole being—with his passionate recollection of the deaths of comrades, with his desire to tell the whole story—is that good men like himself are sent to war as children—men and cope, in decades to come, the best they can with memories of inhuman experience. He speaks of going berserk, of giving vent to rage, but we cannot call him a warrior. He was a citizen-soldier and someone deeply hurt by what he saw and what he did. He speaks briefly and somewhat disconnectedly of the young age of some of the combatants, Vietnamese village kids of 9 or 10 with AK-47's, and of having to kill them, too. He says, "I'm looking at kids who should have been home with their mothers." We are left with the feeling that this is a good man who carries an intolerably heavy burden.

THE WARRIOR'S ROMANCE

Testimonies like the ones in a confessional mode above convey all of the guilt and shame that can be put into words—and rendered viscerally in the body of the teller. The fractures in time that are apparent in these stories speak to the past living side by side with the present. The past returned most powerfully in Alan S.'s narration. It was he who employed the most unusual of genres. Alan does not spend much time with the introductory part of his story, life before Vietnam. We learn a few of the details. He was one of seven children, born into the middle of the pack. He characterizes his family with these words: "I don't know if you'd call us poor, but we weren't rich—we had each other." Thus, Alan establishes relationality as a theme from the first. He also tells us he was "very social" in school. He adds that he was married at age 16, had a son at 18, and was divorced by 19, without elaborating. Like several of the contributors, Alan was bent on going to Vietnam to save his brother from the ordeal. He felt that, as a helicopter mechanic, he would be assigned to a rear area. It appears from Alan's brief introductory account that his brother never saw Vietnam. Things turn out otherwise for Alan. He moves directly into his experiences in country.

On one of his very first days, he and some of the other new soldiers are shocked to witness a helicopter separate from its rotor and plunge to the ground. Seven people died in the crash. Alan says, "That was about the first day—that kind of snapped us into the seriousness of our job there." His job gets deadly serious when he starts flying after two or three months in Vietnam working, not as a mechanic, but as a "wheeler-dealer." This is a fateful move, of course, going from a gopher, who got his reputation early by his ability to obtain quantities of ice, to a crew chief on a gunship. Alan does not really go into this decision of his, once the offer comes to move up. He was an unlikely candidate for warrior, certainly, and he tells us how it made him sick to kill his first man. "I looked him right in the face. We were on the deck. . . . I still see his face. He was surprised, I saw the fear on his face, and he was dead." Alan's captain, an understanding man, explains to him that he had saved somebody's life by killing. The victim was, after all, carrying a weapon, an obvious VC combatant. The captain gives him the option of staying on the ground and working as a mechanic. Alan elects to fly; he will be in battle constantly for the rest of his tour. Alan, however, is not concerned to tell war stories. He speaks briefly of a few events, which has the effect of establishing him in his narrative as a warrior with a warrior's burden of memories. Alan is also a thoughtful man, an insightful man, and an intelligent man. In particular, he is sensitive, intuitive and attuned to the spiritual undercurrent in events. For instance, he frames this account of a sudden perception of the place of God in an evil, violent world within references to the hardening of his heart to the violence.

I started losing all my emotions, the more I went out. I started feeling like a machine, like part of my helicopter. I started not to feel things. I started shutting down. It was like my M-60 was an extension of my arm. I questioned—I don't remember when, but it was during a battle. We were killing them and they were killing us, and I questioned whether there was even a God. Because I couldn't think a God would let this happen. During that same battle, I got my answer. I don't know how I got my answer, why this was happening. There was a big thunder clash, or something, but it wasn't from artillery and there wasn't a cloud in the sky. Everybody heard the noise, but inside the noise I got the answer that I needed. It was like God didn't make war—man made war. And it has to do with his second gift to us. And the gift was unconditional free will. Just that one gift explained everything. . . . At times, somebody might say to me, "God's not on the battlefield," but I don't believe that. He is there, but to put it mildly He's not a happy camper. He can't interfere. But as far as being a machine, I kept on being that way.

Later, Alan explained that God's first gift was life itself. His perception, cast as it is in common-sense language, is not something everyone would endorse; it is, however, perfectly in keeping with the broad approach known as process theology, central to which is the notion that God does not—and cannot—intervene miraculously in the world, that His influence is subtle, a "lure" (the term of Alfred North Whitehead (1979), intellectual father of the process view).

The theme of being shut down, a machine, is significant for the central account of his story, to which he is about to turn. It is equally significant that, while being immersed in the killing and encased in psychic armor to withstand the trauma of violence and loss, Alan remains open to insight and friendship—and intimacy. It will take an exceptional person to penetrate that armor, and Alan's narrative is about to introduce us to the one who, with her love, was able to do so. It would be too pedestrian a representation of this figure to call her his girlfriend. She was to be his beloved. He introduces this long and emotionally laden section of his story with a little war story about a close brush with death. A bullet rips up through the helicopter and nearly severs the pilot's leg; he loses control of the aircraft, which then tumbles through the sky. A chopper that far out of control is considered lost; helicopters are not designed for aerobatics. Alan says, "I was going to die and I was saying, "Good." I didn't want to live the way I was living. I had no emotions, I had no feelings." Somehow they make it back, the copilot flying the ship, Alan using his hands as a tourniquet to stop the blood flowing from the pilot's wound sufficiently to save his life. As sometimes happened after a close encounter of this kind, Alan is given a pass. He goes to a nearby town with a friend, an old-timer named Murphy, whom he refers to as his mentor. They end up at a hotel dating from the days of French colonial rule. Alan has a long, long shower, in fact uses up all the hot water in the place. He goes out onto the balcony. He is mesmerized, as he puts it, by the starlight, the soft breeze, the glow of light around the hotel. "And I think the thing that really touched me was there was no rifle fire, no artillery. It was peaceful. The wind was a strange wind, it was like it was warm. It wasn't hot, it wasn't cool. I was almost mesmerized with my face in the wind."

At this moment two young women come up the stairs. One is dressed provocatively; she quickly leaves with a GI. The other, dressed in a gown, speaks familiarly to Alan. "We were talking about the night and how peaceful it was. She said something I didn't understand. She said she had come for me. I didn't understand that, and we talked." She turns her face to the wind and calls it "God's breath." Then, "She asked me would I be her boyfriend. At that time, boyfriend didn't mean what it means here, it was more like fiancé. And she wanted to take me home. So I said, okay. I didn't know what it all meant." As Alan describes this extraordinary first meeting, he stresses that it meant little to him in any affective way. He was numb. He goes off with the young woman not knowing if he would be killed in his sleep—as happened more than once in Vietnam—and not caring. The two of them go to her house, pass through the front room where her parents are asleep, and into her bed. Alan is impotent; she is understanding, lying on top of him with her hand on his chest. Alan says, "And I never felt a touch like that. It was a gentle but firm touch. And I, I don't know if that was possible. . . . I didn't feel, I had no feeling for her. And she sort of understood; I don't know how she understood." In Alan's story, as we will learn, she has a powerful understanding and an almost mystical grasp of inner meanings, as well as an uncanny ability to communicate feelings. Alan first experiences this when he goes to leave the next day.

And I walked away, and it was like somebody had two eyes on the back of my neck. For some reason I turned around, and the look on her face—I felt something. She looked worried, scared, hurt—whatever it was—I felt something. And it was the first time I felt something for months. And I walked back to her and I said, "Lookit, a soldier doesn't have much but he has his honor, and if I tell you I'm coming back I will come back." And it made her feel a little better.

Alan plans to come back one more time, and that will be the end of it. Still, he says, "I was starting to feel something for this woman. It was like she was aligning all my emotions. She was lighting them on fire. I'd begun to feel for this woman."

Alan had been speaking for over an hour. More importantly, as soon as he began telling the story of his love he started to experience—really reexperience—all the feelings and the smells and the tastes. He is visibly overcome at many points in the telling. He turns away, covers his face with his hands, occasionally seems to sob briefly. This is, as we will learn, a tragic love story. And remembering any part of it, especially when the memories become visceral as they do throughout, brings the end to mind. "It makes me not want to remember," Alan says. At this point in the narrative, Alan elects to stop, promising to come back to finish the story. He does, however, continue for some time in a more retrospective mood. We learn that her name was Su Kho and that her parents were both half-French and, by Vietnamese standards, well off. She had had an American boyfriend earlier, someone who promised to write and to come back, but never did. This had been devastating for her. Then one day, "She felt all happy—she was going to meet someone." This is when she comes to the hotel for Alan. Here, again, "the end seems like it wants to rip in."

Alan returns to the present and to recounting at a distance. He recalls how he had locked the memories of her and the story away for twenty-five years, while in the interim things happened that didn't make sense. He discovered that he had a strange affection for oranges; her father and she, he later learns in remembering, loved oranges, and he used to bring them with him when he visited. Once in the subway, he overhears two Vietnamese girls chatting, and he can follow their conversation though, as far as he knows, he is ignorant of the language. Now, Alan goes on to explain the mechanism he employed to set aside the events he is relating "to deal with it later." He had previously worked out a way of putting things on the shelf when there was not time, in battle, to assimilate them. The story of his tragic love was something that he needed to put away for a long, long time. He decided on twenty-five years. "Twenty-five years, I put it somewhere where I wouldn't have to deal with it." Then, with the help of a student therapist at a V. A. hospital, the door to the memory chamber opens.

> I relived it for four days. It was like a room. In my mind I made a shelf and put all these things that happened on the shelf to deal with later. This particular circumstance was a whole room. I put it in a room with three locks on it. And the door opened and I went in and I relived the whole thing. And everything made sense, everything started to make sense. Not just the things that happened in Nam, but things that happened after. . . . I could smell the smells and taste the food and touch her again. It had to be lived again.

Several days later, Alan comes once more before the camera and picks up the story precisely where he left off. He speaks of returning after three weeks and of her "not very ladylike" greeting; she was overjoyed. We learn that Su Kho was a schoolteacher and quite attached to the children she taught. She had turned the school into a place where they could play and be given a daily respite from the war. We learn about the family and get a sense of how deeply attached to Su Kho's father and mother Alan became, how he'd bring them oranges, and how fond he became of the children. All the while, Alan is able to visit frequently, stretching a three-day pass into ten days as was the practice in his unit, and alternately he is back in the war, in the thick of it. But mostly we learn about the deepening relationship between the two of them. Any war story that works its way into his account he includes to show still another side of Su Kho's character. For instance, he tells her how he had had to kill an American sergeant trapped under an overturned jeep. There was a firefight going on below, and the enemy was closing in. The trapped American would certainly have been captured and tortured to death. The crew must have talked about what they were going to do. It becomes Alan's task to perform a mercy killing. He tells Su Kho, who had sensed that something was bothering him. Her response is a great comfort to him: "He was lucky to have a friend like you."

Su Kho asks Alan to bring her a record player, which he does, of course. She immediately presents it to her father and explains to Alan that that's her dowry. They are officially engaged. Alan, who only knows the waltz, teaches it to her, her feet on his as they dance.

> I'd dance with her—the whole world seemed to stop. And when we stopped the whole world seemed to spin. It was just—it was like when she gave me her love, I would take her love and multiply it ten times and give it back to her, and she would take that love and multiply it ten times and give it back. It was like a game, it was like no end—it was almost like a high. It was heaven and hell. The combat zone was hell and when I was with her it was like heaven, it was like paradise. We more or less were part of each other. Every time I left her, it got more difficult. Because of my relationship with her, if there's such a thing as compassionate killing of the enemy, I think I had that. It's just as easy to give you a head hit or a heart hit—you wouldn't suffer long. That's the way I felt, that was my job. If that's a compassionate way to kill somebody that's what I was doing. I think it was because of her.

Throughout, Alan shifts back and forth between what might be called construct narration and visceral narration, that is, between what we would think of as the normative reformulation as a story of recollected events and, on the other hand, concretely relived material. A transcript of his whole account reveals, however, that even in the latter mode the narrative flow is sustained. Thus, the whole exhibits all the features of constructedness that we expect from literature.

The children who are Su Kho's pupils constitute one element in the story that Alan returns to again and again, along with her parents, narrative strands that go to make up the warp and woof of the fabric of this warrior's tale of true love. There was an orphan among the children, a boy with a fake leg. The limb had been torn from him in a mortar attack that killed his mother and father. According to Alan, in Vietnam an orphan can elect to live with any couple he chooses. This boy, who took for himself the American name Joey, wanted to be adopted by Su Kho; this was impossible since she was not married. He looked to her and Alan as parental figures. One thing that bothered him was the thought that, according to his interpretation of the culture, he would have to go to heaven with just one leg. Alan intervenes.

> He was concerned because if he were to go to heaven he'd go without a leg. I told her to come be my interpretor. I went up to him and I told her to tell him that my God and his God were the same God. And she did. And I told him, "According to my religion you can't kill the spirit of the leg." And she explained that to him. And I took my hand and I guided it around his fake leg like his leg was still there. And she explained that to him. And I said, "Tell him that it'd be as though you can wiggle your toes even though you have none." And when she told him that he got scared. He got petrified. He backed off. He told her that when he first woke up, it was as though he could wiggle his toes on the leg that he didn't have. So he knew what I said was true, that you can never kill the spirit of the leg even though the leg wasn't there. And that you do go to heaven with the spirit of the leg.

It is worth mentioning that this episode is told just after a reference by Alan to one of his most traumatic memories, a baby packaged as

114

a booby trap by the NVA that blows apart before his eyes. It is as if by relating traumatic events to Su Kho Alan could find solace through the story of their deepening relationship.

Finally, she says, "It's time." They go into her bed.

It was dark and there was a candle, and she was on top. She put her hand on her chest and put her other hand on my chest, and she took about three deep breaths. And she moved her head back [and murmured something]. But she wasn't talking to me. So she kind of smiled at me and I didn't know what she was doing. So she took my hand and put it on my chest and she put my other hand on her chest. And she says, "What do you feel?" And I got scared—it was both our hearts beating exactly together. If I had any doubts if I loved her or not, I knew from that time on I was totally in love with her. She called it pure love. That totally took me away, that blew me away. I never had anything like that in my life. Both our heartbeats were beating as one, they were beating exactly the same. And I asked her if she had had that before. And that's when she said that that's pure love. Everything was much easier. We never fought, we never argued. It was like paradise. There was nothing that wasn't possible. Whatever came, we dealt with it together.

Then, abruptly, it is all over; the time comes for Alan to tell of the tragic end that haunts the telling of this magical tale. He arrives on pass to find her mother in tears. She can only say something about the hospital to Alan, who rushes there to be told by a nurse that Su Kho had died there two days before. He will later learn that the VC had targeted her, as they did many young schoolteachers, and that she died in a mortar attack going back into the schoolhouse attempting to rescue Joey. Alan learned about all of this later. At the time, he immediately starts drinking to block the pain, running and screaming, ending up without shirt or boots in a rice paddy, where the MPs find him. He is taken to the hospital, where he stays for a few days, then rejoins his unit, puts on his spare boots, and goes back on duty.

Now Alan becomes one of the revenge-driven berserkers, killing cruelly, unafraid of anything to the point where others feared to fly with him. He goes on.

I couldn't deal with her death. I had to put a date somewhere where I'd have to deal with it. And I remember saying, ten, fifteen, or twenty-five, and I said twenty-five, and I put it away. I put it in a room all by itself in my head—not a shelf. This was a room, and I locked it with three locks. And one was a time lock. And the other two were music. And two years ago, just like clockwork, things began to happen. And this part I put in that room I had to relive. I was in bed three or four days and relived the whole thing, everything—the food, the smells, the tastes, and the feelings. It's like I died all over again.

Alan did go back once more; Su Kho's father was as devastated as he. There was no one to talk to. Murphy, his mentor, had been wounded accidently by a sergeant playing with a .45 and evacuated. Alan's goes on with his account of the memory chamber.

When I went into that room after twenty-five years, she was in one corner—it was like a blinding—she was like sitting down, she was like blinding light—just like looking into the sun, except instead of yellow it was white. And in the other corner, death was there and right next to death was fear. But when I walked into the room to her, I didn't know whether to touch her. And as I was in that room, the sword and shield I had carried all my life were ineffective. Who was that? Grief! He had a stick, and as I was watching he beat me with his stick. And I had to leave the room and shut the door. And that's where it's been. There will come a time when I have to go back into that room. And I know that the things that I've carried in the past are not effective in that room.

Alan explains about the swords and the shield—what do they refer to?

The swords were given to me to defend things like honor, valor, heroism, meritorious achievement—all these swords to use against anything

116

or anybody that objected to it. The shield was given to me by her to protect myself from people trying to use swords on me.

Alan goes on to specify that he carries swords given to him by dead warriors, explaining that "It's like they say, 'Defend my honor.'" Of course, in this way of conceptualizing the world, as Alan confirms, it was Su Kho who, at her death, gave him his shield. In any event, he adds, "in that room neither was effective against Grief." Along the way, Alan is able to make clear that the swords and the shield must be given back. He knows, but does not explain, how to give the swords back; returning the shield is another matter. This process of returning or relinquishing is associated in Alan's view with letting go, which in turn brings him to the related theme of rage—inextricably bound up, as it is, with his memories.

"Let go" is an easy word to say. And to be honest with you, people take that for granted, let go, like it's a thing they do just like that. It's not that easy, for myself or the other vets. How easy it was for me to do that when I was 18, 19 years old, to just let go of something—that was very easy. Why we can't do that now, I don't know. It's just different, it's not easy.

There was a time when I gave control to rage. I've always had control, but in my weakness I gave control to rage and let rage do its dirty work. If you never give rage control, it's easy to control it. It's easy. But you give something else control of you—it bids for that control all the time. I don't know if you can understand that. If you never gave it control, it doesn't know how to have control. Rage is the beast. Rage is—I don't know what you want to call it—the animal. Rage is the subconscious, the id, whatever you want to call it. These are all the same—this is the beast, this is the dragon. There are two sides to each of us. There's the human side and there's the animal side. You can't kill the animal without killing the human. You have to pacify the animal—that's the best you can do, because it is part of you. I don't like my animal, but it is part of me. Even though I may not like it, it is still part of me and I have to deal with it.

117

The retelling of the story of his relationship with his Vietnamese beloved brings back all the memories; this is really a narrative of a reliving experience. One also feels compassion for the stuckness that Alan experiences. He says he's looking for "closure," interestingly enough. These powerful experiences were closed off in the memory chamber for so long; they were so powerful in the living of them. Note, too, that Alan begins his relationship with his young woman in earnest when he begins to feel. The feelings must have been so strong—the young warrior quite changed and shut down by trauma, then these powerful feelings driven by love. In the end comes the tragic loss. We can, therefore, gain some understanding of the potency of the feelings and the waves of emotion that affect the narration. This can hardly explain the genre, however; where the form of this story comes from is a mystery.

In any case, Alan's deeply moving story is a powerful literary document. The quarter of a century that he kept all this in his memory chamber was a period of struggle with a post-traumatic condition for him, a process that will, no doubt, continue into the future. Whether trauma memories are closed off and inaccessible to narrativization or all too available, rendering them into the literary constructs of a life story is a considerable achievement. It represents the possibility of mastering disturbing material through the transformation of somatic memory into narrative memory. Then, too, telling the trauma story is a creative act, and creative acts are healing. There is, however, no definitive cure for the woundings of so long ago, as the veterans' accounts of life after Vietnam attest.

5

BACK IN THE WORLD

■ If you try to say it never happened it will come back and it will disable you. In other words—how can I say this? How tenacious we are that we believe the lie until we know the truth. We are like that, the human race is like that. But that's what happens to you. A lot of people would rather believe the lie than the truth, and I've learned that the truth may hurt. But you're better off knowing the truth. . . . I can't say Vietnam never happened.

Alan S., *The Chambers of Memory*

■ The knowledge of death, of the implacable limits placed on a man's existence, severed us from our youth as irrevocably as a surgeon's scissors had once severed us from the womb. And yet, few of us were past twenty-five. We left Vietnam peculiar creatures, with young shoulders that bore rather old heads.

Philip Caputo, *A Rumor of War*

■ I move my body carefully and watch the ground pass beneath me and hedges and fences move by me until the steps of my house come to me and touch my feet. I experience the sensation that I am at the center of the universe, focused on what I'm doing now. I am looking for peace.

Robert Mason, *Chickenhawk: Back in the World*

119

WELCOME HOME

After all they had seen and lived through in that brief, timeless twelve or thirteen months in the combat zone, the troops came home. They came back home alone, in a plane filled with strangers, alien creatures like themselves. Their welcome home was harsh at best; their treatment, even at the hands of the military, bureaucratic and heartless. "Welcome Home, Returnees" read one banner somewhere. "Your Country is Proud of You" another ran. A steak dinner, a free phone call, and mindless processing out were all the country had to offer. Not only were there no parades, there was not even a debriefing, which might have allowed the shattered selves of the returning troops some chance to begin healing. At the main points of return, like Oakland or San Diego, there were troops of protesters waving signs that wounded anew: "Baby killers!" Having suffered the disorienting, eerie, alien violence of Vietnam, the returning soldiers, now veterans of a different kind of war, were spat upon and reviled as they stepped off the planes onto their native soil. As they had been changed, the world seemed changed, shifted in a hostile, uncaring, vindictive direction.

Home with family was little better. No one seemed to want to listen. Brothers and sisters were perhaps against the war now. Nobody wanted to help the young veterans. Employers weren't interested in whether or not you rose to the rank of platoon sergeant at age 19, that you had led men or had just followed bravely into battle, whether you had spilled your own blood and plenty of the enemy's on freedom's front line. Young Vietnam veterans who sought out the old soldiers in the community were hounded out of VFW lodges, where they might have found solace. Even here they were called whiners and, again, baby killers. They didn't know it then, but the way home was going to be twenty-five years long or more, if they ever reached that longed-for end of the road.

For the young men who would be, or already were, afflicted with

120

wrenching disjunctures of traumatic memories, there was truly nowhere to turn. The nightmares had perhaps started back in Vietnam. What could anyone have thought after experiencing the first flashback, with its smells, and visions of death, and its sinister, threatening enemy figures. Anger would well up and spill over at the most trivial provocation; depression could follow, along with inexplicable tears, feelings of despair and, especially, the guilt and the shame. And then anxiety was a constant companion. You started avoiding crowds, people in general, you closed down, you closed off. You began to isolate. On the other hand, who could explain the urge to rekindle the intense excitement of a firefight that lured young men into dangerous games: barroom fights, wild motorcycle rides, sometimes even illegal acts? Small wonder that relationships with wives or old girlfriends, if they were still around, usually did not last long, just as subsequent attempts at settling down seemed to fail inevitably. The heavy use of drugs and alcohol began, for many, almost at once. Many of the troops in the field in Vietnam had, like Jim E. and others here, stayed purposefully away from intoxicants. They knew their chances for survival were better if their heads were as clear as possible at all times. Later that would change. The number of Vietnam veterans with post-traumatic conditions who do not have a history of severe drug or alcohol abuse (or both) is small indeed. Only Joel D. and Mark A. among the thirty-one veterans who contributed their stories here stayed away from drugs and alcohol throughout the decades since the war. When returning Vietnam veterans turned to the Veterans Administration hospitals, as many of them did in the early years after the war, they received precious little help. In some cases, like Ed W.'s, they were probably harmed further through misdiagnosis and misguided treatment. In one way or another, since the war, the lives of the affected Vietnam veterans were disorganized, chaotic, unfocused, as well as filled with mental anguish, isolation, and suffering. The stories they tell of their lives *after* illustrate this fully.

THEIR STORIES

These accounts speak of the many and varied effects that traumatic experience subsequently introduces into the life of the person. It was well-meaning common sense that friends and family employed when they advised the veteran to put it all behind him. The veterans' stories, however, demonstrate clearly how you cannot leave it behind. It is carried in the gut; it is a visceral thing, which cannot be left behind. Trauma itself is by nature disorienting and has the astonishing ability to remove the person from his or her immediate experience. Yet, while active memory of such events may be fragmentary or missing altogether, the body will keep the score. At the same time, as the contributors indicate again and again in their accounts of combat experiences, the violence of combat has the power to elicit parts of you that you didn't know were there. Several of the veterans refer to the "animal" part of themselves that came roaring out in the midst of battle. So part of you is swept away and another part of you evoked. Once out, the animal does not necessarily go quietly back to the depths of your consciousness to sleep until needed again. It will stir now, long after originating events, perhaps at the slightest hint of danger—nightfall, for instance. It happens every day. Nighttime in Vietnam was especially dangerous; bad things happened to you and to comrades at night. Back home, you rarely get a good night's sleep twenty-five years later. George P.'s characterization is typical:

> I've had dreams of gooks coming up through the woods, and I go out in the kitchen and turn the spotlight on. And it's not there, so I end up staying up. I lie in bed at night looking down the hallway—and I know I'm home. There's one part of me that says, "You're home, what's your problem!" The other part of me says, "Look down that hallway—is someone coming up there?" I still do it today. That's very upsetting.

So not all animals are aggressive killers; some are frightened creatures. Rather, at one point your animal will fight, at another it will
flee. The residual effect represents a disturbance in day-to-day experience. Traumatic experience ruptures the intuitive perception
that events have a natural structure or a sequence. As you carry your
visceral memories forward, their resurfacing again and again dis-
turbs your sense of reality as coherent or at least linked or sequenced
as life unfolds in time. As the traumatic past impinges repeatedly,
you never really gain the sense of living along a coherent, meaningful story line. In fact, disjuncture is your experience; disjuncture
characterizes your story. The accounts of leaving Vietnam and, with
disorienting suddenness, returning to the the world speak of nothing but.

Getting Out—Ed W.

Departure from the battle zone was itself traumatic, another
wrenching jolt, as your day rolled around and you *had* to go. This
was your DEROS, the military's acronym for "date of expected return from overseas," and, no matter what, you were going. Most of
the veterans take special note of this moment, the time they had been
waiting for for a year, hoping against hope just to survive and go
home. Ed W.'s story is especially vivid and very much of a piece, from
the narrative point of view, with his central theme: progressive alienation from friends back home, the other services, the officer corps,
finally from the Marine Corps itself. He introduces this part of his
account with some bitter arithmetic on the small number of troops
actually in the field doing the fighting, which by his quite realistic
appraisal amounted at best to around 10 percent of all the service-
men in the country at the height of the war. He quite rightly points
out that not even all combatants were actually in the bush; some were
assigned to artillery units and to duties guarding rear echelon people.
(No wonder the grunts referred to anybody in the read as REMF's,

rear echelon motherfuckers.) Finally, after getting wounded once, getting stung by a scorpion, and contracting malaria—three times he spent a few days in the rear—Ed gets malaria again. He is hospitalized and finds out to his joy that he'll be going home a little early.

That was New Year's Day in the hospital, which was good, because I saw a doctor, and I only had another month and a half. He said, "You'd better go, you've seen enough—I'm sending you home." I was so happy, I was ecstatic because I was going home. So I only had to stay in the hospital four or five days, and I was happy—this was good. So sitting around the hospital, finally my day came to leave. And they said, "Okay, go out there—your helicopter is waiting." . . . I was finally happy, a lot of my gloom left me. About ten minutes before I was supposed to leave, helicopters come flying in. . . . They were putting out dead bodies on the runway, and the wounded on stretchers coming in, some walking with bandages on heads and arms and stuff. So I ran over, asked, "Who's getting hit, who's getting hit?" And they said, "Fox Company, Seventh Marines." Oh my God! My unit, the one I just left three or four days before. They were getting hit good. I was running around trying to talk to somebody, "Who's hit, how bad?" But most of them were too traumatized. One of them was just—said like, "I don't know, I don't know who's hit or not." So they say, "You gotta leave, Ed, you gotta leave." Naw, I gotta find out—these are my guys. "No, you gotta go, you gotta go." So I had to walk across, seeing all the wounded. I had to walk to my helicopter, which was over there, and I had to walk by twelve, fifteen body bags, dead. And there were still more choppers coming. And all the joy I had, the one joyful day in Vietnam was totally, utterly ruined. They wouldn't even let me leave there in peace—that's the way I left.

Everyone has a story to tell about departure, of course, just as arrival is marked in the mind indelibly. Roosevelt H. was in the hospital, wounded, waiting to leave the country, and the base was overrun. He was able to get his hands on an M-16 and engaged in his last firefight—the day before being evacuated to Japan, where he spent more weeks recovering from his wounds. A few of the veterans, like Syd L. and Joel D., tried to extend but were refused. Steve B. also mentions trying to stay on and being prevented from doing so. His account of departure is brief and seamlessly linked to arrival home and the first disorienting period back in the world.

Getting Home—Steve B.

Steve was a medic who spent most of his tour in a field hospital assisting in an operating room in a tent. His story also introduces along the way a number of themes that are common to the majority of the veterans' memory of their lives after Vietnam.

It was a very—coming home they had me—I was in the surgery tent right up until the last day. And they came and told me it was time to go. I didn't say goodbye to many people and those I said goodbye to, it was a feeble attempt. And we all promised, y'know, that we would get together after we were all home. And I guess it was, maybe, forty-eight hours I was out of Vietnam and standing in New York in snow again. And I was heckled by antiwar demonstrators in between Port Authority and Grand Central. And I was just totally numb, I just couldn't seem to react one way or the other. And I got on the train, and the train stopped in Milford. My particular car stopped in a snowbank, so I had to throw my duffle bag over the snowbank, then jump from the car itself. And made my way down to Milford Center. And it was, it was so weird, nothing seemed the same, nothing—I call it a strange neighborhood syndrome, where everything around you, everything that you've known all your life, everything that should be familiar to you, now all of a sudden it's alien to you. You recognize it but somehow it's just all changed. And I remember hitchhiking in Milford Center to get home, and one car stopped. And I opened up the door thinking he was going to give me a ride. He got angry and told me to get on the sidewalk and don't hinder traffic in the street. And it was almost a feeling like your ears were ringing after listening to loud noises for a year. Now everything is quiet and your ears are ringing. I did quite a bit of drinking.

A couple of days before I left Vietnam, a fellow from Milford was wounded, and I saw him when they were taking him off the chopper and recognized him. So I had to see his mother as soon as I got home to let her know that he was all right. And they lived right up on the next block, up from my father's. I went to see her, and he had been evacuated to Japan and had called her from a field hospital there. He went back for two more tours. I've seen him twice in the last twenty, twenty-five years—I don't know how long it's been now. But I've seen him twice and we've talked for all of maybe ten, fifteen minutes, and he lives twenty minutes away from here. And we never contact one another, and we never try to see one another. I'm not sure why.

But that thirty-day furlough was like being in a vacuum. Nobody knew about Vietnam or cared what was going on, you could sense that right away, and you could sense the hostility in the air. So I got home and I took my uniform off and I left it off. That first day back, I got into the shower and tried to wash and emptied out my father's hot water heater. And I still had some bloodstains on a T-shirt and on my body. I know that ever since Vietnam, I've never been able to get a feeling of really being clean. I can stand under hot water, scalding hot water and lather myself up, and somehow I still feel kind of dirty. And I've had many nightmares over the years about everything that happened there. That feeling of being dirty—I still wake up at nighttime and I'm trying to brush insects off my body and I'm covered with blood. And an incident like that actually happened. It was during mass casualty and I was relieved to go catch a couple of hours of sleep, and I just collapsed inside the tent, and my clothes were all bloody. The insects just—they were feasting on all the blood. And when I woke I was terrorized by all those insects crawling all over me. I could feel the weight of them, there were so many. And I still wake up to this day trying to wipe those insects off of me. I didn't even realize I had a problem with Vietnam.

126

Steve's strange-neighborhood syndrome seems to be something that affected everyone. How could it be otherwise? It began in Nam, that feeling of strangeness. No wonder that, back home at last, your life became chaotic and you started using drugs and alcohol.

Drinking and Drugging—Pat's Story

The vast majority of Vietnam veterans with combat-related post-traumatic conditions also have a long history of drug and alcohol abuse. Pat M. is typical in this way; his difficulties drinking and drugging began early after his return from Vietnam and continued for over two decades. He was in numerous alcohol and substance abuse programs, and certainly had periods of sobriety. This was, however, treatment that addressed only those issues and ignored everything else, which meant that treatment never worked for long. For virtually everyone, however, traumatic symptoms and life events bring back the intolerable levels of anxiety that demand attention to themselves. At this point, you feel as if there is nowhere to turn. You know perfectly well that you're hurting yourself—and those close to you—but you turn back to the things that have worked in the past, worked at least temporarily. If you don't deal with the war, the memories, and the post-traumatic symptoms, treatment remains incomplete and ultimately will fail. It may well fail anyway, but with an integrated approach there is at the very least hope for the future. Pat M. must be given all the credit for persisting in any number of treatment settings until, finally, someone said to him, "Man, you've got PTSD, you're fucked up and it's all about Nam." By the time of the taping, Pat's health had become shaky. He suffers periodic asthma attacks, walks with a cane, and is unable to work. The taping itself was something of a physical ordeal for him. He stopped several times with headache, chest pains, and shortness of breath, but insisted each time on continuing with his story. He spoke slowly and deliberately, seeming to search for the narrative line that would guide him through the story—and finding it!

To have a true understanding of the veterans' narratives of life after Vietnam, it is always necessary to look back at their accounts of life before and, especially, to keep in mind their rendering of their time in country. Pat's story is no exception. He spoke at some length about his life before going into the service. It was a hard life, filled with childhood trauma, including being accidentally burned by boiling water at age 4. Alcohol and children were abused at home, and, as Pat represents his life, things were chaotic and dangerous from the start. In the natural course of events, knowing military service was something he needed to do, Pat joined up with a bunch of friends. In fact, they put his name up for the Marine Corps. He struggled through the rigors of basic and advanced training and ended up in Vietnam as a mortarman. He was quickly given responsibility for the squad. Pat speaks with anguish as he recalls listening on his radio to grunts from his unit begging him to "pump those things, pump those things," that is, to fire and fire and fire rounds in support of troops in the bush under heavy attack. One consequence of this rapid firing was that the mortars could not be retargeted properly and rounds could—and did—end up falling on comrades. Pat also recalls exchanging fire with enemy mortars. This calls for standing your ground and continuing to fight regardless.

> We're shooting out to them, meanwhile these people are shooting in at us. So we're getting hit also, as they're getting hit. And I've got men that run away from the tube, y'know, of course. I did it once in a while, but not all the time—I felt protected, I guess I was in, like, blackouts. Y'know, I stayed there.

This frankness in admitting to human frailty and this unassuming way of recounting heroic acts are typical of Pat's story throughout. He goes on to speak especially of two happenings that sum up and, in important ways, determine how things will go for him when back in The World.

The first depicts the modest hero, saving four men from a burn-

128

ing bunker that had been hit. Ammunition was stored there, and fuses were igniting and spraying sparks in all directions. The whole place was getting ready to blow. Not only did Pat rescue his men, he also went back inside to put the fire out. He explains his actions as something he did without knowing why or what. "I would say I'm in a blackout—didn't know what was going on." At this point in the taping, Pat seems to flag; he complains of a headache but elects to keep going with his story. He finishes his account of this episode thusly: "It ends up I saved four people's lives, but I didn't think anything of it." In fact, this is the second time he has attributed his acts of bravery to "blackouts." In the aftermath, Pat was promoted to corporal and awarded the Bronze Star, a considerable honor for an infantryman. Typically, he says, "It was all right, y'know. It didn't go to my head." Now, after all, isn't what we do without knowing it emblematic of what we are? This is a fateful question for Pat because in another episode he runs away. The unit was getting hit hard, and as Pat is running for cover he spots a captain leaning against a bunker with blood spurting from his throat. Pat runs on, leaving the captain, he assumes, to die. He is haunted by this memory to this day; devastated would not be too strong a word. Such a moment of fear-inspired hesitation, though the *right thing* is so clear, is something we are all capable of. It is also something that could spoil an essential feature of a successful life, the sense that one is basically a good person, that *in extremis* one would do the right thing. Never mind that in combat it is mostly the case that a person's actions are a mix of bravery and something less.

In any event, this moment and much else constitute the core of Pat's post-traumatic condition. Stateside, he was given what the Corps considered an honorific post, attached to a military hospital. One of his duties was to accompany a field-grade officer making the rounds, handing out medals to the wounded. Pat recalls, "Y'know, seeing guys coming back from over in Nam, some with no arms, no legs, blind, it seemed like I was drinking more and more." So begins

129

his life after Vietnam, which for over twenty years will be exceptionally chaotic. Married and, at his wife's insistence, no longer in the service, he worked for a time as assistant manager of a supermarket. And he drank. In fact, he and his boss would sometimes stay in the store after closing and drink beer out of the cooler all night. In the morning they would be found lying drunk in an aisle by the first employees to arrive. His wife is pregnant by then (this is his first year out of the service), and Pat takes up with a young lady who works at the store. She quickly becomes pregnant herself, and introduces him to shooting drugs. "So what I started doing was stealing, money, and eventually you do get caught," he goes on. Meanwhile, Pat was offered an opportunity to become an FBI agent, something he really wanted, but his wife again insists and he does not follow up. Inevitably there is an investigation into the missing money at the supermarket, and Pat admits his guilt. For whatever reason, he is given a deal: just pay the money back and nobody will ever know. So now he owes Grand Union thousands of dollars, his wife is pregnant, and his girlfriend is pregnant. All the while, drug use and drinking continue unabated: "Dope, needles, everything—back in the seventies." First one woman gives birth, then the other. "I was running from baby to baby—I was confused," Pat says. Pat himself, as he tells it, had it right; he felt that it was his time in Nam that was causing all the trouble. Finally, he turns to his family for help. No one believes him when he tells them how bad it is until he goes out to his car to get his works, (his drug paraphernalia) for everyone to see. There follows his first contact with the V. A. hospital. They call it "shell shock" and tell him there is nothing they can do. "The only thing that could help me back then was drinking, so all I did was drink, drink, drink." Meanwhile, he divorced his first wife and married his girlfriend. He would try to stay sober.

Then I'd go back out, robbing, getting money, doing this, doing that. Divorced my first wife, married my second wife, ended up having two children with her. . . . Divorced her, she took everything I had, wouldn't let me see the kids. I was very confused, kept running away, running away. Kept going back to Mom and Dad all the time. They were helping me. . . . My father wouldn't give me any money, he knew what I was doing with it, but my mother would slip me money. I would lie and cheat. I lost a lot of jobs due to my situation. Everyplace I went I stole. First I would be a good boy, work my way up to the top, and before you know it, I'd be down to the bottom. I'd end up bringing drugs into work, selling the drugs, dealing drugs. Then I'd go back to meetings again, last one year, two years. Meanwhile, when I'm sober I'm getting all these nightmares, flashbacks, and things. And I can't figure out how come when I drink and drug I don't see this, and when I'm sober and straight and I see it. And I can't figure it out. . . . And I just kept going to programs, one after the other. And nobody seemed to understand what was going on. No one knew what PTSD was, and I didn't either.

As Pat goes on, it is clear that he intends to tell the whole story. For him the most humiliating episode is just ahead. As he did not spare himself in relating what for him is an unforgivable act of cowardice in combat—he might have saved the man—so, too, he does not relent in accounting for his life after Vietnam. Things go on as they were, periods of sobriety alternating with periods of relapse. His parents die; his mother's passing is what he is intent upon documenting, rather, the part he played at the time. To understand fully the import of what he is about to speak of, it is important to point out that, apparently, Pat was, or tried to be, the family savior. At least, he makes frequent references to attempts at intervening and to making things right as the family falls apart after the death of the parents. How humiliating for a savior to act like anything but, as his mother lay dying.

I was clean and sober for two years then, and I'd go to the hospital to see my mom, and the more I saw her the more I wanted to go out and get high. The more I wanted to, let's say, commit suicide—to be with

131

her, I guess. Finally, we took her to my sister's house, instead of hospice, and took care of her. And she was on morphine, and knowing a drug addict, what does a drug addict do? Yes, I took my mother's morphine—that's guilt. I feel it, I hate it. I took her pills, anything for pain she had I took. You know why—to get high. Off my own mother, I did that. I used to stick the needle into her and then I'd stick it into me.

So the horrors of Vietnam are perpetuated in the course of life after, as the veteran is made vulnerable to further insult quite apart from the active symptoms of his post-traumatic condition. Loss, in particular, is difficult to tolerate, and many of the veterans speak about how they do not "do" funerals. Loss of someone close may evoke a response quite the opposite of Pat's—a "business sort of thing," as Joel D. put it, an automatic numbing to what should be the occasion for emotional release.

Letting Go, Shutting Down—George's Story

So you are either swept away by emotion and experience the self disintegrating, or you shut down entirely and feel nothing, the self hardened to stone. This latter is the most common response when faced with loss or with the ordinary demands that intimacy carries with it, as documented in the veterans' stories. Yet there is never a resolution; there is always a tension between letting go and shutting down. George F.'s narrative is replete with indicators for this pull in these two directions: letting go by the healthy way of intimacy versus shutting down (or off), and now it seems that shutting down has won. George was one of two people among the veterans who told their stories here who did not take the project as an invitation to talk out their narratives with little or no interruption. Several of the veterans came to the tapings assuming that this would be like other research they had participated in, with me asking the questions and them responding. Most quickly sized up the situation and

132

went ahead with an impromptu narrative. George's tape is made up of patches of narrative, each one in response to an open-ended question. His story is, nevertheless, of a piece, coherent, in the way a mosaic is made up of bits and pieces of material that, viewed from a distance, merge into a whole. Although he never details just what happened there, George refers repeatedly to an event back in Nam on the side of some nameless hill. He assumed he was dead, he should have been, everyone else was, but he woke up in a hospital. This constitutes the core event of the story of his time in Vietnam. He spends four months in a hospital and thus finishes his first tour in the country; he can't get rid of the urge to go back. His wife has another idea. George refers again to that hill and his "death" there.

It was a transition, I knew I was mortal now. I still had a semblance of duty, God, and country, but it wasn't as strong as it was before. They wouldn't let me go back to Vietnam because I was on a permanent profile. . . . I realized I'd gone through the worst thing in my life—what the hell was anybody else going to do to me that would compare to that, it would be nothing to compare to that. . . . But like I said, I still had a semblance of God and country. The only thing I wanted to do was go back to Vietnam. I didn't know why, people always asked me why. My first wife— we grew up together—got married between me getting out of high school and going in the army. She just told me she would not be able to take what she had gone through the first tour in Vietnam, and if I was serious about the second tour that she wouldn't be there waiting for me. I acted like I didn't give a shit and went anyway. I don't know why I acted that way. Like I said, she was my girlfriend all three years of high school; we got married, even had a child while I was a drill sergeant. . . . I had all the reasons to stay, but there was still something tugging at me to go back.

And go back he does, intending not to make the same mistakes he made the first tour. First among these, he explains, was getting too close to too many people, people who got themselves wounded or killed or just shipped out never to be seen again.

I just made too many friends the first tour. I didn't want to repeat that mistake, but it's kind of hard—you rely on each other so much that you get friendly with one or two or three or maybe all of them. It was hard. But I thought I managed that pretty well. I guess that was when I first started to shut down.

George's second tour lasts until his commanding officers can no longer tolerate his attitude and a few of his actions. These may be characterized (not his words) as "didn't give a shit, didn't give a shit who knew it." Still the losses affected him deeply, he admits. Back in the U. S. A., George sets off down the random path of dealing alone with the aftermath, until, some months before beginning the advanced treatment program, he attempts suicide by shooting.

I've been so screwed up these last six or seven years. I don't know if I can really understand—I mean, I hear therapists telling me all the time, "You're getting better, you're improving." I don't feel like it. In fact, I feel strongly that once I get out of this program it's just a matter of time before I become another statistic. And I battle that all the time. I mean, I don't know why I shot myself last February, twice. I probably won't know why next time. Fact is, I was in a blackout when I did it, felt no pain, heard no gunshot, woke up in intensive care. So now I've got that haunting me. If I go into another one of these deep depressions, I'll end up blacking out and become just another Vietnam veteran combat statistic.

At another point in his story, George reflects back on all the "bizarre things" he did. He also speaks about how he "pushed the envelope a couple of times, life-or-death type things."

I remember one time, I was tending bar, back in the early seventies. I had a DAV chapter, I was the bartender there. And I had a guy pull a gun on me one night. I just pressed him to the limit to pull the trigger on me 'cause I didn't really give a shit if he did, because I probably would survive anyway. . . . In that same bar, I remember one night talking to another Viet-

■ ■ ■ ■ ■ ■ ■ ■ ■ ■ ■ ■ ■ ■ ■ ■ ■ ■ ■ ■

nam veteran that was so full of shit, did all these courageous things in Vietnam, supposedly, with everybody in the Special Forces down to MACV to almost winning the Congressional Medal of Honor—I just knew he was full of shit. I used to carry a gun in those days. And I remember taking four rounds—it was a five-shot .32 Smith and Wesson —I took four rounds out of that thing. He was telling me how bad he was, and threw it up on the bar. I spun the barrel with that one round in it and threw it up on the bar and said, "Go ahead, pull the trigger." Course, he had sense enough not to do it. And I picked it up and just to show him he didn't have any balls to do it, put it to my head and pulled the trigger in front of the whole bar full of people. And gave it to him and said, "1 went first, now you go." Of course, he didn't again. That was the best night I ever had for tips in that bar. I was thinking of doing it on a regular basis just to get more tips. I mean, that's some of the stupid stuff I've done. And I've done that little game in private, too. Maybe that's what I did that night, too. But that night there were six rounds in the chamber. . . . But the adrenalin pump, it was almost like being in Vietnam. It was getting addictive back then. It's almost like life doesn't have any meaning since Vietnam.

Here is a primary example of the swing from all shut down to fully charged and ready. Moments like these bring you back to Nam and the heightened state of being that is endemic to the combat zone. It takes something like that time back in the bar in Florida to give meaning to life. This brings to mind Tim W.'s lament over the meaninglessness that he has experienced since his "time in the sun," less than three months in and around Khe Sanh, now some twenty-six years later. George seems haunted by his death experience on that hillside—he gives us the very date, February 6th, 1968. In ways that are surely lethal, he seems intent upon recreating that moment, beginning with the irresistible attraction that Vietnam held for him, leading to his signing on for another tour. For George this second period in Vietnam is something he recalls only in fragments. The hillside's spell invades his dreams.

135

I have one that's really bizarre, where I dream that everything that's happened these last twenty-five years is really just the future flashing in front of my face while I'm dying on that hillside in Vietnam. And that's giving me a glimpse of what's to come, and I wake up and realize it's just a dream. But in my dream it seems real, and I feel comfortable with waking up in Vietnam again, y'know, that it was only a dream. It's really weird. You'd think my subconscious mind would say, "Well, you've had this dream before and this isn't reality." But every time I have that dream it just seems it is reality. That I still am on that hillside and all these years since is just my life passing in front of my face as I'm dying.

This is a subtle treatment of the notion that "life is but a dream." Here what is real is death, while time, the historical time where most of us find a home, is merely a figment, a dream sequence about a possible life in the future. How does one live, then, in the world, in the family, dwelling in ordinary time and in an ordinary place? It seems impossible; it seems that arriving at that time and that place cannot be. The splitting of the self that took place *of itself* and *of necessity* in the combat zone is perpetuated back home, where things are neither bound to death nor intensely alive only when death is nearby. Life, meanwhile, is lived somewhere between these two extreme states. The stories told about life, as we weave our autobiographical tales from strands of lived events, reflect the nature of the experience that chance has provided us. Traumatic experience makes for weird braiding and constant unraveling. Close relationships especially seem to keep coming undone. Family life is something that keeps eluding you; this is true for many of Vietnam veterans, but certainly not for all. Several of the veterans whose stories are reviewed here have maintained long-term relationships.

Family Life? Adele and Roland's Story

Virtually all of the veterans who told their stories for this book mention something about family and about the difficulty of reintegrating with family and, in particular, the difficulty of starting and maintaining a family of their own. A few, like Willie W. and Alan S. were married before going to Vietnam. Alan was divorced before going; Willie got a Dear John letter while there. Other veterans speak of children in abundance but also of broken relationships, divorce, little or no contact with children—anything but the ordinary family life they all assumed they would have before going to Nam. One of the veterans, Roland L., appeared with his wife, Adele, for the taping. The participation of this couple in the project was fortuitous. Roland wished to consult with his wife about participating at all, something typical of the mutually supportive relationship that they have worked out over the years. The answer came back, "Okay, but just about life after Vietnam," that is, the focus would be on being back from the war and what life has been like for one veteran and his family. So Adele and Roland's story constitutes a special contribution, a different kind of story with a special perspective on family life. It also represents one couple's construal of what it means to engage in the long struggle with severe and chronic PTSD. Adele, a most articulate and spirited narrator, did most of the talking, especially once the two of them settled into a comfortable way of dividing up the task. Adele would talk but always with a view to what Roland's feelings would be about this or that episode. Several times she looked at him and asked, "Is it okay to tell this one?" Roland always agreed, and she would then launch into an account of an episode from their life together. Roland did provide a brief sketch of his life up to the time of returning from combat in Vietnam. He began, in fact, with a recent event. He had gone in for surgery to remove an old piece of shrapnel from his jaw. The surgeon discovered a bit of bone as well, actually from a comrade who had stepped on a mine and been blown apart in the same incident where Roland had picked up the shrapnel. He adds, ruefully, "They say you shouldn't carry it with you, when something like that hits you." His expression serves to complete the thought: That's really carrying it with you,

137

and what a terrible reminder! Many things happened from the day Roland left Vietnam on a stretcher. The protesters at the airport, we learn, did not make exceptions—they threw eggs at Roland and spat at him along with all the others deplaning. As for the next six or seven years, Roland encapsulates them into these succinct and pointed words:

> Oh, they were fun, I got discharged and started heavy drinking. That was the time I went into the woods for two or three years. And that was my base camp; nobody came to me. I ran into maybe two or three vets, and even then I knew I wasn't going to get close. I was a loner. When I was in the woods I was by myself, more or less like now in the back of my house. For some reason . . . I got fed up with the woods and came out.

Roland's life goes on, chaotic and painful, replete with all the core symptoms of PTSD but without any orientation as to what is going on inside him. Finally, Roland gets a job on Staten Island, where he meets Adele's first husband at work. The couple is having its troubles, which are undocumented here except for Adele's brief notation that her husband was abusive. She has a new baby but leaves him anyway. Roland, by chance, has a place in the same building. At first, she says, "I didn't like him; there was something about him that scared me. I don't know, I think it was the dark side of Nam that I saw, because he's the gentlest, kindest man I've ever known in my life, to me. He's very protective." Roland begins to play a role in Adele's life, a protective, supportive one. At the time, Adele tells us, she was depressed and despondent, with a new baby and a new friend from another world. Roland stayed up with her playing cards at night. She couldn't sleep; he couldn't either. Reflecting back on that first period of their relationship, Adele says, "He thinks he's a monster because of what happened in Vietnam, but in actuality with me he's very gentle and protective. So he needed me and he needed me to need him." Soon enough the two are together as a couple; a bit later, married. Altogether up until the time of the taping in late 1994, they had been in a relationship for sixteen years and have two children together. It hasn't been easy, as we'll learn.

Early on, there were things difficult for Adele to understand and tolerate, even though, as we surmise, she was exceptionally tolerant of Roland's attempts to deal all on his own with the symptoms, the nightmares, the flashbacks, the reenactments, which at one point took on the form of seeking out barroom fights. Meanwhile, there were multiple concerns about their son, Eddie, who began to suffer numerous partial seizures, for which Roland's Agent Orange exposure is indicated. (The family gets medical assistance, thanks to Roland's status as a disabled veteran, but it's not enough.) Somehow or other—she is clearly a resourceful and intelligent person—Adele begins to read books on the Vietnam war. She adds, "I kept trying to get books on the guys and their stories, because I wanted to hear firsthand. Obviously, he wasn't going to tell me anything." One day, out of the blue, she asks Roland to draw a map of the Ho Chi Minh Trail; he is astonished. Finally, Adele finds him a therapist (not easy in those days) who knows something about Vietnam and the veterans' experiences. He is diagnosed with PTSD in about 1981, an exceptionally early date for this. (The diagnosis appeared first in the second [1980] edition of the diagnostic manual used by most psychiatrists and other treaters.) Still, this is only a beginning and really comprehensive treatment for Roland will have to wait for almost another decade. The couple moves to Connecticut, where Roland is from. Here is Adele's account of how life went at the time.

Then, he wanted his own company so he wouldn't have to work for anybody. We thought that was a good idea—well, it wasn't. . . . We ended up split up because he wouldn't pay the bills. He'd pull checks and he wouldn't put any entries because that's the way you're supposed to do it. We don't do anything the way you're supposed to do it. There'd be five or six checks missing and I'd have no clue, because I was trying to take care of the books for him. And people would call and and he'd start a job and walk off and nobody could find him. And even then I didn't know about—because he hadn't come in for treatment or anything so we were still. . . . He would go—oh, way back when, with Eddie even, he'd disappear for a week at a time. He was gone for almost a month when I was pregnant with the middle guy. Just disappeared, nobody knew. He'd go for two or three days. And he was drinking too, just about until I had the last guy, and I said, "I've had enough, no, I can't do this." And he hasn't drunk since. So he hasn't had a drink for—Frankie will be 14. . . . So he's one of the few PTSD guys who doesn't drink or use drugs. So I give him a lot of credit because he's also on no medication— they can't find any PTSD medication to help him.

Life goes on, things going from bad to worse financially. Adele turns to Roland and asks, "Can I tell that one?" She is referring to a time when Roland went and took out a loan of five hundred dollars just to be able to walk in and hand her money.

I realized and confronted him, and he denied it a few times. I guess he figured it would go away. I've learned since then that a lot of denial works for a lot of stuff. So it got pretty bad financially, and he wasn't around much. I think the part that broke me was the silence. See, he doesn't yell. . . . That went on for a long time because we were fighting at Christmas, and I know one of his anniversaries is in November. So I think it must have been, like, October that it started and we didn't talk till, I think, July, when I told him he had to get out. There was total silence. And yet he would sit, stiff—the anger permeates. So the kids would walk around him and we didn't know why. We did not know this came from Vietnam.

This separation lasts until treatment can begin and at least begin to work. They have a heated confrontation, around the time school begins in September, over Roland's not providing any financial support for the children's clothes and school supplies. Then Roland refers to Vietnam for the very first time, in all the years. Adele describes this encounter: "And he said, 'You don't know what it's like to carry dead buddies around with you.' And I think that's what pushed him over the edge because I looked him in the face and said, 'I don't give a damn!'" Adele recalls Roland's telling her that he wanted to kill himself:

> It was a very somber, serious sort of "Help me, if you don't take me back I'm going to kill myself." And at that point I said, "I'm sorry." And he couldn't believe it, but it was, like, I couldn't. It was him or the kids, and I thought at that point I had to take care of the kids. I didn't know at the time, he probably could have and was contemplating it, because Vietnam had gotten so bad.

By this time, the animosity between the two is great, and things could have ended there for the couple. At this crisis point, with Roland at risk for suicide, fellow veterans bring Roland into the V. A. hospital for treatment. Now Roland is able to begin confronting the demons he has carried, along with his dead buddies, since returning from Vietnam. A strained meeting is arranged at the hospital during Roland's stay. A turning point comes during a family night.

> As they're talking, I'm nodding and saying, "Yeah. Wow, I'm not alone." For all those years, before, I couldn't tell anybody I thought I was the only one and he was the only one. You know, nobody knows the pain. ... The clinicians talked, it was, like, a three-hour night. Dr. Johnson went into a great dissertation about what it is, why it is, the physical changes that they've all had—like the adrenaline. ... The families learned a lot that night. I'm sure the staff learned a lot, too, because we were all raring to go. I mean it was a real good night.

Later conversations with another clinician at the hospital help to fill in the gaps. Adele reports especially on one meeting with Andrew Morgan, M.D., at the same time going back to the medical problems that their son encountered and his numerous hospitalizations.

There were questions I still wanted answered, like the taking off on me and the mismanagement of the money and the running out on responsibility. . . . Is that all PTSD? And he said, "Yeah!" And I said, "Really?" And he said, "I don't know his personality before," he said, "but everyone with PTSD tends to have these characteristics." And I had a whole list of other stuff—avoidance. Because all the times my son Eddie was in the hosptial. He was in Mt. Sinai in Manhattan, Bellevue, NYU, for fourteen days at a time. I walked in like I moved in and and left when he came back out and had to get somebody else to take care of the kids because he wasn't around. Nobody could find him, I didn't see him, the other kids didn't see him, and he was gone. And it used to make me angry and everybody else. But, you know, Dr. Morgan said, "This is part of it, the idea of somebody he cares about being hurt or sick, he can't do it, he's gone." So it answered a lot. And then I felt better because I think that changed me. I told him, I felt guilty 'cause I was almost happy, it was like, "You're not just a jerk, you're sick. This is okay, y'know . . . You're just—it's not me." Because my thing was, "I can't make you love me." That was a hard lesson for me to learn because I thought if I loved him enough that would fix it.

Not that things were all in place at this point, of course not. Adele goes on to talk about the rejoining that she and Roland experienced as a process of taking down and putting up psychic walls.

Now, he's breaking down walls and wanted me to come to his side, and I couldn't, because I had learned what he taught me, which is the way he lived. I would react to him. So he broke down the walls, and I had built mine up—for protection. Because you get vulnerable—he would hurt me. And then wear down my walls and put his back up again. So I stood there and I was crying. And you said to me, I remember it till today, I'll always remember it. You said, "Here, you've been calling me all this time, I come flying over, jump over the fence to meet you," he said, "you jump over to the other side." And that's exactly what it was, it was like, "Whoa, don't do this—I can't talk to you. You want me to love you now? I can't, I'm scared to death." But that was '89. And he's been absolutely wonderful.

Still, nothing is as it might have been if Vietnam had never been. Adele and Roland deal with the problems in life as a team. Nightmares, for instance, are something they sometimes handle together. In fact, Adele notes, as she turns to Roland, "I think your nightmares have proven how close we've gotten. Because they used to be hidden from me—now, I'm in them." She gives as an example the first time the kind of participation she has in mind happened. She wakes up with Roland on top of her and whispering in her ear. "Shut off the radio, they'll hear us, shut off the radio!" Adele remarks, "At first I didn't think it was him—this is the one that astounds me the most. I didn't think it was him because it doesn't sound like him." She realizes that she has a role to play here, so reaching over to the clock radio Adele makes it click as if it were a field radio being turned off. Speaking of Roland's voice, she says, "Now, it's nice and gentle and, 'Now it's okay, they're gone.'" An incident like this had happened in Vietnam, a typical close encounter with the enemy at night. Adele remembers wondering about the difference in Roland's voice especially. "He must have gone back because his voice sounded like it did then, we're talking twenty-three years—I didn't think that was physically possible." No one could explain the difference in Roland's voice; Adele's supposition is a likely one—a return in the mind to relive a traumatic event so completely that even changes in the person's physical self are possible. She says:

> You see, I'm not afraid of Vietnam, and I told him that—it can't hurt me. He always, that was his thing, "You don't understand." No, I don't understand, but I'm not afraid of it—I can fight it. I just can't fight him. It's when he turns against me and pushes me away, then I'm powerless. Together, I told him, we can take care of Vietnam because when he can't, I can, because I don't have the fear.

143

Roland likes to say, "If you haven't been there, shut your mouth."
Adele adds,

> but I have been there, over and over for about sixteen years, every night.
> That's what I think would help the guys, well, the guys and their wives.
> Because the wives are powerless—until they let you in you can't do
> anything. . . . If they can just trust you enough to let you be an ally.

Throughout the story, it is worth noting, Adele maintains a positive and even upbeat outlook. She smiles and laughs a lot. It seems
that as long as she has an explanation for things she is willing to try
to deal with them. She is accepting of what cannot be changed while
ready and willing, actually insistent upon, changing what can be
changed. That this characterization sounds like the serenity prayer
from AA lore is no accident. One need only add that Adele seems to
possess the wisdom to know the difference. That there are things
that perhaps cannot be changed is ackowledged by Adele in what
will be the closing statement of the couple's contribution. The subject of revenge has come up, the kind of revenge, usually for the traumatic loss of buddies, that GIs would sometimes extract in Vietnam.
Adele likens it to what she would feel if someone hurt her children
or anyone she might be taking care of, just as the veterans were
taking care of one another. Here Roland interjects a brief comment
that speaks volumes: "It depends on the type of revenge that you
have—what you do." This brings Adele to this formulation:

> There are things he won't tell me because there may come a time he
> tells me something I can't live with, and I don't want that. That was there
> and it was totally different. I don't know what I would do, I can't say I
> would do differently. But they don't—but most Nam vets I've talked
> to, they don't want to open up because everybody else will think they're
> terrible. He thinks he's the most rotten thing that ever walked the earth,
> yet anybody who knows him says what a good guy he is, and he helps
> anybody and he'll do anything for anybody. And, y'know, they don't see

the good anymore, they see the bad. But that was war—they don't go out and do these things now! I mean it's not like they're out hurting and killing people on the streets, because they're not.

This is clearly someone with an intimate and profound knowledge of the impact of trauma on the person and the family. Her knowledge is of the most basic kind, the lived knowing in the day-to-day. Adele and Roland's account illustrates well one of the main functions of telling your story: you sort through events and organize them so that they make sense, at least in retrospect, which is the only perspective that self-narrative has. Not that you can't reflect on the future, speculate on what might be, dream about what you would want to be. Most typical of the endings of the contributors' stories is a certain ambivalence about the future, whether hopefulness is intimated or bleakness foretold.

The foreshortened future, that dim outlook, that sense of everything lying behind you, nothing in front but more suffering, is mitigated in a number of the stories by a glimmer of hope. Most commonly, this is associated with the veterans' children and grandchildren, which yields a theme of rebirth. For Adele and Roland, children have played a role from the very first in their relationship; they had three small children to nurture—and nurture them they have. This cannot be said of everyone, however.

Family Lives?

For instance, George F. speaks of being unable to reconcile himself to accepting the good that might be his through a close, loving relationship with his grandchildren (although, he tells us, he is able to interact spontaneously and lovingly with the children of others). And Alan S. speaks about how he "mimics society," while hugging his children. ("I know if I hug my kids they'll get something out of it—I don't know what. Because I see these other people hug their kids, I want my kids to have what other kids have.") Then, there is Ed W., who spoke of hugging his children from the other end of the room. Richard B., who calls himself "half dead, half a survivor," does not mention children; neither do Bob G., Bobby R., and others. A few of the veterans intimate having outright conflictual relationships with their grown children. The true warriors among the contributors, Joel D. and Tim W., do not make the connection between the new generation and hope for the future. Some of the contributors are childless. Steve B. tells the sad story of how that came to be with him and his wife of many years. He was told by his doctors that, although nearly infertile, this could be corrected. Steve does not tell his wife and, instead, says that there is nothing that can be done. She later learns the truth, and Steve speculates that she will never be able to forgive him for this. Mike V. tells us he has a daughter but that his fatherhood is not acknowledged. He does, however, speak at length of his niece, who for him symbolizes hope and love, now and in the future. Willie W. is quite clear about the connection, for him, between his small children and a sense of hope, while he remains ambivalent about what is to come.

Willie's story is, in fact, a parable of hopes dashed and expectations thwarted, of being an African-American with a vision of a brighter future, of a family tradition of striving, generation by generation, to do better. He was the first in his family to finish high school and was even destined to go to college. Vietnam changed all that; he sees himself as a changed person, as if he were two people.

> I wasn't even the same person. . . . My father and I had a conflict, and before you know it I had raised him off the ground and I was getting ready to put him up against the wall. My mother was yelling at me to stop, but I didn't hear. I think I must have blacked out. After that, I think I lost some of my family—I was like isolated, cut off. We didn't talk much after that. Right now, today, I still feel cut off from my family. It's like, don't speak the unspoken word around Willie, don't start

talking about Vietnam. He goes into another world. That's my interpretation of it. .... I don't really have anything to talk about. .... It's like being two people. The way I was brought up, I could never kill anybody. It's like two people. I am—it's like another person over there, it wasn't me. You know, things I've done. I could go on and on. .... I can't see me doing those things. ·

When asked if he thought he could ever leave that other person behind, he said, on the contrary, that that *other* was the "dominating force" in his life. This is not to say that he is pleased with this. He says, "It kind of scares me because I don't know what that person will do. .... That person lives on the cutting edge. As long as that person is not threatened, it's put on the back burner." The family had high hopes for Willie. Things don't work out, but Willie is able to take some satisfaction from the success of another family member. His account registers the irony of his position as well as an optimistic view of the family's prospects, a modicum of hope for himself through treatment, and motivation deriving in large measure from his desire to be a father to his two small daughters.

> In Vietnam I was at my fullest, I was at my peak of life. I would have gone to college from high school. I was one of the first people in my family—generations—to graduate from high school. I was supposed to pave the way for the rest. And being black—we were a proud family. Oh, we've got one of the guys going to high school, going to go to college. But unfortunately I didn't. But due to my brother—he's in Alaska, he works for the government. He has a daughter graduating from college, she's a veterinarian. And that's the first in the family. We got bogged down a little bit, but, y'know, it's coming out. But unfortunately I couldn't be the one that paved the way—that's a little bit of a letdown. But, you know, it's coming anyway. Can't stop progress.

He concludes, "And I'm sick and tired of being sick and tired—that's why I'm here [at the hospital], I'm trying to get some help, if not for myself, my girls." It seems that, when in telling your story it comes time to contemplate the future, your thoughts naturally turn to children, if you have children, even if you do not. It can be a matter of life and death, as with George P., who clearly does not share Willie's guarded optimism.

> Many times I wanted to put a gun to my head and just blow my brains out and get it over with. And, I mean, I still think of suicide—I don't want to do that to my kids. But who knows, I cannot predict the future, just how much I can take. It seems the older I get the weaker I get, and this stuff is still pounding away at me.

Willie's story is reminiscent of several of those of several of the veterans in that he has a young family, small children. In other cases, the veterans speak of their grandchildren. In any event, it is the appearance of another generation that evokes thoughts about the future and the meaning of life for the person at a critical juncture. Thoughts of the future and of children are one thing; one's place in the universe and, especially, one's relationship to God constitute another, something that several of the veterans found relevant to themselves and their future.

A Higher Power?

Living in and through the natural story of an ordinary life, there are ordinarily guidelines that structure events and predict outcomes. For the traumatized person, whether suffering the post-traumatic effects of childhood abuse or the horrors of war experienced as a late adolescent, ordinary guidelines are often ineffectual. Several veterans make reference to experiences in Vietnam that went, as one of them put it, "completely against everything I was taught." Several make specific reference to things going against everything taught by religion. The majority of the veterans here were raised with at least some religious training, if not growing up as close to the church as Jim E., Mark A., Ray C., and George F. No one but Alan S., among the veterans who contributed their stories, took away from Vietnam anything like a spiritual epiphany or profound theological insight. (In Alan's case, as we have seen, he was afforded the process view that God does not intervene in any gross way in the universe, so it's people's dirty business to make war—and, clearly, against what God would have them do.) Bob G. and George F. address the issue of religion as a guide and support directly. Before turning to their various theological perspectives on life after Nam, I'm reminded of a vignette that Mike V. provides from his very first days home from the war.

As always in the veterans' narratives it is difficult to isolate one episode from its wider context, when it comes to their accounts of life after, in particular. This is so, on the narrative argument, in that as they improvise their stories they feel the influence of something like a narrative instinct to shape parts to whole, thereby creating links between events and generating meaning. So Mike, as he comes to relating his first few days home, harks back to the memories that to this day especially haunt him. The firefight is over; his best friend, Kenny, is dead, Mike helping to carry his body away. He goes over to Brown who was pinned down in front of him and to whom he simply could not throw his rifle, which may or may not have saved his life.

> And I went over to him. I didn't know what I was going to say. What can you say? I couldn't throw him my rifle—I have to live with that. I know there's no way you could give it up, but it still bothers you. And when I touched him he went into convulsions and died. And I looked around, and there was nothing on that hill but death and destruction. It was nothing to fight for. I just wanted it to end, I didn't care if I lived or died, it didn't matter anymore. I just wanted that madness to end. . . . We were in some real heavy fighting till I left.

A couple of days later, Mike is sent out of the combat zone by his understanding company commander, a Captain Draper, in view of

149

the fact he had only a few days left and was "too short to be in that shit." (This was during the Tet Offensive of 1968.) Arriving home in a daze, Mike gets the usual steak dinner, compliments of the U. S. Army, then a taxi ride to the airport. It turns out that his grandfather, who may have been overly stressed with worry about Mike, has had a heart attack, so the whole family heads for Texas, where he and Mike's grandmother lived. Grandfather survives, we learn. Mike has his first experience with the startle response so typical of PTSD, when an air gun in a service station makes a popping noise behind him. "I hit the ground, I hit this filthy gas station floor with oil and stuff, crawling. The guy looked at me like I was nuts. He put the tire on in a hurry. He got me out of there."

All of this is narrated with great economy by Mike, moving us quickly, in a few lines, from a barren hillside outside Khe Sanh to his grandparents' house in Texas where, we learn, it rains hard.

> Also, when I was there it was raining. Down there, it can rain for a short period of time as hard as it did in the monsoon. And we used to dream about taking a hot shower and putting dry clothes on, 'cause you stayed wet for weeks at a time. When it rained like that, I was staying at my grandmother's house, and I ran out to the road, in the middle of her neighborhood. And I was screaming at God, I was calling Him a cocksucker, I was challenging Him to a fight. I was asking Him to get me as wet as He could. And then I went in the house, and—they didn't have a shower—took a bath and put on dry clothes. And I felt so fantastic it was unreal. But every time I walked in the room with my aunt and my grandmother, they walked out of the room. I didn't . . . understand it then.

Mike does not refer to his relationship to divinity elsewhere. The picture he provides of this moment of challenge to the deity, however, exemplifies the alienation from prior religious belief and training experienced by the great majority of Vietnam veterans.

Bob G. does, however, touch on his relation to his higher power, for him a positive one that is essential to his survival and to enduring.

It's unbelievable the alcohol I've drunk. But I finally just couldn't handle it. I was sick and tired of being sick and tired. I was digging a hole so deep that the dirt was falling back on me. I wanted to die for the last twenty years, so bad. But I just couldn't take my own life, I just couldn't hurt my family anymore. What I've been doing for twenty years is hurting my family. I've been staying away from them, been in and out of jail—possession of drugs. I just completely made a mess out of my life. Finally, a year ago I decided to try a new leaf. I put in a new claim to the V. A. for PTSD. The V. A. has guided me back into a little bit of sanity. I got involved with AA and put a higher power back in my life. For the last twelve months I've been getting on my knees in the morning and getting on my knees every night. I don't feel alone any more. I feel like maybe I can pull this off. I have no idea where I'm headed. I'm just following suggestions. I believe that the reason why I'm here right now is my higher power maybe wants me to work with other Vietnam veterans, I have no idea. I still don't want to live, I still don't want to be around people. I don't know if that will ever change. I know that I really can't let go and I know I must. Torn each way—I just go by suggestions.

Bob's words are replete with ambivalence, of course. He feels a change, endorsing his higher power's action in his life, even as he remains symptomatic and torn. He goes on, returning to what he sees as the source of his hope.

And somehow or another it just started working. I asked my higher power for a sign—and I knew he was watching me. . . . I give my higher power all the credit for me being here. It's just amazing to me—I'm 44 years old— that I'm sitting here in this office talking to you. That's a miracle in itself.

A miracle, yes, but Bob wonders aloud if his life is, in fact, a punishment and admits to an old feeling—wanting to die in Vietnam. He says, "I wanted to die in Vietnam from the bottom of my heart. I wasn't happy with myself. I became over there a blood-crazed killer, I loved killing. It was some kind of sick part of me." Love has died in him, he tells us; being around anyone who loves him is intolerable. In fact, Bob questions whether his purpose in life isn't to suffer.

> I just thought for some reason God was picking on me—He wasn't going to let me die. Y'know, maybe I did something a little bit worse than everyone else, and He was going to make me stay here in hell a little bit longer. And that's what my life's been like since I left Vietnam. . . . I haven't liked myself for a long, long time. I don't know if I ever will.

This is where one veteran arrives theologically. As I have indicated, few of the contributors related their lives after to a question of belief or disbelief, faith or unfaith. Most seem to feel that they are cut off from God or religion, either through their actions or because God, in fact, does not exist or is a distant and uninvolved deity.

George F. was raised in a devout Catholic family; he articulates, in his story, an extreme form of rejection of God. His argument is clear and consistent: if there is a God, given the horrors of war, then He is cruel and aloof. I knew something of George's background, and that he was at odds with his family on the religious question. So I asked him specifically to go into the matter of traumatic experiences and religious faith. He indicates that he once did have religious faith, along with a sense of duty to "God and country."

> I truly believed that. I was a good Catholic boy in a good Catholic family. Everything revolved around the church, even our dances, school dances, were CYO [Catholic Youth Organization] dances. We even were given Wednesday afternoons off from public school to go to religious school, Wednesday afternoons. . . . Every Saturday we were at church for confession, every Sunday we were at church for Mass. So the church made up a good part of the week. Three formal days, and Friday night, like I say, every Friday night they used to have a dance for all the teenagers. But I realized that God doesn't play an important role in this life.

It was Vietnam that changed things for George, especially the losses and that one fateful time when he should have died with all the others on that hillside during the Tet Offensive. He goes on:

Because how can He profess to love his children, which is all of us, and allow to see such despair in this world and terror, brutality? I still believe there is a higher power, and from my Catholic upbringing, in that God, I just believe that He is one son-of-a-bitch to allow this to happen. Not only Vietnam, but for eons. So I'm pissed off, and I don't give a shit if that condemns me to eternal hell, because if that's the way He really is I don't want to be hanging around with Him anyway. And if that isn't really the way He really is, I would think that He would be able to understand people like me. Why we feel the way we do about Him, either find understanding and forgiveness and show that He's not a brutal God. Like I said, if He can't do that, who gives a shit? I don't want to be with the bastard anyway. . . .

Even in this program, y'know, ask for your higher power to help you through the PTSD program or drug or alcohol abuse or whatever—and that's bullshit. If He didn't help me in 1968 on the side of that hill, me or the squad or the platoon or the company, why would I expect him to help me now in a PTSD unit to overcome my feelings or help me get away from drugs or alcohol? Why would I expect him to help me now? When he wouldn't help me on the worst day of my life and the worst day of a lot of 18- and 19- and 20-year-old boys on the side of that hill? It's just a matter of using logic.

This is a clear and well-defined theological position: if God, having the power to do otherwise, is willing to tolerate all the suffering in the world, then He must be rejected. It is only a matter of taking still another step to complete this representation of deity as not only possibly indifferent but positively cruel—what's more, a cruel deity that delights in human suffering.

If I could ask Him for one favor, I'd say, "Strike me now, let me go to sleep tonight and just never wake up and do with me whatever You're going to do." But that's not going to happen either because He is a sadistic bastard—that's why He keeps us around. I mean, when the Romans ruled the real world they had to get to the point where they had to see brutality in its rawest form for entertainment. . . . It's even on a higher

153

plane, He's got a whole world at each other's throat providing entertainment for Him.

Should we be put off by George's cynicism? Who would feel privileged to respond in that fashion? The Vietnam veterans constantly
astonish with their profound insight into their experiences; there
seems to be a wisdom that comes with overwhelming trauma. Not
that anyone should envy them that; this is wisdom purchased at too
high a price. (George's vision of God taking amused pleasure in
human suffering is, by the way, reminiscent of a similar passage in
Augustine's *City of God*, where he depicts one of the pleasures of
the Eternal City, the view of Hell with its suffering, which the citizens above may take delight in.) George's rage at God is born directly
of his experience in combat, against the background of a religious
upbringing that hardly could have prepared him for the kind of war
fought in Vietnam. His response, theologically speaking, must be
honored: hatred of God for the terrible suffering that no loving deity
could tolerate, at least, on this quite human perspective. At the same
time, this is a radical form of rejection and subject to rebuttal from
more than one position. At the same time, George's position is one
adopted implicitly, at least, by a great number of the veterans; again,
not to say it cannot be refuted from more than one theological angle,
including, most forcefully, by someone, like Alan S., taking the process view, which says in part that God does not intervene in the
world—no miracles. George's approach does, however, make perfect
sense in a narrative way. As he tells his story, the church-centered
life he depicts growing up constitutes a kind of American icon for
the fifties, one that could hardly accommodate to the stark violence
and wanton destruction characteristic of the Vietnam war, not to
speak of the kind of descent into evil that war, antiguerilla warfare
in particular, represents. In George's narrative we also detect a
powerful undercurrent of despair, despair of a pure and ultimate kind
engendered in him on a hillside in Vietnam, early in February, 1968.

154

How this bleak picture contrasts with the iconographic image from just months before! It would seem that the structure of faith, such as it was, in childhood can never be replaced by another, more suited to a world where evil does dwell and previously unimaginable evil deeds may be encountered and may well be enacted by American teenagers. For those veterans raised according to an all-too-sanitized religious outlook, and for most others as well, the higher power remains an entity difficult to assimilate into a world view that would make sense of the war and of the last quarter of a century. As George puts it, "Religion is a big issue with me because, y'know, it's one of the worst piss-ant issues you can get into."

HALF DEAD, HALF A SURVIVOR

Richard B. is someone who also attributes something to his higher power. He expresses a guarded sense of hope, after years of drug and alcohol abuse and his ongoing struggle with post-tramatic symptoms. Richard experienced a release from addictions, thanks to AA and the twelve steps: "The desire to use was lifted from me." Vietnam, however, would impose itself on him during any period of stress. Meanwhile, he had begun going to Veterans' Centers and the rap groups that meet there, ultimately entering inpatient treatment. Finally, after a period of relapse, he completed an advanced treatment program. Here is Richard's eloquent appraisal of his position over a quarter of a center after leaving the war zone.

Not a day goes by that I don't think about Vietnam, in one respect or another, have a memory. It's unbelievable how one year of my life has affected the next twenty-seven years, or whatever, totally. I feel at times like a part of me died there, and I've been trying to get that part back— or let it go—that I'm half dead already or half a survivor. I don't feel whole. I went through a very extended grieving process, and I think that's over with. Like, I'm not crying anymore, and I cried for a long time. I've done a lot of different things to let it go, come to terms with it. Forgive myself, forgive others. And stop the noise, you know, get some quiet in my head.

There is despair in these words, of course, just as there is a glimmer of hope that there may be peace and satisfaction.

In the veterans' stories of their lives after Vietnam, they refer again and again to never fitting back in, feeling out of place, aliens in their own land. In addition, they frequently refer to the shame that they feel for the things they saw and the things they did or did not do. This is the feeling of being an outcast, someone not accepted in the community. It began in Vietnam, that feeling of strangeness. First, the place was strange, utterly alien to the newcomers. Then there was the combat experience, with its dissociative dimensions. As Caputo (1977) puts it, speaking of his state of mind before making a tragic miscalculation born of nearly twelve months in country with its astronomically high level of combat-zone stress, "Whatever the cause, I was outwardly normal, if a little edgier than usual; but inside, I was full of turbulent emotions and disordered thoughts, and I could not shake that weird sensation of being split in two" (p. 297). So one is split there into two people, and one returns split. The comforting sense of being in your own skin, in your own place, with your own story, that's gone. So you're someone striving to live in the present in this place, at home; at the same time, you're not there, you never left the combat zone. You feel you can't go home again. Then the shock—home doesn't want you back.

You went to an alien place, had alien experiences beyond words there, perhaps had your very selfhood shattered—saw things, did things you could never have dreamed of doing—then went home, an alien creature now whom home was not ready to take back. Thus, you have been unable to maintain the sense of being a whole, undivided self inhabiting your own more or less coherent story. Vietnam happened, as Alan S. says. Just as the country did not wish to make a place for Vietnam in its history, you are forever unable to feel at home in your story. In this way, you must live a random life outside your own narrative history. No wonder the stories that the veterans tell of their lives after Vietnam have a sameness about them—a deadly randomness punctuated with the sufferings that come with a post-traumatic condition. At the same time, of course, everyone's story is different. When your retrospective view is that your life was severed into two discordant parts—before and after—then you are forever uncoupled from your past. There's your earlier period—you could have done something with that, one way or another. Then there's the strangeness and the terror of the combat zone, comprising as it does just one year in most cases. Then, finally, there's the rest of life—adrift, you feel adrift. You no longer possess your own history. Or the history that you see displeases you, makes no sense. You feel disconnected from your own past. You don't even have a very good sense that you had a past, not in the ordinary sense of being able here and now to look back without undue distress and recollect. You might recollect, but you do so from the vantage point of a troubled, suffering present. And you don't really believe in the future. You think you're the only one. Bob G. believed that he was the only 43-year-old Vietnam veteran alive—until he went to D.C. to the wall one Veterans Day and was shocked to see hundreds of veterans like himself—thousands, really. Others knew that there were other veterans—they could assume that. But this was irrelevant because they had the desperately lonely feeling that they were the only one with the symptoms they were experiencing. Imagine having a flashback one day—just like that—and you've never had one, never knew such a thing could exist. Then, too, the nightmares are so vivid, their impact on you so visceral. No wonder you start using drugs and alcohol. No wonder that meaning seems to elude you. Still, with Robert Mason, a helicopter pilot in Vietnam and author of an account (1993) dealing with his life back in the world, you keep looking for peace.

157

6

■ ■ ■ ■ ■ ■ ■ ■ ■ ■ ■ ■ ■ ■

PHIL'S STORY

■ War stories aren't really anything more than stories about people anyway.

Michael Herr, *Dispatches*

■ Vietnam was an experience that will never leave me, ever, ever. It was the place where I was born and the place where I died.

Phil B., *The Chambers of Memory*

The story and the storytelling of Phil B. exemplifies the Vietnam tapes. His is also a fascinating account in itself, quite apart from Vietnam experience. Phil goes more deeply into his childhood than the other contributors, and he makes more explicit the connections between childhood, Vietnam, and life after Vietnam. His handling of the period of his military service and combat duty is, as with all the other veterans, densely structured as narrative. As the other veterans do in a multitude of ways, Phil moves in the direction of the metaphoric transformation of his life story, in his case particularly when recounting his most traumatic experience in Vietnam. In a word, this is a master storyteller. This is not to imply that Phil is any less affected by the traumatic experiences that he encountered, both as a child and as an 18-year-old combat soldier. Nor is it to say that he has detached himself from emotions appropriate to his experiences by way of narrativization of them. At the same time, it is possible to discern the effects of a process of integration and meaning-making in Phil's story, again, as in the accounts of all the veterans. The full text of Phil's story as it was videotaped follows.

PHIL B.'S STORY

Interviewer: It's April 13th, 1994, and this is another of the Vietnam tapes at the V. A. Medical Center, West Haven. Today we're going to be listening to the story of Phil B. Present also are Dr. Maria Goldstein and myself, Bill Chalsma.

Phil: Well, ah, I really don't know what I'm going to say here. I'll just let it unfold here, as it does. My name is Philip B., and I was born on June 22nd, 1949, in New Haven, Connecticut. I've been asked to talk today, about Vietnam primarily, and put it in context of where I talk about life before Vietnam, Vietnam, and life after. I don't know if I can do that in that order, but I'll try. I might jump back and forth a bit, seeing as my memory is somewhat damaged, somewhat, I guess, by a lot of years of substance abuse, so sometimes I don't remember things as accurately as I'd like to. So the best way to start, I guess, is from the beginning.

Like I said, I was born in New Haven. I came from an Irish Catholic family. I don't know what class of people you'd say, I guess, lower middle class, or maybe lower than lower middle class. My first memories go back to the age of 4 or 5. I grew up in a loud, violent family. My first memories are of people yelling and screaming. I remember being very small, crying, being afraid, always wanting my mother. It took me till later to figure . . . they aren't really memories, they're like mental glimpses, little pictures, y'know, that I can still kind of

160

recall, and it took me till I was older to put those pictures into where they made sense to me, y'know, how I got to be how I got to be.

My father, his name was George Francis B. My mother was Mary Elizabeth K. My father was almost 30 years older than my mother when they married. And I never could understand why she married this man. As I go on I guess you'll understand why. My father was an extreme alcoholic, and he was prone to extreme violence when he was drunk. He wasn't exactly a nice person when he was sober, either. He was a very intelligent man, from what I've been told. He had a college education, and he owned businesses. He was a career soldier, he was in the army for 28 years. He was in his late forties when I came into the world. Anything I know about him, other than my own experience, was what people told me that knew him in those days. He was—I guess the man was nuts. I mean that's the only way I can put it.

I grew up in the slums of New Haven. Now we call them ghettos, but back then they were called the slums. And things were never good. We'd always be shuffled around from one tenement building to the next, and I always remember living in buildings that were roach-infested and holes in the wall. And we were always on welfare. My father never worked, and if he did work it wasn't for very long because of his drinking—they'd get rid of him. My mother was just the opposite of father—she was real meek—she was a nice person, but she was no housekeeper, no Betty Crocker. And she, ah, tried to, I don't know, protect me as best she could, but she didn't protect me enough.

Anyways, life like this went on. My clear memories begin, I guess, when I was around 7, 8, or 9 years old. Prior to that time, like I described, I remember not having, always going to the refrigerator and there was nothing to eat. So at an early age I learned to get out of the house and fend for myself, which later in life, especially in Vietnam, would turn out to be a blessing, in a sense. Around 8 or 9 years old, I picked up a shoeshine box. I'd go out every day after school, when I went to school, and I'd shine shoes. And I'd make money to take care of myself and to buy food and whatever I needed. And also help my mother, I'd give money to my mother to help her. And around this time, my mother had another child, my brother George. So at an early age I took on the role of caretaker for my mother and my younger brother.

Even at this young age, it didn't take me too long to have much respect for my father, I didn't know what the word meant at the time, but I didn't have it. The man was a maniac. I can remember endless, endless nights, where he'd come home and start on my mother, start smacking her around. It would wake me up, and I'd go out and get in the middle of it. And then he'd beat on me. I was terrified, I was terrified of this man. And he was the person I was supposed to trust and love, y'know. And so I could see, my first contact with people I should trust in this world were people I couldn't trust. I trusted my mother more, but I guess I harbor some resentment against her, too, because she could have gotten me out of that situation, but she didn't.

Anyways, my father's abuse got worse and worse. Around the age of 7, I think, my mother and father didn't sleep together anymore. She slept in one room and he slept in the other, so I slept in the bed with him. And I remember how it began. One night I was, I was woke up, and I could feel something funny in my rectum. My father was putting his fingers in my rectum. And I didn't do anything, I kind of, like, I was turned away, looking at the wall, and I just kept staring at the wall. But I didn't do anything, and it hurt, but I didn't say anything. I made believe like I was sleeping. I didn't really understand what was happening. I didn't know what was happening to me. . . . I knew it was wrong, but didn't know why or what. . . . I was too young. And things went on for a while, until it progressed to where he would sexually molest me. I became real submissive to this; I didn't, I didn't resist. And this went on for quite a while, a couple of years, until I got to be 9 years old. One of the reasons, I said before, I went out on my own and became a shoeshine boy and got out on

162

my own. It strengthened me. I went out on my own, and I learned
about things, about sex and about right and wrong. And I learned
how to protect myself. I gathered up friends and learned that there
was another world outside of that dungeon that I lived in. About the
age of 9, when he would attempt to do these things, I resisted it. I
didn't know then, but I realize now, that when I put up a fight, so to
speak, when I did resist, when I said, "No, daddy, don't," he must
have been afraid. It must have put fear into him that somebody would
find out. He must have known I hadn't told anybody, because otherwise the law would have been on him or something would have happened. So he stopped, and there wasn't any more of that anymore.

But I guess it did something to me, it broke something. I didn't
realize that then—I was just a little boy—but I can see now clearly
that it set a pattern for me that would affect me all my life. Sometimes it was like a pattern that saved me, literally, like times in Vietnam. But also it made me feel less than, and I progressed slowly but
surely into a mold of being a nonachiever. And if I ever did something, I'd purposely fail. I don't know what the connection is, totally,
what the connection is, but I know it had something to do with that.
I felt, I didn't feel like a victim, but, like I realize now, I was, I was a
little child and I wasn't in control, but for some reason I didn't feel
like a victim, I felt like it was my fault, like I had done something to
have this done to me. And I never shared it with anyone, I never told
a soul. I never told anyone, until I was in my mid-twenties, that this
had happened to me. I don't know why it took me that long. I guess
it was partly embarrassment, partly like I was the only one in the
world this had happened to. Another reason, maybe, was in those
days things like this you didn't discuss. I remember they'd say everyone has skeletons in their closet, that was the kind of phrase, and
you don't talk about things like that. And on the other end, I didn't
know how, how do you talk about it, how do you bring it up and to
who and why, and what are they going to do to me. So I kept it in,
that was the beginning of stuffing feelings, one of the phrases I

. . . .

learned up here at the V. A., stuffing feelings. I started stuffing feelings big time.

And, in a sense, that's a contradiction. For those people who know me well, I don't seem like the sort of person who stuffs feelings; I'm an extrovert. I shit around a lot, I like music, I have lots of friends, and I like people. And if I've got something on my mind, I'll tell you, usually kind of crudely and bluntly. I can be gentle or I can be crude, I've never had a problem dealing with people. At least, like I say, outwardly. So it might sound like a contradiction when I say that I stuff things. I guess what I stuffed was one of the most important things. Another program that I'm involved in, the AA program, they say people like myself have to take a moral inventory of themselves and clean out all the crap. Get rid of it, so you can go on with your life. I guess I cleaned house, but I left some of the worst stock in, the biggest piece of shit in, and that would haunt me for years.

Anyways, after this molesting stuff stopped, I would stay out of my house as much as I possibly could. I was very seldom home, there were many nights when I didn't come home at all, I'd stay at friends' houses and stuff. There was no discipline in my home, so I didn't have to answer to anyone. So, if I didn't come home, and I'm talking about the age 10, 11, and 12. Sometimes I'd be out two days, and my mother didn't say anything to me, and my father didn't say anything either. He was never home—out drinking with his drunk friends or whatever he did, I don't know what he did. So I had freedom, in a sense, that a lot of children don't have. And it taught me how to take care of myself, how to get what I needed.

And I also learned some of the bad traits that a kid learns. I learned out how to shoplift and steal and to con my way to getting what I needed. . . . I didn't think of it, really, as bad; to me it was a survival thing. And I guess when you live in an environment where everybody is doing something, you do those things. Which progressed into my teenage years, 13, 14, 15, and I was a juvenile delinquent. I got into a series of troubles, y'know, with the law, nothing really heinous or evil, but getting caught for stealing cars and breaking into little stores and stealing nickels and dimes and shoplifting. Right about this time, too, I began my career, if you want to call it that, of drinking and drugging.

As I said, inside I felt different, I didn't feel equal to all the others, or as good as. Everybody seemed smarter than me or better looking than me or better at sports or a better talker. I didn't see myself as good at anything whatever; I always thought myself as fair or poor at—I wasn't good at school, I wasn't good at anything. Even if I was good at something I'd play it down. Even to this day, if somebody pays me a compliment, I'll kind of shut it off, pass it aside. I'm quick to give compliments, but I'm not good at receiving them because of my feelings of inferiority or whatever they are.

Anyways, around 13, 14, 15 years old, I hooked up with little boys that were just like me. They came from the same kind of family background, broken homes, dysfunctional families. And we'd find some bum or some older person who'd buy us a bottle of beer, whatever we could find, and we'd go down to the railroad tracks and we'd drink it. And right from the first time, liquor, alcohol, was magic for me. I can remember my first time—I can't remember the first time I tried alcohol, a sip of it or something, but I remember the first time I got drunk. And it was wonderful. It wasn't so wonderful the next day when I was puking all over the place, but the feeling I got from it—it made me feel equal, it made me feel I could do things that I couldn't do without it. I'd be able to talk better. I used to stammer when I spoke—I'm a real hyper person, really hyper. I was extremely hyper when I was young, and when I'd talk, I'd stutter. And I was real self-conscious. Children can be cruel you know, and I'd go d-d-d-d-d-d, when I'd try to get something out, and the other kids would laugh at me. So a lot of times when I didn't know the word or I couldn't pronounce the word I'd bleep the whole sentence, so I couldn't get what I wanted to say across. I couldn't get my information out, I couldn't get my point across lot of times, because I was so self-conscious of my speech. But when I drank, a miracle took place. I was a stronger person, I was more confident, I was everything better, everything. I wasn't afraid of anybody anymore, I felt like a better person. It really seemed to work for me. And I fell in love automatically with alcohol, right then and there. And I couldn't wait until the next time, and I got sick, but that next time came the following weekend. That went on for years. And I guess like most drinkers, most of my drinking was primarily done on weekends.

I went to school when I had to; I hated school. School was an extension of my father. People telling me what to do—they didn't have to live like I had to live—and how I had to act, then I'd go home and I had to live in squalor. Getting disciplined 'cause you didn't comb your hair right or you didn't wear the proper shirt. But . . . it was . . . who were these people to tell me how to live. They didn't have to live as I did. But that's the way it was back then, so I made the best of it. I should say I made the best of it by not dealing with it. And that was another pattern I set up for myself early on in life—I learned how not to deal with things.

When I was 16 years old, and I look back on my life, it seems like I was the one who was responsible for everything, who took care of everything. I cleaned up the house and washed the dishes. I was the one who took care of my mother and my brother. And I was always making excuses for how the house was the way it was. And by the time I was 16, I felt like an old man, like I was in my fifties. And I was still a boy. So when I reached that age, if you can't understand why I was a bit rebellious, then you can't understand me.

By the time I was 16 years old, I didn't need anyone to tell me what to do, especially some Yaley who was going to school, living a nice life. I could easily tell someone like that to go fuck themselves in a heartbeat. It didn't bother me at all. Because of my drinking and this rebellious attitude I developed . . . there was a mean streak that was in me, that was in there. And it came to the surface, and I found that there was power and safety and security in being mean.

The streets I grew up in . . . like most kids grow up their heroes are John Wayne or some famous football player or somebody famous in history, Abraham Lincoln or something—my heroes were the toughest guys on the block. It was the guy who got sent up to prison for murder. And these were my heroes. To me, these kind of people, nobody would hurt them. They were tough. I didn't actually want to be like that, but I admired them. So in my 16-year-old mind, I kind of imitated them in my own way, and it was a con, but it worked. I'd look for the biggest boy I could find—and I knew he was going to beat me—and I'd pick a fight. And he'd beat me. But the word would get around, and the other boys would leave me alone. They knew that if I had the guts to pick a fight with this boy who was going to beat me—this guy's crazy—and they'd leave me alone. And that protected me. But that set me up for a lot of grief and black eyes as life progressed.

In these years, 15, 16, 17, I quit school. I remember this guy, a social worker, involved with my family because we were on welfare, and he said, "You know, you're going to regret this day." I remember at school they told me, Don't bother to come back. I had missed 90 days of the school year. Even if you go to school and get straight A's you still won't pass the course and you'll have to repeat the year, because you've missed so much. And I wasn't interested in school anyways. But this guy took me to school and the principal relayed to him the same thing I'd told him—there's no sense in my going back. So he gave me a ride home from school, and as we were passing the school he said, "Look at those doors, you'll look back and regret this day." And, sonofabitch, to this day when I go by that school that's what I think of, y'know.

It's true I regretted it. Since then, I've gotten my high school diploma. But not having a high school diploma, it was one of those little notches of not being as good as everybody else, not being equal. And because I didn't feel equal, I didn't try to better myself; because I didn't have the high school diploma I would shut myself off from trying to further myself, to, y'know, to pick myself off the ground. So I stayed the way I was, which was fucked up.

Anyways, I was 16 and I quit school, and I was able to get regular jobs. And I did a number of jobs, dishwasher, stock boy, worked in some scumbag factory. And I'd help my mother out, to bring up my brother. Anyways, during these years the Vietnam War was going on, and it was on television a lot. And me, like a lot of fellows in my era, we grew up on John Wayne movies and Rock Hudson, who turned out to be a faggot—can you believe this?—and my heroes were all Audie Murphy types, y'know. It was great to go to the movies and see these guys beat the Japs and kill the Germans and save the world and all that kind of stuff. And for a boy—I was set up— the movie industry had a lot of influence on why I went into the service. So, I'd go home at night and there on TV was Vietnam—live! You could see the troops over there. I was always fascinated by the military. I heard a lot of stories from my uncles, and my father, like I say, was in 28 years. And anyways, I had all these fantasies about being a soldier. And for me, it was probably the only way I could see of doing something good, something important. I didn't have an education, I didn't come from a wealthy family, I didn't have any skills or anything. I don't know if I said those exact words, but that was the thought I had in my mind. If I go into the service, I could accomplish something, somebody would notice me, and I could be something other than a troublemaker, a juvenile delinquent, y'know. So I went down and I enlisted in the Marine Corps. I enlisted in the Marine Corps because I wanted to be the best, I wanted to be a man, to wear that dress blue uniform. And I wanted to be tough and have all the girls admire me, and all those kind of things, y'know. I regretted that a little while later when I got to Parris Island. I got my wish.

In 1967, I joined the Marine Corps, and the Marine Corps was good. As far as Vietnam, which I'll talk about in a bit, I don't blame the Marine Corps. I don't really blame anybody. I didn't really pinpoint who, as far as the way, the political end of it. I was pretty naive about that then, and I guess to some degree I am now. I know a lot of things, but I don't know what I believe. I've got all this information coming at me, from different people, plus my own experience, and I don't know what to believe. It did affect me, but the Marine Corps part of it was good for me. It took the punk out of me, quick.

I went down to Parris Island, South Carolina, and I was introduced to a 250-pound redneck drill instructor. His name was Staff Sergeant Bogmann, and he wasn't a very nice person. He saw right off that I needed some work as far as respect was concerned, and he taught me about respect really quick. A big boot in your ass has a way of motivating you. He made me do things that I didn't think I was capable of doing. Just to show you what your body can do, about the third week of boot camp—they always had us running everywhere, we ran to chow, we ran back, we ran everywhere we went. So one day he got a chair and put it down, and he got our platoon around him running in a circle, and he just kept us running till everybody dropped out. I don't know how long I ran for, it must have been an hour, and anytime you fell out, if you were faking, he'd sort of know, and he'd get up and smack you in the head. And he'd get you back up and you'd run some more, until you literally couldn't run anymore, your body just seized up. I'm really surprised that nobody died from that. But what it did was, that day, the pain showed me that I could tolerate stuff, and it motivated me to know that inside I could do better. And from that motivation, I did really, really well in the Marine Corps. And there were many instances down there, but that one time taught me that I could do things that I didn't know I could do. And it just took that running around in that circle to find out. So I graduated from Parris Island and went on to advanced infantry training in Camp LeJeune, North Carolina.

And I guess I was in the Marine Corps about four months when I got my first leave, and I kind of fantasized about that first leave from the first, even prior to joining. Because that was my badge of courage, so to speak. Now I could go home and wear that uniform. I was a somebody now. And I got my wish. I came home, y'know, with my little suit on, and all the little girls were eyeballing me, and my friends were patting me on the back, and my uncles and aunts were smiling in my face, and my mother was hugging and kissing me. It was the first time in my life that I could remember doing anything to get all that attention just for me, and it felt real, real good. It felt so good that I didn't want to go back, but I had to go back for some reason. I don't know why, but I always felt duty-bound. Maybe it was because of the caretaker part of me that was established at a young age, but any time I did make a commitment to people, nine times out of ten I will fulfill that commitment. If I make a commitment to myself, it would go by the wayside nine times out of ten. But if I make a promise to a person, I'll keep that promise. So I had made a promise to my country, and I intended to keep that promise no matter what it meant. So I finished my leave and I got sent to Camp Pendelton, California, for more training.

Artillery school there, and I learned about sights and coordinates and maps and all these sorts of things that I was going to need to know when I got overseas. And more advanced training. And now they started to get a little more real with us, about what to expect when we got to Nam. Then the reality started to set in, when they showed us films of people getting killed and how to go through villages and how to treat the Vietnamese, the South Vietnamese nationalists. It all kind of—it wasn't a game anymore, y'know. This wasn't the movies, this was for real. And I guess there was some fear.

And I don't know if God was trying to protect me, or what. But I had a week left and I was in staging, which was the last stage before going into combat. We were all geared up and ready to go and I got a letter—correction—I got pulled out of my platoon by a corpsman and he asked me, was I feeling all right? And I said yes. And it turned out that my father and my mother and my brother had contracted tuberculosis. And my father had TB and didn't know it, and he had passed it on to my mother and my brother. My brother had these sores on his neck and under his armpits, and when they took him to the doctor—she just thought they were boils or something—it turned out he had these tumors. My father had it and he gave it to my mother and brother. But I didn't have it. Maybe I was away during the active phase of it. I tested positive, but I didn't have the active disease. So they were all in hospitals back here in Connecticut and I was in California. And somebody started talking to me, some sergeant or something, and he said, "You know, if your family is hurting like this you can get what they call a humanitarian transfer or hardship discharge" or something like that. And it sounded like a good idea to me at the time, 'cause now I knew that Vietnam was waiting for me. I was starting to hear stories from the other guys who were coming back from the end of their tours, and I didn't like what I heard. So I applied for this hardship thing, and my aunts back here in Connecticut went to all this trouble getting all the paperwork for me to get this. So I went before this full bird colonel— here I am just a PFC in the Marine Corps, and I'm in front of a field grade officer. And he sat me down and he said, "Phil, I mean Private, what could you do if we sent you back home? Your people are in hospital. Do you know how much money your country has invested in your training?" It didn't take long for him to talk me into not going home, and I didn't. Next thing I know, I'm on an airplane heading towards Vietnam.

Now I guess we get to the Vietnam part of the story. Vietnam was an experience that will never leave me, ever, ever. It was the place that I was born and the place that I died. I want to explain that. Over there some part of me died; my faith in humanity, my trust, which I didn't have too much of in the first place, died there. Something was born there, too, my ability to survive. Whatever happens, I can make it. This might sound like a contradiction, too, but some part was born there, which was faith in my brothers there. I saw people do things there, I still can't explain why they did what they did, to the point of losing their lives, giving their lives for somebody else. And if you have any feelings you don't forget things like that.

Anyways, the plane landed in Da Nang, in 1968. Just like it was yesterday, I can remember the door of the airplane opening up and that hot air hitting me in the face. Vietnam smelt bad. It smelt like a combination of shit and garbage, and that's exactly what it smelt like. They didn't have any sewer systems over there, and it just smelt bad. It was very, very hot there, hot and humid, they say it's one of the hottest places in the world, and that just kind of like made it smell worse. And when I got off that plane, as soon as I hit the door, bang, and it hit me in the face just like a cloud, and it just opened my eyes up. And I looked around, and it was chaotic, it was a madhouse. People running around, little carts, and little Vietnamese women with six little kids staring at you. Troops all over the place, and helicopters flying back and forth. It's a big panoramic picture in my mind that I remember, that first day as I got off that plane. And I remember thinking, What did I get myself into? I didn't have to be here, I signed up for this, what am I, crazy? Well, they put me in an outfit, 1/11, First Marines, 11th Battalion. And it didn't take long for me to get into the middle of the shit, seemed like wherever I go in life I find myself in the middle of the shit, y'know. I don't know, my destiny or what.

But the first four or five days they kept me right inside Da Nang, where it was relatively safe, with lots of troops, fire-support bases, and you kind of get acclimated to the climate and they give you these little lectures—only bits and pieces I remember, it's so many years ago—till they find you a unit. So they found a unit to assign me to, like I said, 1/11, and I went up to Hill 55. Let's see, it would be northwest of Da Nang. It was a pretty good size firebase. I didn't realize that then, I thought I was out in the middle of nowhere, and I didn't know that this was considered to be a relatively safe place. But for a new guy, I was scared shitless. There was this long road, dusty road, and they put us on these deuce-and-a-half trucks, and they went on this road, and the trucks would travel as fast as they could. The trucks would travel like 65 or 70 miles an hour, and we were bouncing around in back with all our gear and stuff. And the drivers told us that the reason they were driving so fast is because if they hit a mine, the theory was if the mine went off, the cab wouldn't get it, but us guys in back would and the drivers were more important than we were, ha. That's how I was introduced to that.

Anyways, we made it to Hill 55, and they brought me to my unit. And I can't remember the sergeant's name, but he was my immediate leader—King, Sergeant King, he came from Baltimore. He died later—his name's on the wall in Washington. In any event—correction—his name wasn't King, it was Hill, it was Hill. He kind of took me under his wing, the first week I was there and showed me what I had to do, what not to do, where I had to be, and when I had to be there and all that kind of stuff. Most of the time, I just had to stand guard on my perimeter at night, and they kind of let me sleep a lot. To sleep a lot in Vietnam meant four or five hours a night. There would come a time in Vietnam when four hours sleep would be a blessing. But they were kind of nice to me at first, and at night I'd just stand guard on the perimeter of my compound and there wasn't too much action. And tracers would come by, and they'd try shooting at us. And the other guys would say, "Don't worry about it, it happens all the time." And somebody'd try to drop a mortar on us, and they'd say, "Don't worry about it, it happens all the time." And I didn't worry, I fit in. Anyways, I guess I was there for about two weeks, I guess, if I remember right, and I was in my first operation. If I remember, it was called Allenbrook, the operation was called Allenbrook. And I was in a mobile unit, and we packed up all our gear, and we went with a company of grunts and us, and we started moving down this road, going north.

And there was a tree line in front of our compound. If I remember correctly, it was about a click, or two clicks, away in the distance, and we knew that that's where Charlie was, that's where he stayed.

There was, like, this no-man's land out in front of us and nobody crossed it, him or us, and anybody who did was a sitting duck. But we crossed it, and nothing happened, we didn't get fired on, no snipers, nothing, it was a breeze, in fact. So we reached the tree line, and they broke us into three parties. And one party went straight through to the village, I can't remember the name of the village, and the other two parties circled around on the flanks, and we'd all meet in the village—I was in the middle group. And, I guess, we pushed on half a day, and we'd stop every two hours or so for a cigarette, depending on where you were, until we got to this village.

Finally, we got to this village, and we set up a perimeter around it, half of us pointing outward and half of us pointing inward. And a lieutenant and an ARVN officer, acting as an interpreter, and a couple of Marine corpsmen, they went into the village to talk to the honcho, chief of the village. And they went in there and questioned them about the Communists, had they been there, and all this kind of stuff. I don't know what they talked about. And as a good will thing, the corpsmen would pass out medications, to the kids, vitamins or what, I don't know what.

Anyways, we were getting ready to come back in, and that's when the shit hit the fan. Mortars started coming in, and I didn't know what to do. I just knew this was my first firefight. And my eyes were darting around . . . like a camera. Something happens to you when this happens. You're prepared for it, but you're not really. And all your instincts are at their max. You see better than you ever saw, you hear better than you ever heard. And being a new guy, you're trying to keep in the top of your mind all that you've been taught, and you just react. Anyways, mortars were going off all around us, and people were yelling and screaming, and I didn't know what to do. Nobody told me nothing. I just stood there, waiting for something to shoot at, I just didn't, and next thing I know the firefight intensified, and there were tracers flying everywhere. Lot of times, the gooks, our tracers were red color, and the gooks, lot of the time, their tracers were green, and when that happened, it was easy to know which way the enemy was firing from, 'cause they had those green tracers. Lot of times, they didn't though, and theirs were red, too. But this particular time, they were green ones, and I could see, me and this other guy could see where some of the fire was coming from. So we just started aiming in that general direction, but there was a lot of vegetation and stuff all around. I don't know how long this went on for, I can't remember. It seemed like an eternity, but it was probably only about five or ten minutes. And there was a lot of noise, and I really didn't know what the frick I was doing, I just, I did what everybody else was doing. I followed the crowd, and when this other guy started firing toward where the tracers were coming from, that's what I did, too. And I emptied out a few of my magazines, and then everything quieted down and everybody looked around. To see who was hurting or not. And that day we were lucky, because nobody got killed. A couple of guys got hurt. But it made this lieutenant mad, I can't remember his name, but he thought that the villagers knew, that we were being set up. So nothing happened that time, and they pulled us out of there, and we went back to our compound.

Anyways, I went back to Hill 55. And in about a week we went out to that same place again, but this time things were different, at least in my mind they were different. But I felt more prepared, at least a little bit better in that period I was in. So we went back to that village, and it was the same kind of deal. We were broken up into three parts, and I was in the middle party, and I was aiding the mortar people. And we set up the same way, but more secure this time. The lieutenant and the ARVN officer and the corpsmen went into the village, but we set things up more secure this time. The only thing that wasn't different, just like last time, as soon as they went into the village, the shit hit the fan again. It was the same thing this time, but this time I felt more . . . in touch. I just didn't start firing wildly, I waited to see, I tried to look, and I guess my courage got boosted by the guys who were next to me, I kind of watched what they did. That was basically how you learned over there, you learned from the guys who were there before you. This time things got really heavy, and we found out later that there were a lot of gooks, and this time they were NVA and not just VC. So a pretty big firefight came out, and as a result of that we lost two marines that got killed that day. I didn't know them, but they were from the unit right next to me, they were in one of the flank units, and I'd never seen anybody like that before. And when we were coming, they called for a medevac, because a lot of the guys got wounded, and we had to pick them up and bring them to a clearing so the choppers could take them away.

Like I said, I always got stuck in the shit, for some reason or other I was one of the guys who had to carry the stretchers for one of the guys, ah, for one of the guys. And I had never seen anybody who was dead before, and he was like me, you know, he was young, he was 18, and he wasn't all mangulated or anything, he just looked like he was sleeping. And, ah, he just looked like he was sleeping, like he was asleep. And I, like, I felt real sorry for him, and I started to wonder about him, wondering where he came from, y'know. What was he thinking before he died, what was on his mind? Was he scared, was he into it, did he have a girlfriend, a father, a mother, and where did he come from, did he come from California, from New York, or? All these thoughts came. And I didn't realize it then, but I realize it now, I was looking at a human being that died, and he was just a kid, like me, just a boy. And he didn't know what he was doing there, he was just doing what he was told to do like the rest of us. So that was kind of like my first time that I saw anybody like that.

Anyways, a lot of bad things happened, and a lot of good things happened too. I can't remember, my mind seems to be a little blocked right now. Ah, I remember the first time I was frightened by death. I don't know how to explain it but, anyways, it was during the Tet. I don't remember where we were, I think it was out by Phu Bai, I think, but anyways, it was a time when Charlie tried to overrun our position, and I never saw so many of them before. We had a sight that came off this howitzer, a panoramic sight it was called, and somehow somebody had taken it off the howitzer and put it on a post, and you could look down into it and we could see off in the distance. And I could see out there there was lots and lots of gooks, like ants out there. And I'd look around at my position, and there weren't as many of us as there were of them. We knew that there were other units in the vicinity, but the guys in my unit, there was only about sixty or seventy of us in our compound. It was a pretty secure compound, we had three circles of concertina wire around us, claymores and trip wires, and we had four mounted .50-caliber machine guns pointed north, east, south, and west, and then each squad, each platoon rather, that is, had an M-60, and our personal weapons. So I guess we were prepared as best we could. The thing was the waiting. We knew that something was going to happen, but we just didn't know when. And they had these berm watches, 100 percent berm watch, 50 percent berm watches. And 100 percent berm watch, what that meant was that everybody stayed awake. And nobody slept, and that's when they got intelligence that something was going to happen, and so everybody had to stay awake and ready and our shit had to be clean, our weapons. And this kind of wore on a person. And two days of that and you start getting tired and your eyes started playing tricks on you, especially at night, and you'd see something out there and you'd fire, and it was just an animal or a bush blowing in the breeze. And the gooks didn't come, and so I guess they kind of knew that, I don't know if those little bastards knew that or not, but finally they came. It was one particular night, I remember. The first time when death kind of scared me.

Bone-chilling fear. And Charlie came. It was strange, usually they came at night, but this time they came it was almost . . . it was, the opposite of dusk—sunrise—it was like a twilight, this blue light, and they came. The shit hit the fan, there was tracers flying everywhere, and this time they hit us with these rockets, 122 mm rockets. Everybody was afraid of those damned things, they were loud and you could hear them coming in and they made big holes in the ground. And that's how it started. They had two hooches they had built in this compound, and they must have zeroed in on these hooches, because they were the first thing to go. I looked around and saw all this stuff flying up in the air, and the hooches were exploding. And then we started getting small-arms fire and started returning fire. And it was pretty easy, because all the area around us was all flat. And these sonofabitches kept coming right at us. It seemed suicidal to me, because it was right out in the open. I couldn't believe it because these people got inside our compound, they actually got right inside our compound.

There's this part I'm trying to build up to here, there was this Marine. And he was Canadian, in the Marine Corps! I remember he had told me his father was American, and they had moved to Canada, and he was in Korea or World War Two, and he filled his son's head up with a lot of stories about the Marine Corps, and the kid always wanted to be a Marine. I don't know how he did it, but he came to America and he joined the American Marine Corps, to get his citizenship or something, I don't know what the reason was, but he joined the Marines. We always kind of kidded him, like, "Wow, you don't even have to be here and you joined the Marine Corps of all outfits." We used to call the Marine Corps the Crotch. And we'd say, "Eat the apple and fuck the Corps." I mean people talk about the Marine Corps, but when you was actually there the Marine Corps wasn't a pretty place to be. I mean they stuck us in the worst places. Anyways, another thing about this Canadian guy, he was always afraid. He was newer than me, by this time I guess I'd been in country five or six months. And he was always afraid, a real new guy. He'd always wear his flack jacket and his helmet, even when we were back in the compound eating or something. And he was afraid all the time, he kept talking, he knew something was going to happen to him, something was going to happen to him. And we kept telling him, "Don't worry, nothing's going to happen to you." Well, he was right. During this time when Charlie overran our position—they really didn't overrun our position, some of them got inside the compound, but the ones that got inside never left. He was right next to me, about arm's touch from me, and this fighting . . . this place, it was like beach sand—it was in-country but close to the sea and you could smell it. And it was like a beach area that was inland. And when all this was happening he made a sort of "oof" sound, and he fell back and was lying there. But I couldn't look back to see what was going on because everything was still happening Anyways, it ended and by this time it was full daylight. And I looked back and he looked like he was sleeping, his eyes were closed and his hands were, it was almost like they were folded on his chest. It was the way he had fallen. So I looked at him, and maybe ten feet in front of him there was like a toupee, like a wig or something on the ground, and I automatically knew what it was. And as I got closer to him I could see that the whole side of his face and the top of his head got taken off, and it was lying on the ground. . . . I'm trying to think what happened now, he . . . oh, I know, because of the beach sand you couldn't see any blood. It was like a . . . it all sank inside and you couldn't see any blood. So I kept looking at him, I didn't understand, I hadn't ever seen anybody like that. And I kneeled down next to him and I knew that if I looked back I'd see inside his head, and I didn't want to do that, so I kept looking at the top of his head and the side of his face, and I'd never seen anything like that before. Especially for somebody I knew and I'd talked to, and I hadn't . . . and it's like being a little kid who's curious or something, so I had to touch it. And I touched his face, and it was like touching a mask or something, and it bothered me. And I did it, and this sergeant, this gunnery sergeant, he was like in charge of us, he yelled at me, "What are ya doin', what are ya doin'!" And I felt like I got caught doing something really nasty, something real evil. But I don't know why, I had to touch it, it wasn't real or something, I just had to do it. So I did it, so I did. I felt like I had violated somebody. I don't know what I felt. I'm confused right now, this moment. But that's what I did. That's what I did. I don't know, I don't know. But that was like, it kind of, but it all went through me—this could happen to you, this could happen to you.

And from that time, from that moment on, I always felt scared. You know, it wasn't like in the movies where you get shot and there's a little hole in you and you fall down. You get torn apart, your body comes apart, it literally comes apart. And it ain't pretty, it's real weird, especially when it's somebody you knew, somebody you related with, and he told you his story and you told him your story. So from that time on, I guess about halfway through, I was afraid. I always did my duty, I'm proud of myself for that. I didn't chicken out. I didn't take any unnecessary chances, I was no hero, but I did what I was told. Then I kind of lucked out. A while later, there was a back blast on one of the howitzers, it kind of exploded, and I hurt my left ear. And it almost knocked me out. I remember coming to and I couldn't hear, I could see people's mouths moving but I couldn't hear any sounds. And I thought I was deaf. And I remember, I'd been in-country so long that the thought of being deaf was like a blessing. It meant that I could go home, and anything was better than being there, anything, even being deaf. And that's how your mind gets. But I wasn't deaf. The sound was so loud it kind of, like, screwed my hearing up a little bit. But three or four days after this happened, I got an earache, and it was excruciating pain. My whole face was just pumping with pain—I was really hurting. So they sent me back to Da Nang, and they drained out my ear—I'd gotten an infection—and they gave me a few days to kind of chill out—that's what we say now, I don't know what word they used then. But anyways, I got some time to regroup, and after that they never sent me back out on the line again—I don't know why they didn't.

It wasn't because of anything bad or I chickened out. One of the corpsmen told me it was because of my ear, they didn't want to damage it anymore. So I had, maybe, I can't really remember, four or three months of in-country time left, so I stayed in the rear. Funny thing about Vietnam, there really wasn't any rear. There was some truly shitty places to be but there wasn't any good place to be; there was no front line, so to speak. There was fighting going on everywhere you went, there was worse places than others, and I was lucky, my last few months there, I didn't have to be in the worst places. So I became an ammo technician, so I became sort of a supply guy. I was in charge of ammunition, going to the ammo supply places and going to pick up rounds and powder, and I had a little power, in the sense, if there was a five- or six-truck convoy, I would have to pick the guys to go on the run with me, guys for shotgun on the trucks. So that gave me power, the guys I picked got to get off the compound. So they'd get to go with me and not be in a foxhole all day or something like that, and then if we did it really fast and I had a certain time to do it in, we got to fuck off. And there was whores and it'd give us time to get laid. And we'd get to Da Nang, and the Air Force guys—I mean, compared to us, they were all clean and they had polish on their boots, and they got to eat real food. They had hot water for showers. And they felt sorry for the guys in the field, and they'd trade, if they needed stuff that we had available, like certain kinds of ammo. They had good stuff—food, and books, and paper and pencils, and stuff we couldn't get and, of course, the girls—we wanted sex. So I got to be important, 'cause I gave guys the opportunity to go back to the rear.

Anyways, I finished my tour in Nam. And I lucked out, I didn't get hurt or nothing, except for the one experience I just related. When I hear some of the stories of the other guys, like pilots who got shot down and spent nine years in prison and stuff—I dunno, I probably would have killed myself. I don't know if I could have handled that. But I did my time, I did my time, and I got out of Nam, alive and in one piece. So I went back stateside, and, like I said, over there, something died and something was born. Over there, the something that died was stronger than what was born because now, I don't know, I didn't care much any more, nothing mattered, nothing mattered anymore. Life was meant to be dealt with on a daily basis, and get what you can get and that was it. I didn't have any plans for the future. I wanted to do my time in the Marine Corps and get out, and that's what I did. I did well though, I had real high proficiency and conduct marks, except for the last four or five months I was in service. I had a year and a half to do when I got back, when I got stationed in Camp LeJeune, garrison duty.

And I didn't like it down south. There was always guys singing songs about losing their cow and honky tonk, and I just couldn't handle North Carolina. So I talked to some gunnery sergeant, and he told me that if I volunteered—and everybody tells you in the military, don't volunteer for anything. But he said, "Don't listen to that bullshit, you want to get out of here?" And I said, "Yeah, anything's better than hanging around here with all these redneck dudes, y'know. They don't like us guys, us Yankees." So I volunteered and I went on fleet duty. And that was good, that was my best experience in the service. If I would have stayed in the military I would have stayed in the Navy. They're clean, and it was nice. And I was on board ship, I was on two ships. And it was kind of neat—I was primarily a CPO kind of aide. I had it real easy, what I volunteered for, and this officer—I can't remember his name, Ellenberg, I think it was—he said they were grooming guys like me for embassy duty. The marines guarded all the embassies around the world, and before you do that they put in this kind of job and it was kinda neat. I just stood aboard ship in my duty belt and with my little hat on and my dress blue pants, and I opened up doors for people. And saluted a lot. And as a result of doing that when we went into port—starboard side would go on pass one night and port side another night, but I went on pass every night and it was nice. I had it made in the shade. And we traveled all over the place. We went to Colombia, Panama, Brazil, I mean just all over the place. And I liked it. And it was an extended cruise, oh, about seven months, all around. Finally we came back into LeJeune again, and like I say, I didn't like it there.

And my drinking picked up. As soon as duty was over, I'd go to the base NCO club, and it was cheap to drink on base, y'know, so every night I would get drunk and I'd come back and fall asleep and get up the next day. And this was repetitious, getting drunk every day. And this went on and on and my attitude started changing. Where before I didn't want to do anything to blemish my record in the Marine Corps, now I just didn't care anymore. Plus, more guys were coming back from Nam, and their stories were getting worse and I was starting to realize that we were getting fucked. And like I said, I don't to this day know where to pinpoint the blame but I knew back then, at 20 years old, that the blame belonged somewhere. Somebody was fucking up and we were the ones that were getting the shit thrown at us—it was the troops. And it was really a bad time, if you all remember, y'know, everybody was demonstrating against the war and saying that we were all baby killers and stuff. And we were getting fucked by the government and our own people were shitting at us, you know. I mean we couldn't win to lose. Nobody wanted to admit he was a Vietnam veteran. Now everybody walks around with their hats on, and they make movies, and the wannabes. But then, nobody wanted to be, nobody wanted to know us—we were like outcasts. That's how it was for a long time after that.

Anyways, my attitude in the Marine Corps changed and I started getting in trouble, like one time I threw a phone book at a second lieutenant, and I got wrote up for that. And a short time later, I came home drunk one time and fell asleep in my bunk and almost started a big fire in the barracks, and I got wrote up for that. So my CO called me in and asked me what the story was, and my father had died about this time, I got emergency leave, which wasn't really a heartbreaker for me, you know. But the CO thought that that's what the pattern was about—I was screwing up 'cause of my father dying—and I just let him believe that because I didn't really know. I didn't know anything about Post-traumatic Stress Disorder, I didn't know the fuck about nothing. I just wanted to get out of the Marine Corps. I'd had enough of inspections and polishing the bottom of my shoes, and ironing my underwear, and marching around, and I just didn't want to do that no more. So I had about three months to do, and all the combat veterans, if you had less than a year to do, you could get an early out. So I was first in line—sign here—and, man, I was first in line. So I got out.

And I got out with an honorable discharge, which was a blessing, 'cause the V. A. saved my life, so I'm glad. So I went home. And when I went home, it got worse. Now my father was out of the picture—he wasn't anything to lose anyways. I remember when I came home, walking in the door, and my brother was, oh, about 9, I guess. He opened the door, and he was dirty. My mother was sitting at the table, and she was bombed, crying to herself. The house, the apartment, was a shambles, looked like nobody swept the floor in a month. And I saw it, and, man, it was like this wave of depression hit me, the first day! I mean the very first moment I walked in. I said, ah, man, part of me wished I hadn't left Camp LeJeune. I could have reupped, ha! At least it was clean there. I could feel the depression, it was like a physical thing. And I got angry, I didn't know what to do with the anger, though. I couldn't take it out on them; I felt sorry for them but at the same time I was mad that I had to be with them. I tried taking care of them for a while, but I just couldn't do it.

I tried to get a job, but I just couldn't hold it. If the boss'd tell me something to do, I'd tell him to go fuck himself. I didn't feel like I had to answer to anybody anymore. I felt like everybody owed me now. I know that's not a very mature or right way to feel about things, but that's how I felt. My whole life up to that point was just dreary, and the only fun and good things I had was when I got in trouble, when I was running around breaking windows and getting into gang fights and getting drunk in somebody's cellar. Those were my good times. Everything else was TB and alcoholism and beatings and sexual abuse and state welfare, and it was all the pits. And the Vietnam War, and people telling you what to do, these pompous fucking peacocks, telling me how to live. Who are you to tell me how to live? You weren't over there, you don't know. So I tried to be a carpenter, and they said, "You can't be a carpenter because you don't have a high school diploma." And I said, "Well, Jesus didn't have a high school diploma either, and he was a carpenter." But they always had a reason, whenever I wanted to do something, and they'd say, "Well, Phil, what do you want to do?" And I'd say, "I want to do this." And they'd say, "You can't do that." Well, what the fuck did you ask me for? And so I didn't have much patience anymore. I didn't have a lot to start with, but now I let everybody know I didn't, and I just couldn't hold down a job. And I felt embarrassed. I wanted to work and I wanted to have money in my pocket, but I just wore out. Like, I'd go get a job, and I'd get some shitty job in a factory making minimum wage, you know, and after two weeks or two months I couldn't take it any more. I said, Look at this I'm breaking my balls for 79 dollars a week working Saturdays and things and getting all scummy and everything, and I couldn't take it. And I felt like I deserved more, but I didn't know how to get it, you know. I know that nobody should hire me because I wasn't skilled at anything, but I felt that the country or somebody owed me something for going to Nam, and I thought that that would help me, that having that piece of paper, the honorable discharge, combat veteran and everything, that somebody would say, "Hey, man, don't worry, we're going to train you and we're going to get you a good job with benefits and all." But that never happened. It just never did happen. And it didn't take me long to figure out that, y'know, with a quarter and my honorable discharge I could buy a cup of coffee. Those nine ribbons that I wore didn't mean anything, except to me and maybe other Nam veterans. They didn't open any doors for me at all. As a matter of fact, I remember for a long, long time, except with other Nam veterans, never even telling anyone that I was one. I remember lying on applications for jobs, and not even mentioning the fact that I was a Vietnam veteran. It was taboo. We were all nuts, we were all no good, we couldn't be trusted, we were all crazies. Well, some of that's true, but we thought that we would get some kind of honor or some help, but we didn't get any help at all. We got just the opposite, we got shit on and swept under the rug. And other veterans from other wars, at first they thought we were all crybabies—they've changed their minds since—but at first they said, We had to go to war but we didn't cry about it. But they got accepted when they got home, they got a job, and the government helped them buy houses and did things for them. It didn't do nothing for the Vietnam veteran. Nothing, I mean absolutely nothing. Up until, maybe the last seven, eight years they've done things for us. But I mean, you've got to do something for a guy when he's 21, not when he's 41, you know what I mean? When you're young, when you're still starting. If I had what I have now I probably wouldn't have gone through a lot of the things. Anyway, I couldn't hold down a job, I couldn't take orders from anybody. If somebody'd yell at me, I'd just quit. I'd just, "Fuck you and your job and I'm out of here." And I'd run off to my bottle and my drugs.

And all these years my drinking and drugging just progressed. I got to the point where I couldn't fill myself up enough. I'd drink so much I'd drink myself sober, and that's no exaggeration, I mean literally, I'd drink myself sober. I'd literally—I'd be drunk and I'd drink and I'd be sober. And then start over again—this is really the truth. And then I got introduced to syringe, in about the mid-seventies, and I picked up heroin, shooting crystal methedrine. And that did something to me, it was like living on the edge. Every time I shot speed, I had to shoot enough where I thought I was going to die. Sweat would come off me, my heart would start racing, the hair on my arms would stand up. And there was something about it, about almost dying that turned me on. And I continued to do this and my body started to deteriorate. I started to get skinny, and I got these big sores on me. And I wound up here a couple of times. In those days they didn't have drug treatment here, at this V. A. Medical Center, all they treated was alcoholism. So I came under the pretext that I was being treated for alcohol, and I'd stay a couple of times, and they put me on the psych ward, and I never stayed too long. I didn't trust the V. A. As far as I was concerned you guys were just an extension of the government, which you are. And at that time there wasn't any PTSD, they didn't even invent the term yet. There was no PTSD, and every time I went on a psych ward they put me with schizophrenics and manic-depressives and here I was wandering around in a sea of . . . psychotics, and I knew what I was, who I was, I didn't think I was Napoleon, I wasn't talking to Spock and pink elephants. I just had all this anger in me and I was really, really depressed and I had a lot of anxiety, but I never, really, really lost touch with reality, where I would get lost or something like that, unless I was under the influence of drugs. As I'm talking about this, we're talking about a lot of days, two decades this went on, twenty years; it's a long time. And there are a lot of days in twenty years, and a lot of hours and minutes in all those years of suffering, of not having anything and feeling useless, and cutting myself open with razor blades and cutting my face up with glass and . . . getting into fights, and begging for dollars to get some drugs, hurting so bad I had to get high. And every so often, I'd kind of clean up my act for a little while, you know. I'd come up here to the V. A. Hospital for about two months, maybe a month and a half. Get a little healthy, you know, go out there, make a new commitment, get a job, working at some shitty place. I started painting, I got a trade finally, and so I could make a better dollar. But I still couldn't make a commitment to myself, I had no desire to better my future. I just wanted to make it through the day, make sure I had enough money for booze and cigarettes and drugs and that was it. And any kind of, like a relationship, with women or something, was scary to me. I didn't want any responsibility, I didn't want to answer to anyone, take care of anyone—I did that already, remember? I don't want to do that anymore. And so that's how I lived for all those years. Sleepless nights. One of the problems that haunted me for a long, long time, was that I couldn't sleep. And people that I knew used to laugh at me, "What do you mean you can't sleep—you stay in bed till three o'clock in the afternoon." That's 'cause I couldn't sleep till eight o'clock in the morning, my patterns were all fucked up. I couldn't sleep, I was always hyper—I couldn't calm down. And people would say, "Phil, why don't you calm down?" I felt like strangling people when they said that to me. Calm down—I can't—I just did a hundred dollars worth of heroin and I can't calm down. I'd do a whole handful of barbiturates, and I can't calm down. You're telling me to calm down. I'd come here and these doctors would say, "Calm down!" I don't know how, make me, show me, I want to calm down. But they couldn't calm me down, it was unbelievable. I felt like I was banging my head against a wall. "You got to tell us what bothers you, y'know." So, I'd tell them what bothers me—what bothers you—I'd tell them everything, I'd tell them anything they wanted to hear—now calm me down. And they tried a dozen different kinds of medications on me. I can't remember half of the names, Trilafon and Thorazine and Haldol and Lithium, I can't remember the names of half the drugs they tried on me—none of them worked, y'know.

Anyways, this leads up to now, I guess, right? Ah, now. In the last . . . nine years. I know why I can say nine years. I have a little daughter. About ten years ago I met a woman and fell in love and like that. We had a child, and I didn't want children. My family has a hereditary disorder called Huntington's Chorea, and we were advised—that's how my mother passed away, part of the story I left out. That would take an hour in itself. And it scared me, this disease, children can have it. But, anyways, my ex decided that I was going to have a kid, and that's that. So I have a daughter. And when I saw this little baby, like, the caretaker kind of came back, only not quite the caretaker before, where I was pressured into it. Now I felt willing. Not that this was a miracle thing, where it changed me. But since the child's birth, little by little, my determination to find out why I am the way I am and how I can get better has grown. It may not seem that way to some people, because I wound up in here a period of time and went out and started using again and got myself all screwed up and came back again, and so on. But I knew in my heart and head that when my daughter Mary was born the part that died in Nam came back alive. And started to grow. But it just didn't happen like that. And this last time I was out on the street, I had an apartment here in West Haven, Connecticut, and I was drinking and drugging like I always do. But now that I'm older, I'm 45, I burn out faster. And because I learned in psychotherapy and the 12-step programs, I've learned that when I do these things I shouldn't be doing them. That I've got to take responsibility for my addiction, for my mental illness, my PTSD. I know what I have, I have some tools now to deal with it. I know my early warning signs. If I ignore them why should I expect anything good to happen? In other words, what I'm trying to say, I don't have any excuse any more to fuck up. I have a beautiful little daughter. I have some tools. And I do have—it's not tunnel vision anymore. There's hope now. And what more can anybody ask for. I mean, there's people in this world who have no hope at all. I mean none. No matter how hard they try, no matter how much potential they have, they're not going to get it. There's some sucker out there stuck in a wheelchair, y'know. No matter how hard he tries he's never going to get out of that wheelchair. Some blind guy is never going to be able to see; there's no operation that will fix his eyes. You see? And I don't have that problem. I've got a situation that I just haven't worked out yet, y'know, and I have the ability to do that, and I've got the resources. And this time when I came in I accepted the fact, really accepted, not just acknowledged, the fact that I have a chronic mental illness. That's not my fault, like they say. I didn't ask for it. But I got it, and that's the facts I have to deal with, and I'll always have it, just like I'll always have alcoholism and drug addiction. But I don't have to live in misery because of it. There's things I can do on a day-to-day basis to improve the quality of my life. Ah, I didn't start the Vietnam War, I was just one of the players in it. And I did my duty to the best of my ability, and I have a right to feel proud. I'm proud to be a Vietnam veteran, I'm proud to be an American. I like this country; I wouldn't go anywhere else. I mean, we have our fucked-up problems and everything, but this is where it's at, right, the good old USA, y'know. And with PTSD and my anxiety attacks and my drug addiction and alcoholism, I'm going to try to make something happen for myself. And I feel confident, more confident than I ever felt, that it's my turn to reap some of the goodness in this world. I've suffered long enough, and I don't expect to leave this world alive, you know. We're all going to die, but I don't have to live like I'm going to die tomorrow, like I was all those years, because of something that happened to me when I was a kid, because of something that happened to me on the battlefield. I wasn't in control of those things, but I am in control of me now, at least to some degree. Nobody's really in total control of themselves, but I'm in some control of myself and for that I'm responsible. And I won't, ah, deny myself that chance anymore. When somebody gives me a compliment now, I'm going to say thank you. I don't want to get bigheaded or anything, but on the same token I deserve some respect, y'know. And I had to start respecting myself, not just others, I had to start learning how to love Phil. And the more I do that, the higher my head—when I walk down the hallways of this institution now, I can't get from one end of the building to the other without five "Hello, Phil's." And that ain't something phony, that's people see something in me. People like me, and I don't think people like you for nothing. I'm not a phony, they know that I'm a real deal and that I deserve respect and that I deserve to respect myself. That I've got a lot of . . . knowledge about life and pain, and I can share it. That's basically what I'm doing here today with this film. I didn't come up here to be dramatic, to try to impress anybody, to make a fool of myself. You told me that by doing this video thing it might help somebody someday. Well, that's good enough for me. I don't even know the person that might see this film, if anybody ever does see it. But if he does, whoever that person is, I hope it helps you. And if anybody is looking at this film, and you're some student, and you're wondering if the Vietnam War was worth it, I don't know of any wars that are worth it. But they happen, they're part of the human condition, and people hurt and suffer because of them. I don't know if there's ever been a good war, has there? Vietnam was especially dirty, and it ruined a lot of lives, it took a lot of lives. And I won't say now that it ruined my life, it ruined a part of it. But I've been lucky enough and blessed enough to . . . salvage what's left of my life. And part of that's because of this government finally got around to helping us guys out. And put some therapists and people in our lives that sincerely care for us. They're helping us out; they're not holding us back, they're pushing us forward. And so we're lucky for that. And that's about all I've got to say.

7

. . . .

MAKING SENSE OF IT ALL

- Traumatized people calculate life's chances differently. They look out at the world through a different lens. And in that sense they can be said to have experienced not only a *changed sense of self* and a *changed way of relating to others* but a *changed worldview.*

  Kai Erikson, *Trauma*

- So often in the war I felt an utter dissociation from what had gone before in my life; since then I have experienced an absence of continuity between those years and what I have become. As a teacher of philosophy and a would-be philosopher, I strive to see at least my own life as a whole and to discover some purpose and direction in at least the major parts. Yet the effort to assimilate those intense war memories to the rest of my experience is difficult and even frightening. Why attempt it? Why not continue to forget?

  J. Glenn Gray, *The Warriors*

- Combat trauma destroys the *capacity* for social trust, accounting for the paranoid state of being that blights the lives of the most severely traumatized combat veterans. This is not a selective mistrust directed at a specific individual or institution that has betrayed its charge, but a comprehensive destruction of social trust.

  Jonathan Shay, *Achilles in Vietnam*

193

▪ The hardest earned and most fragile accomplishment of childhood, basic trust, can be damaged beyond repair by trauma. Human beings are surrounded by layers of trust, radiating out in concentric circles like the ripples in a pond. The experience of trauma, at its worst, can mean not only a loss of confidence in the self, but a loss of confidence in the surrounding tissue of family and community, in the structures of human government, in the larger logics by which humankind lives, in the ways of nature itself, and often (if this is really the final step in such a succession) in God.

Kai Erikson, *Trauma*

▪ If PTSD must be understood as a pathological symptom, then it is not so much a symptom of the unconscious, as it is a symptom of history. The traumatized, we might say, carry an impossible history within them, or they become themselves the symptom of a history that they cannot entirely possess.

Cathy Caruth, *Trauma*

▪ The deepest fear of my war years, one still with me, is that these happenings had no real purpose.

J. Glenn Gray, *The Warriors*

▪ Not a day goes by I don't think about Vietnam.

Richard B., *The Chambers of Memory*

THE BODY KEEPS THE SCORE

Having experienced overwhelming trauma, whether a single event, like an auto accident, or the kinds of unremitting violence that combat in Vietnam entailed, the survivor is faced with the task of assimilating traumatic experience to life now and in the future. It might do as well to speak of digesting trauma, for the body will take in its own visceral memories of events (as Bessel van der Kolk [1994] has documented in a series of books and articles, including his review of the somatosensory response to trauma, "The Body Keeps the Score"). The body itself makes its own attempts at accommodating the often devastating effects. The nightmares that are a regu-

194

lar feature of post-traumatic conditions may be seen in this light. Richard B. tells of night visitations of the horrors of Vietnam (which do not reflect any actual event that he encountered in country).

> One of the nightmares I had, and I've had it through the years, and I don't know why but I'm murdering innocent people. One was in a classroom, half Vietnamese and half American soldiers facing each other. And a Vietnamese gets up and says he doesn't want us here, and then I get up and I shoot him. And the other Americans start shooting, and we massacre a lot of people. But one of the themes is that I'm butchering or murdering, unjustly, innocent people. In some cases somebody will, like, sort of do something minor to me, and I retaliate by massacring them, butchering them. It used to scare me because I felt like I was a bad person because I was having these deams where I was committing atrocities. I didn't understand it. And I'd wake up screaming sometimes. One recurring theme was that I was being sent back to Vietnam.

Richard speaks in detail about his years of drinking and using drugs. He speaks of a time when he took pills in an attempt to commit suicide. He tells us, toward the end of his story, he has no secrets; he has told us, if not everything, enough to know him as a sensitive and intelligent person who, as a very young man, had serious misgivings about being in Vietnam and about America's role there. This is someone who attempted even then to make sense of it all. Still, he was unable to come home from Nam. He tells us how he had periods of some success and some periods of sobriety. He adds, "But what I noticed over the course of my sobriety, whenever a crisis occurred or a loss, I went crashing back to Vietnam."

Richard's nightmares are better understood when we learn that, as an MP, he was often required to pick up stray dogs and get rid of them. He recalls:

> We had to police them up, and we were told to shoot them. And there was one time, when I was with another guy, and a dog was in a pit—it was

195

very deep. And we both fired—I don't know who hit the dog. But I didn't like doing that. And there were times when I sold the dogs to the Vietnamese for five dollars. That one time we shot the dog, there was a bunch of Vietnamese, and they just charged—to get the meat—they just charged it. So there were a few times when I just sold the dogs to the Vietnamese.

He recounts a number of times when he felt outraged at the treatment of the Vietnamese by the American soldiers, as well as being profoundly disturbed at the actions of the civilian and the ARVN (South Vietnamese military) personnel who lived and worked around the area in which he served. His military assignment would have put him regularly in contact with native civilians and with prisoners of war. What he sees and is asked to do lodge deeply in his body, many episodes and details dwelling there with no conscious memory of them. Angry and disgusted, he crosses a line that, for him, was definitive. He kills an innocent creature quite intentionally; his own sense of innocence dies as well.

I was in the jeep and I was at that garbage dump, and there was a dog eating garbage. And he must have been thirty, forty yards away. And for no reason at all, I put my rifle on the hood of the jeep, took careful aim, and fired one shot. I hit the dog, and he flipped over on his back. All four legs were trembling in the air. And I did this out of total disgust. Actually, when I got out of the service I told somebody about it. And they said, "You did *what*?" And I forgot about it. Like, I knew I had shot a dog, but I didn't know the details. Then a couple of years ago I saw the whole thing, you know, vividly. I saw how the dog died and everything. But I think that was my frustration at the whole situation. And I think my innocence was shattered, and in a lot of ways I became the very thing that I hated. And did some things that I wouldn't normally do. I just wanted to get out of there.

Here, I think, we see the very process of struggling to assimilate the story of a life, its trauma in particular, to some narrative framework of meaning. First, the body does its work by means available to it, the nightmares and flashbacks, the intrusive thoughts, as then the man attempts to come to an understanding. Traumatic history does not prevent him from improvising for the camera a finely crafted narrative; in this, his story is of a piece with those of all the narrators here. A major accomplishment of the telling is the fashioning of an account that will, if not set to rest, at least partially accommodate remembrances of overwhelming experiences twenty-five years before.

TRAUMA STORIES AS NARRATIVE

Apart from telling of extraordinary events, the veterans' stories exhibit extraordinary structural integrity. Taken together they draw most frequently on a simple overall design that moves from days of innocence and late adolescent enthusiasm and daring, to shocking and traumatic events in Vietnam, then to years of disorganization and distress, often involving broken relationships and addictions. Finally, this commonly heard Vietnam story may end with the beginning of a healing process, with accounts of some success in treatment and the birth of hope in some sort of future. The rebirth of hope is often linked in the veterans' stories with the coming of a new generation. Thus, there are to be discerned in the Vietnam tapes archetypal or, to use Crites's (1971) term, "core stories," having to do with a very young man's descent into the chaos and violence of war, his personal involvement with evil, followed by rejection by his people, personal disintegration, and years of struggling with the aftermath. The narrative may move toward renewal, marking the beginning of possible redemption for past knowledge of evil. This is a life story told as a developmental tragedy, which often ends, nevertheless, on a note, however faint, of hope. It should also be recalled that several of the stories the veterans tell assume unanticipated forms: the Warrior's Tale, the Confession, the Warrior's Romance. Finally, several of the veterans' narratives unfold under the shadow of feeling unforgiven, a feeling of being forever tainted. As Jim E. remarks at one point, "It just doesn't go away." Even the hope of redemption is absent.

The trauma narrative views a life differently; meaning seems harder to come by, connections much more difficult to make. This may be seen especially in the disjuncture felt in the veterans' stories between what went before Vietnam and the rest of life. Childhood and growing up may seem long ago and far away; as time goes on we look back for different things. Often we return to those times looking for a pattern, which is to say looking for motivation of what comes after in the story. From among the many items available in the annals of childhood and youth, we will select what fits the present story best. As we look back, we tend to search for early indicators of hopes, plans, aspirations, particularly for evidence of earlier versions of later outcomes. For the Vietnam combat veteran, the hopefulness and aspirations of youth must seem empty and devoid of narrative relevance. *Nothing* worked out as youth would have had it, and that is the reality of the matter. Therefore, *nothing* can serve to make complete narrative sense of what came after. In particular, there is no way that the themes of youth, in the narrative of the veteran, could have served to prepare the 18-year-old grunt for the experiences that awaited him in battle. When telling this story the narrator looks back and sees nothing that goes before, other than what, in fact, went before. It doesn't matter whether that was an ordinary life growing up or one marked by poverty, abuse, or loss. There is no obvious set of narrative links such as one looks for in constructing a life story. Triumphing over catastrophe has its own narrative structure: The promise of youth—then the catastrophe, an accident perhaps, sudden reversal—ultimately an overcoming, triumph over adversity. For the veteran, there is no certain, satisfying narrative resolution. Most represent themselves as ordinary kids with ordinary aspirations and prospects. Their catastrophe—Vietnam—shatters their lives to such a degree that not one triumphs in any fundamental way. For two decades most were overwhelmed by the aftermath, making the first part of their stories irrelevant. Some do tell of limited success, like Steve B., who climbed the corporate ladder doggedly before the past caught up with him. A few others speak of some success in life, often telling also of how they managed to lose what they had gained. From today's perspective, the veterans look back past combat experiences and through the long symptomatic days that followed and struggle in their stories to see narrational patterning and structural motivation for what happened immediately after the abrupt close of growing up. A few of the narrators are beneficiaries of what appears to be an innate energy that can seem manic at times. They are able to speak with enthusiasm of their youths, while many others seem simply to be resigned to finding no particular meaning in the beginning of their stories. A few are simply mournful as they recall that distant time. Always the sense of a life cut in two, before and after, remains.

So we can read the taint, see the shadow cast by Vietnam back onto personal history. This is the dead hand of the future reaching back to stifle the past, giving the stories a sense of a foreshortened past. The narrative moves that are made to align the beginning with whatever particular middle and end are ultimately meaningless. Rather, we get mostly a recognition of the lack of alignment, as the veterans speak again and again of the inadequacy of their forevision of what military service would be like and of their sense of why they were fighting in Vietnam. This renders their accounts of childhood and growing up ironic; the very structure of their stories demands it. A narrative disjuncture is encountered right at the outset of the telling. How could there be adequate motivation for what is to follow? If the life narratives of the Vietnam veterans represent, as Lawson (1988) maintains, a kind of *Bildungsroman* (i.e., the narrative of development from youth to maturity), then their stories are ones that exemplify prolonged struggle to achieve developmental success. Only

Phil B. seeks to connect then and now explicitly: "How I got to be how I got to be." But even he makes no pretense that any of this makes any definitive sense. The veterans' life stories do all have structural coherence, however, in that they all exhibit the narrative flow, thematic sequences, and genre-specific shape that are characteristic of the life story.

THE SELF AND THE STORY— TELLING AND HEALING

Everyone has a story to tell, we are told. We look back on our lives and naturally see things in their narrative order, identifying causal relationships, linking the periods together, making sense by making a story. This is hardly to say that we can approach this formative task fancifully or that we can ignore the memory of pain, guilt, shortcomings. When the story to be told is of traumatic events beyond imagining, the position in which the person finds himself is an untenable one. There are factors working to silence the story. These may be internal, involving dissociation, repression, or memory loss of any kind. Then there is the guilt and shame often associated with trauma, even when the person is in no way responsible for events or when caught up in situations, such as combat, where doing violent harm to others is an inevitable outcome. "Survivor guilt" is a term that oversimplifies and dismisses complex human interactions. Again and again, Lawrence Langer (1991), author of a study of videotaped Holocaust testimonies, refers to survivors who are bound by guilt over events beyond their control or ken. Repeatedly, in the Vietnam tapes, the veterans speak of guilt over events that took place in a radically different context but with strikingly similar psychic outcomes. Whether it is Myra L., who could not give up her last crust of bread to a dying man (Langer), or Mike V., who could not give up his M-16 in the midst of a firefight, with lethal consequences for a friend, the survivor continues to blame himself or herself, perpetually burdened by what Langer calls "tainted memory." And tainted memory is slow to speak.

The internal restraints on telling such stories were reinforced powerfully for the Vietnam veteran by his country turning away, calling him a murderer, spitting upon him; even his family did not want to hear. "Put it behind you! Get on with your life!" he was told. Both internal and external barriers, then, must be overcome for the story to be told. The internal barrier that the veterans find hardest—all but impossible—to surmount is the feeling of having crossed the line, of having transgressed beyond where forgiveness could be granted. Forgiveness may be admitted as a possibility, as something, say, God might extend. Forgiving oneself is another matter. The taint of radical transgression is indelible, it would seem. That one may nevertheless live and even make progress in treatment, may even go on to feel easier living in one's skin—that is a possibility, judging by the struggles that the veterans have endured and the generosity and goodness that they are capable of. Is this so because the veteran has told his story? Or is he able to tell his story because of the healing he has achieved? Certainly, it is a matter of a dynamic interaction between the two things, as well as a gauge of the innate nature of what we might call the narrational imperative.

We human creatures may well be described as storytelling beasts; we have an instinct to respond to any kind of experience by narrativizing it. Healing is one function of telling your story. There are other reasons for the trauma story to be told and heard. There is the need to document events, of course. The Vietnam War was and remains of historic importance for the country; the many effects that it had and continues to have on the life of the nation are important to know and to ponder. The veterans' stories are, indeed, not without historical and political implications; by and large they condemn the war, either explicitly or by implication. The Vietnam tapes, however, are about the individual, about trauma and its lasting effects on the person, and about the potential for rebirth in telling your story. In fact, in their telling the narrators enacted both the devastating and lasting impact of combat trauma on the individual and, often, the glimmer of hope that seems to motivate them to continue to seek healing. At the same time, the structuring of one's personal history into a comprehensible narrative is personal in a fundamental way; self-narratives are the means by which personality is both created and manifested, as well as the way in which self-understanding is made possible. We all tell stories about our experience of life to others and also to ourselves, so there is an ongoing creation/recreation of personality at stake. The audience for our stories will affect profoundly their form and their import. Life stories about traumatic events place special demands upon the teller. Yet the event of the telling is of extraordinary importance for the individual; silence will preclude healing and serve ultimately only as the grounds for retraumatization. Thus, the listener's role and his or her responsibility are of utmost import. Stories are told *to* someone *at* some point in time, *in* some appropriate place.

THE TELLER AND THE LISTENER, THE COMMUNITY AND ITS STORY

An account of any human experience implies a teller *of* and a telling *to*. The event of the telling is a dynamic and interactive thing that generates a powerful link between the two—teller and listener—who participate in the creation of self-narrative. In turn, your telling of your story to an *other* will contribute to a collective story of your community. The stories the veterans told tend to merge into one story, when viewed from a little distance and a certain narrative angle of vision. This is the way it always is; one's own story amounts to a contribution to the lore and the traditions of the community. Not that there aren't stories and stories; some stories interact more dynamically with the Communal Story than others. The narrators of *The Chambers of Memory* take their place in the Vietnam literature and yield nothing by way of force of authenticity *and* eloquence of expression. The scene of the telling proved to be a powerful motivator; the video camera, a signifier for the seriousness of the project—to document the veterans' lives, organized as they are around overwhelming trauma experienced in combat. This ritualized setting also became a place for healing. Healing for a person may come from the telling of his or her story by way of reorganizing and reevaluating traumatic events, as most treaters believe. Any healing of the old psychic wounds must come also through the linking effects of telling one's story, linking from teller to listener and, beyond, to the community. As Shay (1994) indicates, the strands of social bonds are torn for the soldier in combat, just as new and intensely felt bonds are woven among combatants. One could still attempt to communicate with one's comrades, though it was in an impoverished, if blunt, language. "It don't mean nothin," the grunt could pronounce over any indignity, death, or atrocity. That may have made things seem okay then; it did nothing to banish the pain and anguish that was to be carried forward into the future. Healing the broken link between the traumatized person and his or her world is a central principle, perhaps the most critical one of all, in the overwhelming majority of approaches to the treatment of psychological trauma. Kai Erikson (1995), who studied the effect of the Three Mile Island nuclear disaster on the surrounding community, is especially alive to the way that trauma tears the social fabric and the tissue of family life and saps the individual of a sense of continuity, finally destroying the sense that one is, after all, a part of a larger spiritual community. Linkage in human community is made in large measure through language, through stories exchanged. In this way, telling your story to a compassionate listener, someone who can truly listen—which means being able to hold part of the hurt—is how the self-narrative comes into play in the healing process.

Does the suffering experienced by the tens of thousands of very young men in America's war in Vietnam have any meaning, or have these happenings no real purpose, as Gray (1970), reflecting on his own experiences in World War II, fears? Cathy Caruth's (1995) characterization of individuals' traumatic past as symptomatic of history is suggestive. The perspective of the individual person is always limited; what experience brings by way of traumatic personal history may be a burden he or she cannot carry—no one could. And it just doesn't go away (Jim E.'s words); it "protrudes" (another of Gray's formulations). Meaning is impossible to come by for the traumatized, at least anything that would make things all right again. What the survivor can do for the rest of us, for the community, is to allow what is personal hurt to be communalized—as narrative—by telling the story. I think again of the words of Thich Nhat Hanh (1993), a Vietnam veteran himself and a spiritual healer: "We are the light at the tip of the candle. . . . We know what war is. We also know that the war is not only in us; it is in everyone. . . . We must share our insight, not out of anger, but out of love" (p. 92). In collecting the stories for this book, in thinking about them, in trying to come to terms with them, I have come to believe that we must honor the suffering portrayed in them and cherish these and other accounts as a history we all may share.

AFTERWORD

■　■　　■　　■　　■　　■　　■　　■　　■　　■　　■　　　■　　■

Some More Background

The project that preceded this book has its own history, which is, among other things, the history of my own involvement in or avoidance of the Vietnam War. A few years too old to be subject to the draft during America's Vietnam period, I had done my two years in the U. S. Army in what now seems like another era altogether. Kennedy was running for president, or about to, and people did occasionally mention Vietnam. "Advisors" were being introduced into the civil war going on there, a level of involvement that Kennedy would escalate as president. A sergeant I worked with, a veteran of the Korean War, told stories about being pulled away from his office job there and sent directly to the front, during the Chinese onslaught that was threatening to push the Americans and their allies into the sea. Another draftee once commented that, what with the way things were going, we might all end up in Vietnam one day. For a moment, my desk-bound complacency was broken. And there was the time that I attended the annual show for the graduating class of West Point, staged every year at Aberdeen Proving Grounds, where

I was stationed. I recall helicopters swooping in firing rockets and, especially, the Gatling-type .50-caliber machine gun that sat on a tripod pointed at a target 50 yards away. I'm sure there were other things equally impressive in their way, but I don't remember. At the time, I had no idea that I was looking at a preview of most of the basic hardware to be employed in America's long involvement in Vietnam. (The Gatling gun, mounted aboard the military's version of the DC-3, would be called "Puff the Magic Dragon" in Vietnam, a modernized instrument of death wedded to an antique airplane.) Then, subsequently, there was the day-to-day, week-by-week unfolding of this unwieldy, ever more bloody involvement that actually began at the end of the fifties and would end for America in the third year of the seventies.

Meanwhile, my personal narrative had me in graduate school, starting a family, getting a first academic job, then a second, then looking for work, not finding any, working marginally in publishing, doing freelance translations, finally beginning training to become a therapist. This last turn in what had been looking like a random path brought me to the West Haven, Connecticut, V. A. Medical Center, where one of the inpatient treatment units was devoted to healing the psychic wounds of the Vietnam War carried by thousands of U. S. veterans of that now seemingly pointless conflict. Among the random baggage that I carried onto the unit as a psychology intern was a background in literary studies, rapidly eroding fluency in Russian, and an interest in writing a dissertation about people's personal stories of their traumatic histories. I already knew something about that from working with severely abused children, listening to their stories, and to their mothers' accounts of their own often extremely traumatic lives. So I found myself a clinician working with Vietnam veterans on what may well have been the country's most intensely organized, highly motivated healing community, masquerading as an inpatient psychiatric unit. This true community of veterans was known officially as the National Center for PTSD.

. . . .

A Ritualized Setting

The unit turned out to be an ideal setting for the project. The PTSD unit at West Haven was certainly one place that the healing represented by transforming traumatic memory into narrative memory could take place. The treatment program there developed over time, beginning in the late 1980s, in response to the needs of the thousands of Vietnam veterans suffering from post-traumatic conditions. Treatment specifically for war trauma was, at long last, becoming available throughout the V. A. system. The unit at West Haven would be different, however. Dr. David Johnson, a psychologist there, was responsible for shaping the unit from the first, and he put his stamp on every aspect of it. David had formerly been a drama student; he returned to this background in fashioning the program, which, among other things, featured drama therapy, a discipline that he himself founded. The veterans in the advanced phase of the program, a fourteen-week sequence, would participate in a variety of dramatic exercises, culminating in the creation of a one-act play derived from their own histories. The play would be presented to the public as part of the final phase of their stay. These performances were on a professional level and, in fact, were powerful dramatic experiences. In addition, a series of rituals, or ceremonies, were an integral part of the treatment, progressing from an initiation ritual and ending with a ceremonial return to the world and to family and friends. In addition to more traditional group and individual therapy, there were also psychoeducational presentations, rather like academic lectures; music and art therapy; as well as instruction in relaxation techniques and cognitive approaches to dealing with stress. Throughout, there was an effective blending of what clinicians refer to as cognitive therapy (using your mind to manage your emotions) and more emotive transformation of traumatic memory into creative activities, of which telling your story is one of the significant functions. Altogether, the unit became a ritualized place for healing, rather like a sanctuary or a refuge for retreat from the world. The place and the people associated with it became a community. Even as a trainee I felt a part of this great project and looked upon the work of the community more as a mission or calling than a learning experience (which it also was, of course). In this setting the videotaping of life stories was completely at home.

Unfortunately, this vital healing center serving as a home for the hearts of hundreds of Vietnam veterans was closed in 1996 as a result of an administrative decision to convert PTSD inpatient units to outpatient services throughout the V. A. system.

The Vietnam Tapes

The tapings provided an opportunity, as one of the contributors said, of telling the whole story, from beginning to end, with Vietnam as the central, organizing period. The project, as it was formulated, did have a structuring effect on the narratives, naturally so. The point is a simple one, but significant: the listener and his or her motivation will profoundly affect the form any story takes. I, then, occupied the privileged position of being there as listener and witness; we tell our stories *to* someone and, in an important way, we fashion our stories *with* someone. The context for telling your story, therefore, includes the listener/witness as well as the setting, in this case the PTSD unit. The instructions, really the suggestions, to the veterans included telling their stories in their own words and taking as much time as they wished. It was also said to them that they had taken part in events of historic importance to the nation and that "future generations" would want to know about their "ground level" experiences in the war. Finally, I would say, "So think of it as a three-part account. Consider life before Vietnam as 'Introduction', then Vietnam as 'Chapter One,' and life after as 'Chapter Two.'" The veterans were urged to put the emphasis on either of the two main sections, Vietnam or after. As a result, the veterans' accounts of their early years tended to be brief, with several exceptions, while most spend more time on their war experiences than on their lives after. In no case was there anything like major skewing of emphasis toward either period. (See Phil B.'s story for an example of someone who provided important material from early life and who treated the two later periods with almost equal emphasis.)

In addition, the role of that other presence in the room must be considered—the video camera. The equipment available was primitive; the quality of the tapes produced, far from ideal. Nevertheless, the effect this recording device had was unanticipated by me. It is difficult to overstate its power, I really want to say its spell, for its effect seems almost magical. It is fascinating for me to compare the two interviews I did on audiotape in preliminary work on the present project. The stories that resulted were in ways similar to those elicited in the Vietnam project, yet different. It was as if these first two narrators were talking to me and the tape recorder was there as an aid to the task at hand. With the video camera, the communicative dynamic is radically different; it is as if the narrator is speaking mostly to the camera. This was especially true during the bulk of the recording session, when the veteran was telling his story without any prompts or inquiries. Several of the veterans spoke directly into the eye of the camera, without a sidelong glance at the "interviewers." The veterans were told, in effect, "Sit down in front of this video camera and tell your story. The camera's rolling, you keep talking." In some cases, particularly in Alan S.'s, Mike V.'s, and Jim E.'s tapes, the speakers seem to be in a trance-like state. It was necessary to interrupt Jim after nearly two hours of his story, just as he got to the after-Vietnam segment. The hour was late and the tape was running out. He was amazed; it apparently seemed to him that time had slowed down for his story. Alan S.'s story was recorded over a total of three sessions and runs nearly five hours in length. Again, he seemed unaware of the passage of so much time, and he told me a month later that he did not remember the taping. Thus, the videotaping itself seemed to convey solemnity and evoke a certain testimonial realm of discourse, as well as sometimes inducing what may well be considered a trance state. The topics of the telling themselves acted as stimuli to evoke memories of extreme intensity; the setting organized the themes and invested the whole with import beyond the individual and the moment. The results were rewarding. Every one of the participants spoke eloquently, whether in a more plain-spoken style, like that of George P., or in a more literary language, like that employed by Willis W.

Taking a Narrative Approach

In looking back on the veterans' stories, I was struck again and again by the seemingly native narrative skill with which they are constructed, exhibiting all the structuring and devices of "literature." How I came to see the veterans' narratives has to do with my background and my interest in the more literary approaches being applied to narrative material amoung certain practitioners of academic psychology, deriving from the postmodern position that has held sway in literature and philosophy departments going back as far as the early seventies. To make this part of my story as short as possible, suffice it to say that I began with hermeneutics, the philosophical approach to perspectivism that has influenced what is referred to in psychology as *constructionism* (itself the stepchild of deconstructionism). The hermeneutic position seems to me to be one that is natural to the human situation, and it captures much of what is specifically derived for applications in psychology. It speaks to reconciling differences and to living with difference. It addresses the issue of the implicit interrelatedness of whole communities and of individual persons and provides a way of accounting for the ways in which communities and individuals may be enriched by encountering otherness. It recognizes the implications of assertions about the constructed nature of reality. Living within a knowledge boundary, examining with critical skepticism what one knows, and approaching what one doesn't with a sense of the significance of boundaries and an openness toward what is alien may be called the hermeneutic attitude.

People's stories are told to another. The telling is a dynamically interactive process, as I learned almost viscerally sitting with thirty-one veterans (and the wife of one of them) listening and witnessing their stories. The understanding I have of this interactive dynamic, surely hermeneutic in nature, is heavily indebted to Mikhail Bakhtin and his *dialogism* (see Todorov 1984 and Holquist 1990) and Martin Buber's (1958) I–Thou theology. (Perlina [1984] formulates the many similarities between the two.) Chessnick (1990) asserts, with Heidegger and Gadamer in mind, "that meaning in a dyadic relationship is generated by language and resides not in the mind of individual speakers and writers but in the dialogue itself" (p. 269). This is essentially the view expressed in numerous works by Bakhtin (1984), for instance: "Truth is not born nor is it to be found inside the heart of an individual person, it is born *between people* collectively searching for truth, in the process of their dialogic interaction" (p. 110). A final point suggests itself—the person as text. If all meaning is made, in the final analysis, within the intersubjective field of linguistic exchange resulting in a text, then are we not left with the feeling that something is missing? A text, after all, seems like it would be a pale version of the whole person. The problem here, it seems to me, is precisely in the desire to have the whole person. How would this be possible? In fact, the drive to possess another in his or her totality is a mark of an obsessional, pathological striving doomed to fail. We mediate our interaction, our fusion of horizons, and a part of us remains unarticulated. It may be said that it is a question of looking in the wrong place to seek meaning within the individual in any event, as indicated above. The recent turn toward narrative studies in the human sciences in general involves a concern with the interpersonal field in which narratives live and, therefore, with their context. One "text" encounters another, and the scene in which this meeting takes place (hermeneutics' region of *fused horizons*, constructionism's process of *co-construction*) has a profound impact upon the meanings that emerge.

Two other sources of inspiration for the work that has gone into constructing—actually co-constructing—this book must be mentioned. The first is the literature on the Holocaust memoirs (oral histories and video testimonies). I owe a great debt of gratitude to the work of Dori Laub and to James Young's (1988) *Writing and Rewriting the Holocaust*, in particular. Young is alive to the meaning of Holocaust narratives—as narratives—and to the human and historical significance of them. He eschews the mystifying complexity and opaque jargon of much postmodern criticism, which he sees as obscuring the text rather than illuminating it. On the other hand, he himself practices a sensitive hermeneutics that permits the narrator of traumatic personal history to emerge as a human being caught in inhuman circumstances with an individual, human perspective on real events. Thus, the teller is seen as engaged in a consequent act and, as it were, embodying both a particular moment in history and a meaningful contemporary moment that contributes to a society's or a culture's sense of its place in the universe. The rhetoric of the survivor's account is to be taken as data about both events narrated and the narrator's role in making meaning for self and others, now and in the future. It is by this latter function that we come to have deeper understanding not only about past events but about the world in which we live as well.

This is to say that history is made, a construction, which is not the same as saying that it did not happen, that it may be a fiction, or that actual events are irrelevant to ongoing dialogical existence. The function of documentation may be to establish the facts, as in a court case, but in taking or making testimony as a function of making of— that is, constructing a representation of—history through some procedure, the procedure itself is all that may be documented with certainty. Young (1988) makes this point in speaking about documentary film.

> We find that the aim of filmed testimony can never be to document experience or to present fact as such. But rather it is to document both the witness as [he or she] makes [his or her] testimony and the understanding and meaning of events generated in the activity of testimony itself. [p. 159]

And he writes:

> By examining the process of making testimony, we are able to shift our emphasis away from a putatively normative product of testimony to the activity of witness. This is making witness, reminding us that it is made, not just transmitted, and that we . . . are part of this making. The aim here becomes to document the witness, the witness's memory of events, and the transmission of this memory—not the events. [p. 123]

These are the standards to which I attempted to adhere in the making of the present volume.

In addition, a number of feminist thinkers who base their psychological and sociological writing on the study of narratives of all kinds have also exemplified an attitude that is quite compatible with my intentions here. Their work, while not used directly in fashioning consideration of the veterans' self-narratives, is nevertheless also one of its inspirations. The exception to this is, for me, a significant one, Inger Agger's (1994) *The Blue Room*. Agger is a Danish clinician and researcher who has worked with trauma victims, many of them refugees, and published important works on the subject of trauma and testimony. *The Blue Room* is an account of Agger's meetings with some forty emigré women from the Middle East and Latin America, refugees from political oppression and, in most cases, the victims of authoritarian patriarchal cultures as well. These women came to Agger and shared their stories with her. In the process the writer is changed and she begins to hear the diverse stories as one narrative. She emphasizes both the healing function and the political implications of testimony, in particular testimony as part of a purposeful gathering together of self-narratives. She writes:

> As testimony, the traumatic story can thus be integrated and perhaps also given new meaning: the private shame can be transformed to political dignity. It can therefore become a source of new knowledge . . . and at the same time heal the wounds inflicted. [p. 10]

Agger's elegant study has been an inspiration for the present work throughout, including the arrangement of it into its seven sections. Of special relevance is the way in which Agger accounts for her own role as "participant-observer" in the process of meeting with the other, listening with compassion, and serving as coordinator of what verges on becoming a single trauma story. Agger does not, however, pay particular attention to the narrative features of the stories she is privileged to be recipient of. This is the framing perspective of *The Chambers of Memory*, the true creators of which are the veterans who so generously participated in its making.

Further Thoughts, Looking Back

From the vantage point of 1998, twenty-five years after the American withdrawal from Vietnam, the war seems to fade into another era. We have an Ambassador in Hanoi now; Vietnam is courted by multinational businesses as a rich source of cheap labor and a potential market for the electronic gadgetry and trendy footwear that seem to proliferate when things open up in previously closed societies. They've closed the PTSD unit in West Haven; Vietnam veterans now take tourist excursions back to Nam. It all seems so long ago and far away. Yet for those profoundly affected by their combat experiences—and who wouldn't have been—the war and those long twelve or thirteen months in country linger, sometimes ominously, in memory. Jim E.'s words come back to me often: "It just doesn't go away." Veterans who have gone back have reported being deeply moved by the experience. They speak, some of them anyway, in terms of a healing. They have embraced their counterparts in some cases. The war is coming to be viewed as a traumatic event for all concerned. The veterans who spoke their stories for the project rarely mention the enemy; several do, however, note that the North Vietnamese troops were highly trained and efficient fighters. Yet the American story is only one chapter of a much longer history for the Vietnamese themselves. It was a devastating one, and one that brought untold losses to them. This viewpoint, occasionally expressed by survivors with PTSD, is rendered with soldiers' grace by Harold Moore and Joseph L. Galloway (1992) in their book, *We Were Soldiers Once . . . and Young*. Moore was commanding officer and Galloway a journalist with the troops during the first major battle of the Vietnam War, in the Ia Drang valley, October and November, 1965. The encounter really consisted of a series of skirmishes, with the worst fighting taking place between November 14th and 18th after the 1st Battalion of the 7th Cavalry unsuspectingly landed among a huge element of North Vietnamese troops. Altogether during the entire period three hundred and five Americans lost their lives. Moore and Galloway dedicate their classic account to these comrades. They also add:

> While those who have never known war may fail to see the logic, this story also stands as tribute to the hundreds of young men of the 320th, 33rd, and 66th Regiments of the People's Army of Vietnam who died by our hand in that place. We who killed them pray that their bones were recovered from that wild, desolate place where we left them, and taken home for decent and honorable burial. This is our story and theirs. [p. xxi]

May this accounting of what I came to call the Vietnam tapes represent as well a tribute to the untold thousands of victims of all races and nationalities of the bloody decade of America's active involvement in that distant land that still figures so vividly in the haunted memory of old soldiers, wherever they are.

REFERENCES

■ ■ ■ ■ ■ ■ ■ ■ ■ ■ ■ ■ ■ ■

Agger, I. (1994). *The Blue Room.* London: Zed.

Barker, M. (1981). *Nam: The Vietnam War in the Words of the Men and Women Who Fought There.* New York: William Morrow.

Bakhtin, M. (1984). *Problems of Dostoevsky's Poetics.* Minneapolis: University of Minnesota Press.

Buber, M. (1958/1987). *I and Thou.* New York: Collier.

Bilton, M., and Sim, K. (1992). *Four Hours in My Lai.* New York: Viking.

Caputo, P. (1977). *A Rumor of War.* New York: Ballantine.

Caruth, C. (1995). Introduction. In *Trauma: Explorations in Memory,* pp. 3–12. Baltimore: Johns Hopkins University Press.

Chessnick, R. D. (1990). Hermeneutics for psychotherapists. *American Journal of Psychotherapy* 48(2):256–273.

Crites, S. (1971). The narrative quality of experience. *Journal of the American Academy of Religion* 39:291–311.

Diagnostic and Statistical Manual of Mental Disorders (1994). 4th ed. Washington, DC: American Psychiatric Association.

Engel, S. (1995). *The Stories Children Tell: Making Sense of the Narratives of Childhood.* W. H. Freeman.

217

Erikson, K. (1995). Notes on trauma and community. In *Trauma: Explorations in Memory*, ed. C. Caruth, pp. 183–199. Baltimore: Johns Hopkins University Press.

Foa, E. B., Zinbarg, R., and Rothbaum B. O. (1992). Uncontrollability and unpredictability in post-traumatic stress disorder: an animal model. *Psychological Bulletin* 122(2): 218–238.

Gray, J. G. (1970). *The Warriors: Reflections on Men in Battle* (reprint of 1959 edition). New York: Harper Torchbooks.

Herr, M. (1991). *Dispatches*. New York: Vintage.

Holquist, M. (1990). *Dialogism: Bakhtin and his World*. London: Routledge.

Karnow, S. (1991). *Vietnam: A History*. New York: Penguin.

Kovic, R. (1976). *Born on the Fourth of July*. New York: Pocket Books.

Langer, L. (1991). *Holocaust Testimonies: The Ruins of Memory*. New Haven: Yale University Press.

Lawson, J. (1988). Old kids: the adolescent experience in the nonfiction narratives of the Vietnam war. In *Search and Clear: Critical Responses to Selected Literature and Films of the Vietnam War*, ed. W. J. Searle, pp. 26–36. Bowling Green, Ohio: Bowling Green State University Popular Press.

Lewis, L. (1985). *The Tainted War: Culture and Identity in Vietnam War Narratives*. Westport, CT: Greenwood.

Mason, R. (1993). *Chickenhawk: Back in the World*. New York: Viking.

Moore, H. G., and Galloway, J. L. (1992). *We Were Soldiers Once . . . and Young*. New York: Random House.

Nhat Hanh, Thich. (1993). *Love in Action*. Berkeley: Parallax.

O'Brien, T. (1969/1973). *If I Die in a Combat Zone: Box Me Up and Ship Me Home*. New York: Laurel.

Olson, J. S., ed. (1987). *Dictionary of the Vietnam War*. New York: Peter Bedrick.

Perlina, N. (1984). Mikhail Bakhtin and Martin Buber: problems of dialogic imagination. *Studies in Twentieth Century Literature* 9(1):13–28.

Puller, L. B. (1991/1993). *Fortunate Son: The Autobiography of Lewis B. Puller, Jr.* New York: Bantam.

Remarque, E. M. (1928/1956). *All Quiet on the Western Front.* New York: Fawcett Crest.

Santoli, A. (1981). *Everything We Had.* New York: Ballantine.

Shay, J. (1994). *Achilles in Vietnam: Combat Trauma and the Undoing of Character.* New York: Atheneum.

Todorov, T. (1984). *Mikhail Bakhtin: The Dialogical Principle.* Minneapolis: University of Minnesota Press.

van der Kolk, B. (1994). The body keeps the score: memory and the evolving psychobiology of posttraumatic stress disorder. *Harvard Review of Psychiatry* 1:253–265.

Whitehead, A. N. (1979). *Process and Reality.* New York: Macmillan.

Young, J. E. (1988). *Writing and Rewriting the Holocaust.* Bloomington, Indiana: Indiana University Press.

INDEX

■ ■ ■ ■ ■ ■ ■ ■ ■ ■ ■ ■ ■

Index